Advance Praise

This book analyzes Indian social enterprises to yield valuable lessons for successful, sustainable, context-sensitive and inclusive development more generally.

—**Hilary Silver**, Professor of Sociology and Urban Studies, Brown University

This book nicely illustrates the challenges of organizations that tackle problems grounded in particular normative and power relations that cannot be targeted just by technical innovations and quick fixes.

—**Christian Seelos**, Stanford University Center on Philanthropy and Civil Society

This book and the case studies it contains contribute valuable insight into how social enterprises pioneers in India have experimented, learned and, in the author's words, started to create much-needed alternative social realities.

—**Jessica Seddon**, Founder and Managing Director, Okapi Research

SOCIAL
Entrepreneurship

Bulk Sales

SAGE India offers special discounts
for purchase of books in bulk.
We also make available special imprints
and excerpts from our books on demand.

For orders and enquiries, write to us at

Marketing Department
SAGE Publications India Pvt Ltd
B1/I-1, Mohan Cooperative Industrial Area
Mathura Road, Post Bag 7
New Delhi 110044, India

E-mail us at **marketing@sagepub.in**

Get to know more about SAGE

Be invited to SAGE events, get on our mailing list.
Write today to **marketing@sagepub.in**

This book is also available as an e-book.

SOCIAL
Entrepreneurship

Working Towards Greater Inclusiveness

RAMA KRISHNA REDDY KUMMITHA

Los Angeles | London | New Delhi
Singapore | Washington DC | Melbourne

First published in 2016 by

 SAGE Publications India Pvt Ltd
B1/I-1 Mohan Cooperative Industrial Area
Mathura Road, New Delhi 110 044, India
www.sagepub.in

SAGE Publications Inc
2455 Teller Road
Thousand Oaks, California 91320, USA

SAGE Publications Ltd
1 Oliver's Yard, 55 City Road
London EC1Y 1SP, United Kingdom

SAGE Publications Asia-Pacific Pte Ltd
3 Church Street
#10-04 Samsung Hub
Singapore 049483

Published by Vivek Mehra for SAGE Publications India Pvt Ltd, typeset in Sabon 10/12 pt by Zaza Eunice, Hosur, Tamil Nadu, India, and printed at Chaman Enterprises, New Delhi.

Library of Congress Cataloging-in-Publication Data

Name: Reddy Kummitha, Rama Krishna, author.
Title: Social entrepreneurship : working towards greater inclusiveness/by Rama Krishna Reddy Kummitha.
Description: Thousand Oaks : SAGE Publications India Pvt Ltd, 2016. | Includes bibliographical references and index.
Identifiers: LCCN 2015049020|
  ISBN 9789351508847 (hardback : alk. paper) |
  ISBN 9789351508830 (epub) | ISBN 9789351508854 (ebook)
Subjects: LCSH: Social entrepreneurship–India.
Classification: LCC HD60.5.I5 R43 2016 | DDC 658.4/08–dc23

ISBN: 978-93-515-0884-7 (HB)

SAGE Team: Aditi Chopra, Saima Ghaffar, Megha Dabral and Ritu Chopra

Contents

List of Abbreviations

AIF	American India Foundation
BASIX	Bharatiya Samruddhi Investments and Consulting Services Ltd
BNGVN	Bhagini Nivedita Gramin Vigyan Niketan
BoP	Bottom of the Pyramid
BPL	Below Poverty Line
BSE	Barefoot Solar Engineer
CCCTP	Career Centric Computer Training Programme
CfW	Cloth for Work
CM	Chief Minister
CSIM	Center for Social Initiative and Management
CSR	Corporate Social Responsibility
DBS	Development Bank of Singapore
DFI	Development Finance Institution
EDI	Entrepreneurship Development Institute
EISPL	Enable Indian Solutions Private Limited
EOP	Employer Outreach Programme
GDP	Gross Domestic Product
GIZ	German Agency for International Cooperation
GoI	Government of India
GRIPS	Graduate Research Institute for Policy Studies
IBM	International Business Machines Corporation
IIIF	India Inclusive Innovation Fund
IIM	Indian Institute of Management
IGNOU	Indira Gandhi National Open University
IIT	Indian Institute of Technology
INR	Indian Rupee
IT	Information Technology
JNU	Jawaharlal Nehru University
MDG	Millennium Development Goal

MGNREGS	Mahatma Gandhi National Rural Employment Guarantee Scheme
MoU	Memorandum of Understanding
MSME	Micro, Small and Medium Enterprises
NGO	Non-government Organization
NIVH	National Institute for the Visually Handicapped
NMIMS	Narsee Monjee Institute of Management Studies
NSTEDB	National Science and Technology Entrepreneurship Development Board
OBC	Other Backward Class
PwD	Person with Disabilities
RRWH	Rooftop Rainwater Harvesting
RTE	Right to Education
RWHT	Rain Water Harvesting Tank
SBI	State Bank of India
SC	Scheduled Caste
SDG	Sustainable Development Goals
SE	Social Enterprise
SEBI	Securities and Exchange Board of India
SHG	Self-help Group
SO	Sustainable Orientation
SPOs	Social Purpose Organizations
SROI	Social Return on Investment
SSCWE	Sikkim State Chief Water Engineer
ST	Scheduled Tribe
SWRC	Social Work and Research Centre
TBI	Technology Business Incubator
TISS	Tata Institute of Social Sciences
UGC	University Grants Commission
UK	United Kingdom
UNICEF	United Nations Children's Emergency Fund
UNU	United Nations University
UoH	University of Hyderabad
USA	United States of America
USAID	United States Agency for International Development
USD	United States Dollar
VDC	Village Development Committee
VEC	Village Education Committee
VEEC	Village Energy and Environment Committee
VGB	Village General Body
WISE	Work Integration Social Enterprise
WPS	Work Place Solutions
YSMD	Young Students Movement for Development

Preface

The book starts with a sociological assumption that both social exclusion and inclusion in social contexts are manifested by social actions. Further, it goes in deep to understand how exclusions, which exist in a variety of social backgrounds, are being addressed using innovative attempts by selected interventions. The discussion sets to project that it is just about time and space that decides inclusion and exclusion where human interventions are capable of making a shift. However, factors such as intentions and passion to make the shift and create a necessary dais for rolling out positive ideas are what matters the most to promote alternative social realities.

As we move forward reading the book, we realize how various social problems destroy social bonding and create havoc for groups who have been labelled in the recent past as socially excluded. The deprivation and exclusion they experience have led them to lose their dignity and destroy social bondage within families, communities and social settings in which they live. On the contrary, the failure of institutional mechanisms, resource constraints and imbalances that arise during the resilience building process are causes for concern. However, different ways of addressing these problems using various innovative ideas, processes and institutions by a dedicated group of individuals bring hope about possible ways of altering the conditions. These individuals approach problems from a first-person perspective and integrate themselves within the communities who suffer from the problem. Such individuals who are known as social entrepreneurs establish institutions which are dual edged to create both social and financial values. Such a practice is fuelled by the social entrepreneur's immersion or direct experience or visualization. The processes involved and the ways communities have been facilitated to join hands with each other have manifested momentum for both communities and social enterprises to build inclusive societies in which the participation of different social groups is ensured. Further, such social fabrication unleashes societies from social hierarchies in order to build inclusive social order.

The interventions while addressing concerns of social transformation undertake attempts to focus on sustainability orientation. In order to ensure such transformation, community participation has been opted as a benchmark where the excluded communities play an active role in their own inclusion process. This process not only enhances the skills and capabilities of communities but also their dignity. The book further explores the processes and innovative ways adopted by both communities themselves and social enterprises to question the status quo. While exploring such processes, it is found that new partnerships, collaborations and social structures have been facilitated to create impacts that benefit the marginalized. The sustainability orientation that social entrepreneurship is capable of bringing on board in addition to social innovation is discussed in detail. The various strategies that social enterprises adopt to cultivate their ambition to advance in mobilizing resources required apart from other established methods offer rich insights into understanding what it means to achieve organizational sustainability. The book then goes on to develop a framework to understand various phases involved in the process of social entrepreneurship. The framework is expected to assist a budding social entrepreneur to learn and understand what brings success in social entrepreneurship. Further, the framework offers a novel understanding of the processes involved in achieving social value and systematic social change.

The research in the beginning opts for a dialogue to understand various arguments and debates pertaining to analysing the concept of social entrepreneurship which has been in practice for quite some time. Recently, this concept has started receiving attention from different stakeholders while the ecosystem is being built to strengthen the presence of social entrepreneurship and scale innovations initiated in the process.

The work in this book carries out an in-depth analysis of innovations and processes created by social entrepreneurs to attain social transformation in four different social contexts in India. The processes include bringing together communities—which were immersed in the vicious circle of social exclusion—to address their own social problems through skill development and innovative service delivery. On a larger scale, the book is expected to fill the gap in terms of contextualizing or developing a framework based on social enterprises that come from both rural and urban contexts.

Acknowledgements

The book takes inspiration and energy from a variety of individuals and institutions. Without active support from a rigorous and active institutional environment, it becomes quite difficult to produce quality research. Fortunately, in line with me, the book project has travelled to four unique academic environments where I met several scholars, intellectuals and friends who contributed, both directly and indirectly, to complete this mammoth task. Though the project started as part of my doctoral research, due to enormous interactions, suggestions from various individuals, exchange of ideas and knowledge, the book subsequently became a different project than the one which I deemed to publish. It was altogether a continuous process of learning and reflection. In the process, I owe my gratitude to a variety of individuals. I have committed to mention here all those who helped me in the process.

I should first start with my guru, doctoral supervisor and mentor Professor Sudarshanam Gankidi, from whom I have not only learned academic knowledge and wisdom but also several life skills. His humanistic nature has influenced my behaviour and I am sure that it promises much more. As a teacher during my masters and then supervisor, he became my source of inspiration with whom I have shared ideas and thoughts numerous times. Besides my guru, Professor Sudhakara Rao has always encouraged and supported my career plans. I approached him several times for his help and support, since we first met in 2007. Initially, as the Director of the Centre for Study of Social Exclusion and Inclusive Policy where I completed my MPhil and then as a doctoral committee member, he guided me in every step of my research endeavour. Both of them showed me the right path when I fell short of ideas and encouraged me. I met Professor Krishna Reddy when he joined the Centre for Study of Social Exclusion and Inclusive Policy as the successor to Professor Sudhakara Rao. He also offered me enormous support and critical perspectives on my research. He was mostly unhappy with my work and always wanted me to do more in-depth research and contribute to scholarship. His critical overview—which is based on his vast knowledge— helped me to correct myself and move in the right direction.

My other well-wishers and teachers, including Dileep sir, Dr Ramdas, Dr Rani Ratna Prabha and Dr Ratnam, have always encouraged me whenever I needed their support. In fact, if it was not for the discussion I have had with Dr Srinivasa Rao of Jawaharlal Nehru University (JNU) and Dr Nagaraju Gundemeda from University of Hyderabad (UoH) when they visited the Tata Institute of Social Sciences (TISS), publishing my work into a book would have never materialized.

I happened to meet Professor Satyajit Majumdar, the Chairperson, and Dr Samapti Guha, the Coordinator of the Centre for Social Entrepreneurship at TISS, when I started to work at the Centre in 2011. In fact, they both gave me an opportunity to involve myself in the business and management of an academic environment. It came at a time when I had no idea about management concepts due to my social science background, whereas the study of social entrepreneurship requires both social and managerial understanding. This engagement at TISS has helped me to balance my knowledge on multiple paradigms that social enterprises are expected to fulfil. At TISS, I met Zubin, Saini and Nadia, with whom I had lunch-time discussions and exchange of ideas that were really useful to sharpen my knowledge. The student-led social ventures and class-room interactions have further enriched my understanding about social entrepreneurship.

The book took shape when I moved to the Institute of Advanced Studies, United Nations University, Yokohama, as a postdoctoral researcher supported by the Japanese Society for the Promotion of Science (JSPS). I joined the Institute of Advanced Studies at United Nations University when it was in a transition period and was later renamed as the Institute for the Advanced Study of Sustainability. Initially, I was expected to work with Professor Govindan Parayil, the then Director, who gave me an opportunity to engage myself with the Institute. Then I met Dr Manu V. Mathai and Mahendra with whom I had several interactions and day-to-day discussions to develop the book project. My informal interactions with Elu and Shipli were also useful. As a result of the transition, I was expected to work with another scholar, Professor Jose Puppim de Oliveira, the then Assistant Director and the Editor of the journal, *Public Administration and Development*, who was always helpful, encouraging and prompt to respond to my never-ending requests for help and support. Professor Atsushi Tsunami, the Deputy Director of Science, Technology and Innovation Policy at the National Graduate Institute for Policy Studies (GRIPS) acted as my host researcher and made sure that the entire administrative procedure was smoothly conducted during my stay in Japan.

I would also like to thank the three experts, Professor Christian Seelos, Professor Hilary Silver and Dr Jessica Seddon, who took out time to read the book and write short reviews (advance praise).

Altogether, the book took shape in four institutional environments namely, the UoH, GRIPS, TISS and UNU. There are numerous individuals who supported this work. They took care of all my administrative needs smoothly. At UNU, it was Ms Taeko, Ms Mihoko, Ms Sayo, Ms Makiko and many other friends; at GRIPS it was Ms Mika, Ms Yokoyama and Ms Sawaji; at TISS, it was Sujata Tupe, Unmesh, Manali Patel and Alka Chawan, and at last, at UoH, it was Gupta, Prakash, Suresh, Chandu, Uma, Padma, Raju and Khan who responded positively, sometimes, to my endless requests.

It is needless to state that friends and well-wishers played a key role in shaping up my daily life and contributed to enrich my knowledge and passion. I tried to avoid thanking all of them individually, but in the end, I could not resist myself. I take this opportunity to thank Ashok Dara, Bala Krishna, Bijayani Mishra, Balakrishna, Brahmaiah Choppara, Chaitanya Jawaji, Chendu Kodivaka, Chintala Venkatramana, Harshavardhan Reddy Kummitha, Jacob Kalle, Mochesh, Nagaraju Koppolu, Nagaratna, Nani Babu, Naveen Kolloju, Poonam Agarwal, Prakash Chittoor, Prasanth Kumar Munnangi, Rajasekhara Reddy Yatam and his wife Siri, Rama Krishna Devata, Ramanjaneyalu Dasari, Ravi Kolleti, Santosh Hanumala, Satri Veera Kesalu, Satya Kiran Adapa and his brother Siva Krishna Adapa, Seema Mahapatra, Ujwala, Venkaesh Madepalli, Yasmeen and others. I would also like to thank my grandparents Subbamma Pulicherla and Pera Reddy Pulicherla, my parents Tirupathi Reddy and Padmavathi, my aunts Ravana, Hymavathi, Ankamma, my uncles Srinivasa Reddy, Venka Reddy and Subba Reddy, and my cousins Srikanth, Pavani, Teja, Surya and Chendu for their love and affection.

In the end, I would like to thank several other institutions that provided much needed help. While the Development Bank of Singapore (DBS), India, contributed a part of the research grant to undertake some part of the field research, the Japanese Society for Promotion of Science offered much wider support with a friendly academic and research environment at the United Nations University in Japan. In addition, the social entrepreneurial teams, their employees, communities and the other respondents in the four field sites receive my deepest appreciation.

In the end, I would like to thank the SAGE team including Aditi Chopra, Elina Mazumdar, Supriya Das, Sutapa Ghosh, Saima Ghaffar, Megha Dabral, Shambu Sahu, Sharmila Abraham, Shreya Chakraborti, Savitha Kumar, Tanvi Kawatra, Kitty Mahapatra, Smrithi Sudhakaran, Merin Jose and other team members for their continuous inputs to improve the quality of the book. In fact, their continuous support has not only enriched the quality of the book but their suggestions have inspired me to undertake several rounds of revisions that resulted in fine-tuning the content.

Introduction

*Exclusion is a tragedy and inclusion is a bliss;
everything is human cultivation.*

Recent developments over the concepts of social exclusion and inclusive growth have opened up intensive debates and discussions on the role of various factors in the developmental discourse across the globe. Global experiences show that the tragedy of exclusion is not limited to any particular section of population or a geographical area. This scenario becomes visible as we start identifying and defining social contexts associated with the hierarchies and deprivations in a variety of social contexts. For instance, starting from Europe, the deprived and the downtrodden have been brought under one umbrella to name them as 'socially excluded' which opens scope for defining all segregations and exclusions as a single unit (Silver and Miller 2003). Such demonstration is based on a utopian paradigm that argues for equal participation of every human being in social processes.

In United States, pushing certain sections away from the mainstream society, who are termed as 'outer classes', is a predominant phenomenon.

This proves the magnitude and multiple dimensions of social exclusion (Silver 1994). It does not require any introduction to explain the sorrows of the Africans who are often denied minimum access to basic needs (O'Brein et al. 1997). There are several sections of people who are excluded in the process to advance human existence. For example, the Indian experience of exclusion is stratified on the basis of caste, class and gender (Kummitha 2015). In addition to region-specific exclusions, larger problems such as poverty, employment and exclusion based on gender continue to affect the social functioning. The trauma that exclusion results in is incremental in nature which has the potential to degrade the basic human existence. With these examples, the imperative outcome contextualizes the social realities of exclusion into two categories: (a) some of the exclusions, in certain contexts, have been attributed to the historical formation of societies; while, (b) most of them have roots in the modern developmental discourse.

From global experiences, it is found that the tragedy of exclusion is expanding to every corner of the world (United Nations 2010). As a result, strategies drawn to reduce the drudgery of the poor and the marginalized, including the Millennium Development Goals (MDGs) and the post-2015 Sustainable Development Goals (SDGs) strategy, highlight the need for inclusive and sustainable societies to ensure comfortable life not only for the present population but also for the future generations (Brundtland Commission 1987). However, failure of the State to address needs of a larger section of population in various parts of the globe is the biggest cause for the current social scenario. It becomes more relevant especially among the developing and least developed nations. In addition, the increased population across the globe, especially in the developing countries, should also be held responsible for the aggravation of problems. For example, in the beginning of 20th century, the total population of the globe was a little over 1800 million, whereas by the end of the first decade of the 21st century, it reached to 7,100 million which is about four times larger when compared to the previous century. Unfortunately, major population growth has taken place in the least developed countries due to which people are stuck up in chronic poverty for generations. It is largely due to the failure of the State to promote or utilize the capabilities of its citizens in order to ensure a dignified life. The United Nations (2004) estimated that the population would further reach to 9 billion by the end of the 21st century. This is a sharp five times increase from the earlier century. The drastic increase of population means increase in consumption that results in natural resource exploitation and associated environmental problems including climate change, environmental degradation, etc. (Blowfield 2013). In addition, the problems get manifested when the systems responsible for utilizing human resources and addressing the concerned problems fail to recognize the need for allocation of resources, providing basic amenities and opportunities to excel the capabilities. Though it is not desirable, so far, the developmental trajectory has either ignored such needs or has rather failed to facilitate strategies to promote capabilities of the deprived who are trapped in the chains of exclusion.

Despite the ostensible efforts from the current economic system that drive certain growth in terms of pushing few sections out of the exclusion trap, the disparity between different classes continues to take its worst form. For example, a total of 50 per cent population share just less than 5 per cent of the global income (Bornstein 2004). Taking it to further lower, the system also aggravated natural environment which resulted in new social problems including climate change, environmental degradation, ozone depletion and land degradation (Blowfield 2013). The overall scenario with regard to exclusion and deprivation is contemplated as "... half the population on the planet struggles to survive on less than \$3 a day and half of them live under harsh conditions of extreme material deprivation and food insecurity" (Davis 2002, 9). Moreover, over three billion people around the globe are poor, despite their engagement in full time employment. Apart from their employment and income figures, their socio-politico-economic condition and cultural status are uncannily endangered.

On the other hand, it is believed that the modern technologies, which contribute for human advancement, also play a certain role in the social and environmental collapse. In addition, there are terrible diseases such as swine flu (H1N1) and HIV and man-made disasters such as war and terrorism that offer a stressful effect. The social and natural acts affect the basic survival of certain sections in which the poor and deprived sections fail to negotiate with the so-called trends created by both natural and man-made disasters. So, the human civilization and development goes on to contribute to social stratification that serves as a threat for a healthy society. The classic understanding of the scenario is that there is an uneven distribution of wealth, welfare benefits and infrastructural facilities on the one hand, and on the other, human and environmental disasters that talk about uncertainty of human existence on a larger scenario.

Once again, let us understand the role of the State in dealing with such situation. In spite of severe social disasters, there remains a case where all sections can be equally protected, provided that a strong policy mechanism and social commitment from the State is guaranteed. However, in the current scenario, State policy is largely driven by corporate interests, where the scope for minimizing social segregation is limited. Thus, it multiplies social problems and expands the neoliberal space (Hirway 2012). In this milieu, the role of the State has been reduced to a mere spectator. The unaddressed social problems and consequences result in distress and promote unrest that speak about the failure of the State (Austin et al. 2006; Dees 2001; Guclu, Dees and Anderson 2002; Nicholls 2006c; Peredo and McLean 2006; Thomson, Alvy and Less 2000; Weerawardena and Sullivan Mort 2006). This situation has widened disparities among different sections of the population. As more people experience poverty and deprivation not only in material condition but also as a matter of negligence from a passive State, the situation further reduces to a stage where expectations of the large, yet excluded, sections are ignored. This further pushes the State to ignore the interests of marginal sections due to corporate lobbying for those whom neoliberal economic conditions offer invaluable support. Due to this turmoil, sometimes people may get re-excluded[1] (Kummitha 2008) as they are not in a position to articulate their own problems.

The Emergence of Third Sector and Need for Its Innovative Existence

The third sector, which came into existence in response to address some of these social problems, so far, initiated several activities through dedicated organizations initiated for the purpose. Various activities initiated by these organizations have been made possible due to the changing nature of civil society, especially in terms of generous contributions from various players. In addition to munificent monitory support, both voluntary and intellectual support has been quite supportive for the growth of the sector. Though the initial efforts from the sector have been impressive, due to the adverse social contexts, the space created for inclusion has been overpowered by social realities.

In addition to such dynamism that creates a counterproductive environment, the efficiency of the sector has been compromised. Issues such as lack of professionalism, shortage of skilled employees, nepotism, lack of accountability, transference, top-down approaches, carrying forward the agenda heavily set by donor agencies and compromise on the mission due to pressures from

---

[1] Social re-exclusion is seen as a process whereby the excluded sections, which are in the process of inclusion, are forced to face exclusion again through deliberate or non-deliberate social processes or state policies.

philanthropists have always attracted the sharp attack on the sector (Wallace 2003). This trend has facilitated expectations and planted seeds for its downfall. Once praised for their commitment and social impact, the third sector has been subjected to sharp attacks by the civil society.

There is an increased belief that most of the organizations in third sector have failed to address the global problems. In spite of its growth in terms of the number of non-governmental organizations (NGOs) that came up in the last couple of decades, the sharp increase in the number of people who are trapped in exclusion and deprivation have left no scope for these organizations to serve and address their problems. As a result, in the United States, there has been a 36.2 per cent growth in the non-profit sector in the last few years (National Center for Charitable Statistics 2007), whereas in India, there are about 3.3 million non-profit organizations at present, which is almost one organization to every 400 people (*Indian Express* 2010). In addition, as discussed, the unprofessional practices and conventional methods adopted by the third sector organizations have always been a major concern. Yet, there is no significant evidence to claim that the quality of life of those who have been served by these organization has increased and such transformation is sustained. Due to the growth in the sector, it is evident that these organizations are forced to compete for the limited financial resources available from the shrinking philanthropic institutions. Wallace and Chapman (2003) have elucidated that the competition "leads to the mushrooming of claims that NGOs make about what they can do with relatively small amounts of money" (p. 9). There are growing indicators to prove that quality of assistance is what probably is required, not the quantity. However, there are lack of institutional reforms to improve such quality (Fowler 1999; White and Woestman 1994). It is found that the NGOs spend huge percentage of the donations collected on their administrative costs than on the actual process of benefiting the downtrodden. For example, NGO watchdogs in India state that more than half the money raised by the sector is being misused in order to mostly support high administrative costs to run the organizations and their activities (Bhowmick 2010). Fowler (2000b) believes that NGOs need to relinquish their current static role as intermediaries whose objective is just constrained to provide charity-based services. It is especially relevant in the current scenario of declining aid provision from internationalized system that has so far promoted patronage, dependency, pathological institutional behaviour and financial malpractice (Eade, 1997; Gould and Amaro-Reyes 1983).

In a nutshell, the overall perception about the sector has transformed from a mere saviour of the social order to a burden on the system. For example, a majority of the people believe that the non-profits have failed to address significant social problems (Silverthorne 2008). Further, they have been viewed as inefficient, infective and unresponsive (Dees 2001). Simultaneously, there is a growing demand from stakeholders and donors to explore and adopt strategies to achieve innovative and sustainable solutions which may be embedded within the local cultures (Haugh and Talwar 2010). However, on the other hand the donor-funded initiatives are obliged to work in traditional methods to show quick results and impact. Though time and again these organizations attempt to resist funder attempts to structure the behaviour of the organizations, in most of the cases, they fail to do so due to the rigid systems in place. Ebrahim (2003) opined that there is not much that organizations can do in such scenarios.

Thus, in order to negate with the complex systems in place and address social needs efficiently and viably, organizations need to embrace a professional approach for development (Devine 2003). Such approach may include ability to manage, ability to renovate, effective internal governance, strategic thinking, transparency and accountability, which put together contribute to sustainability discourse that has been overlooked by civic organizations so far (Aldaba et al., 2000). At this juncture, there is a greater need to revamp the third sector by adopting various innovative practices that could assist it in regaining its credibility. Beyond the credibility issues, third sector needs to negotiate ways in which its operations have been initiated. In addition, in order to demonstrate its credibility, there is a larger need to focus on alternative means of capacity building and fund raising and adopting innovative methods in order to achieve rapid, yet sustainable social change. Hence, there is a greater need to adopt advanced methods and understand the need for a sustainable third sector with innovative ways of service, process and product delivery. With this background that emphasised on the current status of the third sector, the next section focuses on the environment which enforced the need for sustainable third sector. It further proposes a larger picture which emphasizes the need for building a sustainable social order.

The Sustainable Third Sector

In the last section, we discussed that the trends such as increased social problems and decreased welfare provision including failure from both state and civil society posed a strong challenge to the existing third sector to explore new ways for unlocking its potential. In addition, since past three decades, especially when the report of the Brundtland Commission—*Our Common futures*—was released, sustainability has been seen as a significant convergence in the successful development debate (Devine 2003). The debate spread to the organizations, initially ranging from corporate and business to third sector. In response to such debate, it is identified that a set of social purpose organizations (SPOs) gained a significant growth and visibility by adopting sustainability as their central mission (Salvado 2011). These organizations have not only aimed to achieve sustainability in society, but have also shown strong commitment for embarking on their own sustainability. Sustainability of organizations, in general, refers to a broader agenda that emphasizes on (a) continuation of organizational existence, (b) continuing its activities and creating impact and (b) generation/mobilization of resource from local sources. In a much detailed explanation, it refers to the enhanced ability of organizations to secure and manage resources sufficiently and innovatively that will optimize effective operation of the organizational mission and value creation (Cannon 2002).

Among all, financial sustainability of the organizations occupies a predominant role. USAID (2008) opines that financial sustainability "is a state in which an institution has a reasonable expectation of covering its costs for the foreseeable future through a combination of donor funding and locally generated income" (p.2). It further states that in the event of donor funding declines, financial sustainability of the organization may be attained through a variety of methods including, but not limited to cost control and income generation etc. It may also be understood as "an evolution towards a balanced amount of funding from governmental subsidies or grants, membership fees and small funding projects" (Sarriot et al. 2004, p. 31). The earned income strategies within the SPOs have become a departure point for strategic transformation of the industry where social organizations undertake business ventures in order to promote the mission of the organization through their entrepreneurial activities.

In other words, organizations work towards achieving their social mission while exploring earned income strategies (Alter 2006; Boschee and McClurg 2003; Drayton 2006; Fowler 2000a; Yunus 2006). This change in the nature of functioning and resource allocation has brought a new approach called social entrepreneurship into practice, and the organizations that deal with the innovative approach have been termed as social enterprises. The approach of social entrepreneurship talks about adoption of innovation and business skills for achieving sustainable social transformation. This approach is expected to stimulate the 'lost' glory of the third sector.

While the adoption of social entrepreneurship within third sector is an impressive move for addressing social problems and fostering alternative social realities, there is also a growing interest among donor-dependent organizations to adopt sustainable initiatives that foster organizational sustainability. However, it is identified that such transitions may result into a massive resistance from both for-profit and non-profit sectors. For example, Tony Wanger has been astonished by the resistance that he came across from both for-profit and non-profit sectors as his hybrid venture in Minneapolis tried to create a business and carry out a social mission by employing people who were economically disadvantaged (Boschee 2006). Hence, social entrepreneurs while employing new ways to unlock the potential of the sector need to manage the resistance they may come across in the process from different stakeholders.

The in-depth understanding of social entrepreneurship as an approach or organizational form reveals that the primary motive for initiating a social venture comes from addressing a significant social problem (Mulgan 2006). The process aims to create value for society through promotion of sustainable solutions to neglected societal problems (Zeyen et al. 2012).

Fowler (2000a) and Borzaga and Defourny (2001) opine that social enterprises move beyond the focus of current institutional logics and aim to transform social settings. The social firms focus to make both social and financial returns on investments, while the mission is not compromised (Letts, Ryan and Grossman 1997). Traditionally, non-profits, which used to undertake activities that impress donors to get grants, have started to employ the current approach towards social value creation. The creation of social value is advanced by the financial value creation principle through mobilizing resources in innovative methods against the predominant grant seeking behaviour. Anheier (2005) denotes that as part of the social entrepreneurship approach, the resources generated may be of three kinds: monetary, in kind and labour. While monitory resources include grants, donations, fee from services or revenues earned by undertaking different activities, resources in kind include donated food or equipment, and labour includes both paid and/or volunteer support. They come in three modes: (a) from public sector including grants and contracts, (b) private giving that includes foundation grants, business or corporate donations as part of their corporate social responsibility (CSR), individual grants and philanthropy and (c) private fees and charges including fees for service, sales, membership dues, etc. The interaction among these three modes of sources may be complex in nature where an increase in one form may result in a decrease in other. For example, philanthropic donors rarely show interest in funding social ventures which have market penetration.

When we talk about sustainable orientation (SO) in social sector, the financial sustainability aspect aims to bring value addition, which is a crucial factor that attracts non-social entrepreneurial organizations to transform their existence towards sustainable value creation. The SO in the current context of social entrepreneurship is related to achieving financial sustainability of social organizations, using market-based mission-centric approaches. The adoption of entrepreneurial principle in third sector environment may not necessarily reduce the gap between entrepreneurship that creates business and social entrepreneurship which advances social value (Barendsen and Gardener 2004). Kathleen Buescher, President and Chief Executive Officer of Provident Counseling Inc., explains the various advantages that come with making money by social organizations:

> The beauty of making a profit, as we've been able to do during the past 15 years is that, you can do a lot with the money, you can do what you want to do. You can do it how you want to do it for as long as you want to do it and you don't have to make anybody happy except your own Board and staff. You don't have to meet anybody else's expectations. That's a very freeing idea, and once you feel it, you don't want to go back to the confines of any other type of funding.

It is not simply about generating finances or achieving self-sustainability; rather, it is about freedom to do things that are well suitable for the mission. This is one of the crucial aspects that social entrepreneurship essentially brings on to the table. If the financial resources are available for any organisation to spend on achieving the mission without relying on other decision-making bodies expect its own board, the working on achieving mission becomes quite interesting. However, sometimes the attempts to balance between financial and social value creation may fail altogether. But it could emerge as a successful departure point for future activities. In fact, the penetration with communities and local environment in the first instance ensures that the aspirations are not compromised. Overall, the SO brings resources on board without compromising on the mission and objectives of the organization. However, in order to bring social change and build sustainable ventures by raising resources locally, social enterprises would need to balance between multiple, yet contradictory, value creation. Such value creation may force social enterprises to employ risks and innovations and contradict with existing systems. It is simplified that the image of social entrepreneur has been projected as risk taker in times to act innovatively and resourcefully (Bornstein 2004; Dees 1998). Adler (2006) denotes that "Whereas money motivates some people, meaning is what inspires most people" (p. 496) and the prominent leadership challenge today is not restricted to motivate them, but to inspire (Harding 2006; Westall and Chalkley 2007).

While it is emphasized that social entrepreneurship as a process promotes fundamental social change (Mair, Robinson and Hockerts 2006; Waddock and Post 1991), it is also conceived that it enables incremental improvements within the efficiency of non-profits (Chell 2007; Dees 2001). There is a strong feeling that the social problems can be better dealt by social ventures than traditional non-profits as the approaches and efficiency levels that the former adopts creates value addition (Dees 2001). Accordingly, the role that the social entrepreneurs play in the global market is significantly increasing. A wide spectrum of investors started showing interest in the field with an optimistic view to get blended value on their investment. Impact investing is now emerging as a strong focal point in social entrepreneurship investment. According to a global impact investment[2] market study, investors started to show keen interest in social entrepreneurship market, as it is 'in its infancy and growing' with an investment tune of up to USD4 billion in 2012 alone (Saltuk, Bouri and Leung 2011).

---

[2] Impact investing is a form of social investment that has seen light in the recent past. This investment is meant to provide financial support to organizations or individuals with the aim of addressing social or environmental problems while adopting market-based solutions (Brandenburg 2010).

Further, it is claimed that the field would play a decisive role in the markets. For example, it is estimated that the impact investment will grow to 1 per cent of global assets under management every year (Monitor Institute 2009).

The approach of market penetration is expected to fill the gap where resources are limited, and in fact it is seen as a classic solution for the financial constraints that the social sector faces (Anderson and Dees 2006). Boschee and McClurg (2003) state that the earned incomes remain unparalleled among other means of incomes. This allows organizations to be self-reliant and focused with clear strategies. A business-like approach promises efficiency, accountability, discipline and creative resources assembly that enable social ventures to achieve their mission. Such a move may pave a way to end the problems in both social and business sectors, such as reduced funding in case of the former and the failure of the latter to address social and environmental problems (Alvord, Brown and Letts 2004; Cho 2006; Nwankwo, Philips and Tracey 2007). The intention to adopt SO is to diversify the funding available for SPOs, reduce their dependency on donors and largely recover the costs incurred to run a programme from stakeholders involved or various other processes that may be developed from time to time (Alter 2006). In a number of cases, cost recovery may include cross-subsidized models where the people who can afford pay the fixed fee while the poor and deprived pay nominal fee or no fee. It leverages those who can afford to pay for the necessary needs of those who cannot. This also means that the organizational focus is not restricted to maximize financial value but to create social value. This maintains balance in society where both the rich and the poor understand prosperity and limitations of the other. For example, Aravind Eye Care System runs its eye care programmes based on the cross-subsidized model, whereas TOMS, a well-known shoe company donates a pair of shoes for children in need against a pair of shoes purchased by a customer.

Though there is a gradual agreement about social enterprises becoming sustainable through exploiting market opportunities, there is no agreement about how to determine an organization as a social enterprise. How much percentage of income should be market-based? While there is no agreement or consensus about such criteria, the social enterprise unit in the United Kingdom (UK), which was established to promote the sector, has stressed that a significant part (usually 50 per cent or more) of the total income must be market-based for an organization to become a social enterprise

(Defourny and Nyssens 2010). This is just a referral which is to explicate the rigor that an organization needs to adopt in order to become a social enterprise based on financial resources exploitation. However, there are other perspectives too for defining social entrepreneurship which we will take up as the discussion moves forward.

Within the SO, there is no agreement upon when the market-based initiatives became benchmark for social organizations to enhance their efficiency. However, there is evidence to claim that non-profit organizations generated incomes in the early 1900s. For example, Fundación Social in Columbia—established in 1911—aimed at generating and applying incomes to foster social change. The research claims that it includes, but is not limited to, producing goods and services to benefit low-income households by establishing viable business (Fowler 2000a). Macro economic context plays crucial role in supporting social enterprises to emerge. For example, there are three contexts where social entrepreneurship could possibly take place: (a) the liberal economy, in which the market mechanism is considered as the best way to share and maintain economy and social justice (e.g., the United States economy); (b) the cooperative economy, in which the State plays an important role in redistributing wealth, and markets are controlled by the regulatory interventions (e.g., most European economies); and (c) the informal economy where neither the State nor the market can create wealth and maintain social justice but instead affiliation to social groups determines the creation and distribution of wealth and justice (a good example is India, but many countries in Latin America and Asia are also an example for this type; Mair 2010).

Though adoption of business-like approach will reduce dependency of non-profits on donor, and philanthropic actors (Alvord, Brown and Letts 2004; Cho 2006; Nwankwo, Philips and Tracey 2007), money- making orientation alone may create tensions. As many non-profits are embarking on new business skills to adopt business-like orientation, the concern rises about the possible mediocre roles that they may end in, in case if money making alone becomes their priority (Collins 2005). In addition, usage of the business language such as 'scaling', 'replication' or 'maximization' have been overemphasized in social entrepreneurship research which may lead to adverse conditions, if adoptive environment is not created for such a transformation (Mueller et al. 2011). Nevertheless, the societies at large are enthralled by the financial commitments of social enterprises and their promise for SO to transform society (Mair, Robinson and Hockerts 2006).

This vague discussion on social entrepreneurship in this introduction part leaves us in a certain uncertainty. There is a need to further understand the concept and analyse its credibility through the existing literature and explore different prevailing schools of thought. The first chapter will deal with further deliberation about the concept of social entrepreneurship followed by a brief understanding about the current study, its objectives and research questions. In addition, a short discussion about the methodology adopted for conducting the research will also be dealt towards the end of the next chapter.

1

Background and Conceptual Overview of Social Entrepreneurship

We learned that social entrepreneurship promises to advance inclusive societies through innovative approaches, practices and institutions. We further discussed that the recent global and financial crisis have enhanced the momentum for the practice of social entrepreneurship as various governments, markets and ecosystem started to support the field as an alternative for the so-called 'developmental dilemma' that the current financial and social order create (Lehner 2011, Zeyen et al. 2012). The promotion and practices of social entrepreneurship altogether blurred boundaries among the State, markets and civil society. Traditionally, the Welfare State is expected to deliver welfare, the market ensures production, accumulation and creation of jobs, and civil society focuses on the articulation of interests and shaping broad societal agenda (Stryjan 2006). However, the social enterprises originate with inspiration from practices of both social and business sectors. The practice of social entrepreneurship broadly encompasses a business model that civic entities adopt while addressing social issues. Under this process, innovative mechanisms, market-based approaches and income generation activities may be listed to name a few strategies that advance the contexts (Lehner 2011).

The term social entrepreneurship was first claimed to be coined in the 1970s (Banks 1972), whereas it started to gain momentum after the 1980s (Dacin, Dacin and Matear 2010; Short, Moss and Lumpkin 2009; Nicholls 2006c). However, until a decade ago, the concept of social entrepreneurship, social enterprises and social entrepreneur were rarely found in the development sector, and in academic and policy discussions. Social entrepreneurs are the people who initiate or undertake the process of social entrepreneurship with the social enterprises they create. Social entrepreneurship in the recent times has become a buzz word and its practices are considered to fall under a broader list of organizations which exist to create social value. Accordingly, it is not clear within the circles of social entrepreneurship what alone constitutes social entrepreneurship. In other words, due to the excessive usage of the word in multiple directions, it is quite unclear what matters for the practice of social entrepreneurship. Despite the lack of direction, the terminology now occupies a significant role in all the three areas (social, environmental and economical) through their innovative attempts to promote social order (Defourny and Nyssens 2008).

Social Entrepreneurship as a Social Phenomenon

Social entrepreneurship is a phenomenon, the central driver of which is focused towards addressing a social problem (Austin et al., 2006). To pin it down further, social entrepreneurs create social value through sustainable solutions for unaddressed social problems in order to stimulate social change (Mair and Marti 2006; Nicholls 2006b; Nicholls and Cho 2006; Tan, Williams and Tan 2005). They foster alternative realities through their passion, commitment, skills, teams and approaches. The alternative realities speak about social inclusion, advanced social positioning and social value creation. The process of social entrepreneurship takes place when some person or a group of persons come together in order to address social problems from where some kind of social value is created (Peredo and McLean 2006). Creation of social value may refer to attaining social justice, altering the bonds that manifest social exclusion and adoption of social innovation that results in social and environmental sustainability which contributes for larger social transformation (Hill, Kothari and Shea 2010). Though the social problems tend to be different in different contexts, the intended outcome of the process is to create social value in one form or the other.

Thus, the process of social entrepreneurship is a result of interactions and the contexts in which they operate (Mair and Marti 2006).

Nicholls (2006c) narrates that the social entrepreneurship discourse follows the demand and supply principle. For him, both the demand and supply result in the need for emergence of such organizations to revolutionize markets, governments and civil society. As a matter of demand, issues pertaining to social exclusion, environmental degradation, income inequalities, unemployment, inefficiency of government and markets to address basic social problems etc. become the major concern, whereas when it comes to supply, improvements in the lifestyle of the people, better education, health and living conditions respecting the voices of the deprived and the excluded in decision making etc. are a few instances (Nicholls 2006b). All such factors influence the socially conscious individuals who have been alarmed by the need for creating such an inclusive social order.

There is disagreement among the scholars about the process social entrepreneurs employ to achieve social transformation; for some scholars, social entrepreneurship refers to the creation of positive social change, regardless of structures or processes employed. Dees (1998) demonstrates that social entrepreneurs are concerned with reconfiguring resources in order to achieve specific social objectives, and their success is measured by the extent to which they achieve 'social transformation' (Alvord, Brown and Letts 2004; Bornstein, 2004; Pearce 2003). In the process, they may develop business ventures in order to substitute a part of their expenses; however, they continue to rely on philanthropy and government subsidy to achieve their mission. For others, social entrepreneurship refers to earned income strategy to achieve a social mission (Boschee 2001; Oster, Massarsky and Beinhacker 2004). Within this dialogue, social enterprises fully depend on the entrepreneurial-approaches that they opt for in order to achieve intended social outcomes. This includes in most of the cases creating institutions that are capable of being both commercially viable and socially goal oriented with a mission-centric approach (Amin, Cameron and Hudson 2002; Leadbeater 1997).

Boschee (2008) opines that from the financial resource point of view, social entrepreneurship could be explained using two institutional forms, which include (a) usage of allied sources:organizations that depend on multiple sources of resources that can be facilitated through a combination of philanthropy, subsidies and earned revenue, and (b) organizations that seek self-sufficiency which can only be achieved through earned revenues

(Boschee 2008). Prominent adoptive measures from different streams that social entrepreneurship practice adopts include (a) strategy of adopting earned income stream in order to balance support from other sources, (b) the adoption of business-like skills, (c) redefining stakeholder participation through more democracy and accountability and (d) creation of multiple-bottom line approach (Hockerts 2006; Lasprogata and Cotten 2003; Peredo and Chrisman 2006; Spear 2006; Wallace 1999). From a variety of distinctions in defining the concept, it is to express that social entrepreneurship has been attributed as an important process of social, economic, political, cultural and environmental wealth creation (Leadbeater 2007; Spear 2006; Steyaert and Hjorth 2006; Shaw and Carter 2007).

Social entrepreneurship gets visualized in both the existing and the new organizations created for the purpose. Hence, in order to promote social entrepreneurship one may not need to initiate a new venture within the coded philosophy to discover, define and exploit opportunities, where existing organisations may also move forward with an innovative way to create or to enhance social wealth (Zahra et al., 2008). Accordingly, the role of social entrepreneurs gets manifested by reducing or eliminating the causes and consequences of market and State failure. While social enterprises are familiar for their dual focus on social and financial value creation, (Austin et al. 2006; Certo and Miller 2008; Nicholls 2010) in the end, successful social enterprises are considered to be those which demonstrate both social and financial returns with a priority towards social focus (Thompson and Doherty 2006). Whereas organizations deal with environmental focus, deliberate up on triple bottom line that encompasses environmental value in addition to social and financial value (Bridges and Wilhelm 2008). The surplus made as part of social enterprises is reinvested in the prime purpose on which organizational mission is focused or it can be used to improve the working environment or living conditions of the stakeholders. In this approach, there is no scope for shareholder emphasis or profit distribution. In order to emphasize this aspect in principle, social enterprises make surplus rather than profit (Fowler 2000a) because the profit element may drift the focus against the prime mission, whereas the surplus principle creates the ownership for all stakeholders involved.

Dees believes that value creation is the basic driver that encourages social entrepreneurship. Value creation consists of blended value where social and financial value coexist. In addition, when it comes to social entrepreneur as an individual, he/she is the one who adopts earned income strategies to demonstrate social objectives and differs with a traditional entrepreneur in two important ways: their earned income strategies are tied directly to their mission and they abide by a blended value creation principle, as discussed (Dees 1998).

In spite of the innovative engagements that the process of social entrepreneurship unveils, there is a grave disagreement over the meaning of the term which leaves the debate inconclusive within academic boundaries and among practitioners (Hill, Kothari and Shea 2010; Mair and Marti 2006; Nicholls 2006c; Nicholls and Cho 2006; Ormiston and Seymour 2011; Pearce and kay 2003). Hence, let us analyze various significant debates on the meaning and definition of social entrepreneurship and draw a working definition that would form the basis for the current study.

Mapping Social Entrepreneurship in the Existing Dialogue

Due to the intense academic and research interest and its adoption in the field, the concept of social entrepreneurship has been defined in a variety of ways. As a result, the meaning and understanding of its practice and implications for social value creation are diversified (Chell 2007; Dees 2001; Nicholls 2006c; Nicholls and Cho 2006; Peredo and McLean 2006; Shaw and Carter 2007; Sullivan Mort, Weerawardena and Carnegie 2003). It is further opined that the term social entrepreneurship is poorly understood and that such confusion and lack of agreement among various stakeholders is a significant short-term barrier for the growth of the sector (Martin and Osberg 2007). Social entrepreneurship, as a research and academic discipline, is scattered across multiple academic research fields. The involvement of researchers from an array of disciplines including management, taking the lead, economics, sociology and policy studies, etc., has resulted in broadening and thus liquidating its scope. Short, Moss and Lumpkin (2009) offer a comprehensive dialogue that lack of a universal definition must be attributed to the emergence and growth of the term from multiple academic fields. The practitioners and their advocates have also failed to determine a structural definition that dictates boundaries for the field. This situation could be attributed to the complex combination of 'social' and 'enterprise' which generally contradict with each other (Salvado 2011). In addition, the range of organizational models and processes it adopts to address broader social problems make it more difficult to arrive at certain decisions. The whole scenario becomes much devastating when attempts are made to define 'social' in social entrepreneurship (Mair and Marti 2006) due to complex structures involved. The other possible reason is attributed to the overemphasis on 'enterprise' orientation in ventures by scholars from management studies and economics, who attempt to monopolize the concept with their contentions to prove that both economy and financial management will tackle all problems in the society as a whole (Salvado 2011). In spite of the differences among scholars and practitioners about drawing a boundary, there is an overall agreement about the social value it creates and benefiting stakeholders rather than certain individuals (Thake and Zadek 1997). This leaves a contention with the existing entrepreneurship practices, the interests of which have always been driven by personal motives or shareholder interests. However, as discussed earlier, entrepreneurial professional ethos such as, creative vision, innovation, leadership and passion, etc., have been the key attributes that are derived from practices of entrepreneurship to achieve social change under this hybrid approach (Thompson, Alvy and Lees 2000).

As discussed so far, due to the overemphasis on the practices of entrepreneurship in social entrepreneurship, defining social entrepreneurship has been largely focused on entrepreneurship theory and the key issues associated with it such as opportunity recognition, opportunity exploitation, wealth creation, investment, etc. (Austin et al., 2006; Dees 2001; Mair and Marti 2006). Though it becomes quite relevant to include such terminology as social ventures are expected to be entrepreneurial, there is a need to make sure that the systems in place to articulate for social aspects take the lead.

There is a need to draw our attention to the adoption of innovations in several aspects starting from idea generation to creating entrepreneurial orientation. For example, Nicholls and Cho (2006) argue that it is not sociality and/or market orientation alone that facilitate social entrepreneurship, but also innovation which makes impossible possible. Thompson (2002) projected that social entrepreneurship is considered to be a vehicle to address the social needs that were for large part of the time undermanaged by all levels of governments. It is a "process involving the innovative use and combination of resources to pursue opportunities to catalyze social change and/or address social needs" (Mair and Marti 2006, 37). When it comes to operations or working of social enterprise, it is defined that social enterprises operate on a worker-centric approach where needs of the workers are taken care of with decentralized planning. Largely, workers are considered as equal stakeholders and the opinion of employees is respected in planning and operations of the venture. Accordingly, cooperatives are also broadly considered as one form of social enterprises (Fedele and Miniaci 2010).

One of the virtues of social entrepreneurship is that it permits different experiments to be conducted for exploring better ways of serving social needs (Dees 1998). According to the international social entrepreneurship non-profit organization Ashoka:

> The job of the social entrepreneur is to recognize when a part of society is not working and to solve the problem by changing the system, spreading solutions, and persuading entire societies to take new leaps. Social entrepreneurs are not content just to give a fish or to teach how to fish. They will not rest until they have revolutionized the fishing industry.[1]

Ashoka's explanation and its involvement in the field experiments spread across the entire spectrum within the social entrepreneurship discourse. For Ashoka, any social value creating activity is considered to be a social enterprise which is folded in its simple explanation of the phenomenon that 'everyone is a change maker'. Such assumption further complicates understanding of the concept. Moreover, Ashoka is well respected in the field for its efforts to nurture and create systems to foster social entrepreneurship. Thus, the stand on which Ashoka opts to define social entrepreneurship is a puzzle for many researchers to tackle.

Dees (2001, 1) refers to social entrepreneurship as, "The passion of a social mission with an image of business like discipline, innovation, and determination." The business-like discipline influences entrepreneurial ideas in social venture and innovation in practice ensures both reach and determination which make sure that the experiments are likely to be successful. Social entrepreneurship creates different

---

[1] www.ashoka.org (accessed 9 December 2015).

organizations/institutions/ventures which bring sustainable social benefits for overall social development in general and for a specific target population in particular (Fowler 2000a). It may comprise of both for-profit and hybrid organizations. Even in case of those organizations which adopt for-profit motive, the surplus created by the venture would be reinvested to tackle the needs of weaker sections for their inclusion. In such cases, it loses its credibility as a for-profit venture and continues to operate as a hybrid organization, that is, social enterprise (Hibbert, Hogg and Quinn 2002). The European Social Enterprise Research Network envisages that:

> [S]ocial enterprises are not-for-profit private organisations providing goods or services directly related to their explicit aim to benefit the communities. They generally rely on a collective dynamics involving various types of stakeholders in their governing bodies, they place a high value of autonomy and bear economic risks related to their activity. (Defourny and Nyssens 2008, 204)

However, due to the different organizational forms it could embark on for attaining larger social interests, the development of such organizations is governed and influenced by specific laws of the land which may dictate its adoption.

The global experience indicates that most social entrepreneurs come with professional, well-educated backgrounds and are trained as bankers, teachers, doctors, social workers, nurses and lawyers etc. (Bornstein 2004). The innovative practices they undertake show that they are not those who frequently shift from one task to another; they would not leave initiatives that they undertake until they make significant changes. In the process, "They combine innovation, resourcefulness and opportunity to discover new ways of doing things" (Wong and Tang 2006/07, 627). Thus, their innovative existence determines to adopt a variety of practices required to achieve the change.

Skoll Foundation, a key player in the social entrepreneurship ecosystem denotes that social entrepreneurs reflect the following characteristics:

1. Ambitious: in order to tackle major social/environmental issues.
2. Mission-driven: aiming at social value generation against creation of wealth. In case a social enterprise is operating in a for-profit mode, wealth creation may be a part in the whole

discourse of social entrepreneurship but it simply does not become the end. Wealth created through the enterprise would be invested in a social mission.

3. Strategic: among the key strategic attempts by social enterprises are (a) opportunities to improve social system, (b) creating solutions for the unsolved social problems and (c) inventing new approaches that create social values.

4. Resourceful: resource management is one of the vital components of a social enterprise. Mobilization of political, financial and human resources are the significant breakthrough processes that the social entrepreneur has to adopt in order to run a venture smoothly.

5. Result-oriented: at the end, social entrepreneurs are driven to produce measurable returns in terms of triple bottom line in socio-economic and environmental aspects. These results transform dreams into realities and promote well-being of those involved.[2]

The novel explanation of social entrepreneurship is that social entrepreneurs see promising opportunities where others only find problems. For example, their overall intention is to see villagers as part of the solution rather than passive beneficiaries of solutions initiated in the process or a cause of the problem (Bornstein 2004). A number of authors have emphasized the hybrid nature of social entrepreneurial activities as incredible (Boschee 1998), whereas others argue that social entrepreneurship can take place equally well on a not-profit or a for-profit basis. In general, creation of social value holds priority in a venture, while economic value creation is necessary, but not simply enough (Mair and Marti 2006). Apart from the social value created, social ventures aim at hampering social realities which minimize social participation of certain sections for whom an alternative is framed in the form of value created. Very often, social needs addressed by social entrepreneurs such as, food, shelter or education, find difficulty in capturing the economic value. Even if customers are willing to pay, yet they are unable to pay a small part of the price for the products or services because of their financial incapability (Seelos and Mair 2007). Thus, the dynamism at both micro and macro levels influences and articulates

---

[2] www.skollfoundation.org (accessed 9 December 2015).

the existence of social entrepreneurship. The social entrepreneur is expected to create such dynamism to adopt him/herself to the local realities and to foster the envisaged change.

Schwab Foundation, which is another well-known key player in the social entrepreneurship ecosystem, emphasizes that social entrepreneurship is

a term that captures a unique approach to economic and social problems, an approach that cuts across sectors and disciplines grounded in certain values and processes that are common to each social entrepreneur, independent of whether his/her area of focus has been education, health, welfare reform, human rights, worker's rights, environment, economic development, agriculture, etc., or whether the organisations they set up are non-profit or for-profit entities.[3]

The foundation further clarifies that this unique approach distinguishes social entrepreneurs from rest of the initiatives or organizational forms meant to create social value. It distinguishes among three varieties of social enterprises while selecting the social entrepreneurs for its awards. They are (a) leveraged non-profit ventures, (b) hybrid non-profit ventures and (c) social business ventures. Leveraged non-profit ventures operate on multiplier effect and continue to depend on outside philanthropic funding, whereas hybrid non-profit ventures adopt some degree of cost recovery methods through the sale of goods and services to different sections of the people in a cross-subsidized model. In addition, they may also depend on other means of resource mobilization including loans, grants and quasi equity. Social business ventures are typically businesses that produce social or ecological products or services for a cross section of people. Though profits are generated through its sales, mission and vision of the organization remains focused towards creation of social value. They aim at reaching a large number of people who are in need through generated income. Accordingly, profits are reinvested into the mission of the organization.

There are plenty of ways in which the concept of social entrepreneurship has been defined, although these definitions most unlikely form a normative basis. However, there are scholars who

---

[3] http://www.schwabfound.org/content/what-social-entrepreneur (accessed 9 December 2015).

developed a different viewpoint where they argued that developing a universally accepted concept for social entrepreneurship is most likely not possible. For example, Choi and Majumdar (2014) articulate that it is neither feasible nor plausible to achieve consensus for reaching a unified conceptual framework that is applicable across the field. Thus, they emphasize that social entrepreneurship be seen as an essentially contested concept. Gallie (1956) argues that there are a number of concepts that exist in academic scholarship which would open up to endless discussions and disputes among scholars to define their concrete existence. It is argued that there are seven reasons that restrict the possibility. These seven reasons include: (a) appraisive character, (b) internal complexity, (c) innumerable describability, (d) openness, (e) contested agreements between the aggressive and defensive scholars, (f) original exemplar and (f) progressive competition (Collier, Hidalgo and Maciuceanu 2006). However, it is also necessary to remember that defining boundary is an essential context for developing theory for any phenomenon (Gartner 2001). Thus, there is a greater need to adopt better ways for understanding the phenomenon. Accordingly, EMES European Research Network came up with a set of four entrepreneurial/economic dimensions and another set of five indicators to determine social dimension in order to draw boundary for social entrepreneurship. The economic dimensions include (a) continuous production or selling services, (b) high degree of autonomy, (c) significant level of economic risk and (d) minimum amount of paid work where volunteers take active role. Whereas social dimensions include (a) an explicit aim to benefit a community, (b) an initiative launched by a group of citizens, (c) a decision-making power not based on capital ownership, (d) a participatory nature, which involves various parties in the activity and (e) a limited profit distribution (Spear 2002). In the end, it is to emphasise that the social dimensions reorient or monitor the presence and evolution of economic factors.

Social enterprises operate in markets where no major player wants to enter. In fact, the failure of markets to enter into such contexts conceptualise the essence of social entrepreneurship. Social enterprises would go for most disturbing and difficult sectors in which, generally, businesses do not care or show interest to involve. In the process, they deal with the untouched potential in markets such as low-income customers and the most excluded in order to create visible social value. For example, SELCO, a Bangalore-based social enterprise, identified the lack of electricity for poor communities as a market gap and started to address the problem by adopting solar technologies. As stated in the Bottom of the Pyramid (BoP) theory proposed by Prahalad (2006), social entrepreneurial actions are driven to fill the market or social gap in the BOP markets where the poor and the deprived live. They adopt social innovations in product/service development and implementation in order to improve the conditions in which they work (Drucker 1999; Leadbeater 1997). It emphasizes that unless such attempts are not accompanied with a certain level of planning and passion, they may be exposed to significant setbacks. While the successful ventures will have the first-mover advantage due to the risks they undertake (Shaw and Carter 2007), the failed attempts offer valuable lessons for those involved and for the next generation social entrepreneurs.

Ideally, it is to understand that social entrepreneurship offers scope to address social problems in an innovative way and upgrade the existing non-profit sector to the next level where sustainability is given importance while not compromising on the mission-centric operations. Hence, it is to consider that any economic value generation as part of the social enterprise is to ensure sustainability which in turn is directed to benefiting society (Ormiston and Seymour 2011). With this background, Dees (1998) opines that social enterprises (a) adopt a mission to sustain and create social value, (b) recognize and relentlessly pursue new opportunities to strengthen the mission, (c) generate continuous innovation, adaption and learning, (d) act boldly without being limited by resources in hand, and (e) exhibit enormous accountability to the constituents served and for outcomes created.

In order to further analyze the concept, there are two well-known schools of thought in the popular literature that narrates the growing divide in the sector: (a) social entrepreneurship school of thought and (b) social innovation school of thought. Dees and Anderson (2006) take the credit in promoting the social entrepreneurship school of thought which is considered to be quite dominative school of practice and research in the US and Europe. This school builds upon a notion that generation of income is a significant factor for social enterprises to achieve social mission. It goes with a belief that social enterprises are linked to generation of income through their market participation (Alter 2002; Haugh and Tarcey 2004; Nicholls 2006a). This is to improve their commercial activities in support of their mission, which may include (a) non-profits undertaking commercial activities, (b) non-profits establishing commercial entities on their own, or (c) non-profits partnering with commercial entities. On the other hand, the social innovation school of thought was developed by Ashoka. This school emphasizes upon social entrepreneurship in Schumpeter entrepreneurial meaning. Accordingly, social entrepreneurs are considered as change agents as they propose new combinations that enlarge social impact; however, such combination may or may not have any relation to generating incomes. This may happen by introducing a new service, a new method of production, a new form of organization or a new market. Hence, the, legitimacy of social entrepreneur may depend upon outcomes and impact rather than questions related to incomes (Alvord, Brown and Letts 2004; Bornstein 2004, Kramer 2005; Cohen 1995; Dees 1998; Leadbeater 1997; Mulgan et al. 2007). However, organizations once proven to be successful on social innovation school can transform themselves towards social entrepreneurial school over a period of time by adopting entrepreneurial approaches.

A typical social enterprise opts for a strategy upon successful completion of selecting its mission and vision based on a problem or opportunity identified, exploited and explored. The working of social enterprise gets strengthened with required resource mobilization and building new partnerships within the ecosystem. Like any other business, ecosystem building is a crucial area of interest in order to promote the social entrepreneurship field. Especially for an industry like social entrepreneurship which has special inputs and skills needed, its growth and effectiveness may be enhanced by creating a strong ecosystem that supports the field (Nelson 1994). Social enterprises have to wisely create new networks and connections in which they may need to invest time and efforts in order to ripen the results (Granovetter 1973; Burt 1992). Partnerships with various stakeholders including donors, volunteers, government, suppliers and fellow social entrepreneurs are crucial for the success of a social venture (Brooks 2009).

For example, Backman and Smith (2000) argue that survival of the non-profit sector depends upon its capacity to foster relationships with key stakeholders such as members, community volunteers, private donors and other organizations in the sector. Such requirement has facilitated the bonding among the organizations involved. It is also found that social enterprises create such networks to build their resource base. Earlier research argues that social enterprises by collaborating with communities achieve a win-win scenario where both communities and social enterprises benefit (Kummitha 2016).

Accordingly, resource-based theory argues that firms network and participate in collaborations in order to advance their sustainable market advantage (Barney 1991). However, when it comes to firms, resource-based theory argues that firms network and participate in collaborations in order to advance their sustainable market advantage (Barney 1991). The networking, in case of social entrepreneurship, is driven by four reasons as indicated by Wei-Skillern et al. (2007). These four reasons include (a) resource scarcity (Boschee and McClurg 2003), (b) growing competition for the scarce resources (Nicholls 2006a), (c) a growing societal appetite for greater efficiency (Chell 2007; Dees 2001; Wallac 2003) and (d) an increasing demand for documented performance (Ebrahim 2010).

We have so far agreed that the societal needs, resource constraints and raising expectations from society enhance the need for existence of social entrepreneurship. Kummitha (2011) clarifies that the social enterprises can be further classified into two categories: (a) area-based social entrepreneurship and (b) issue-based social entrepreneurship. The objective and mission of an area-based social enterprise is to empower people who reside in a geographical arena in which a social enterprise is operational. Barefoot College in Rajasthan, India, is an example for an area-based social enterprise. That means, the area-based social enterprises work on more than a single issue and contribute for holistic development in a chosen geographical location. However, the objective of the other model is to provide services to stakeholders on a single social issue. It means, the enterprise only involves in a single issue or producing a goods or facilitating an innovative attempt to reach out to the poor. It allows the venture to get deeper into the magnitude of the issue. In the case of issue-based social enterprises, their geographical reach would ideally be greater as the scaling is considerably easy. Aravind Eye Care System in India is a unique example to elucidate the issue-based social entrepreneurship.

With this background and analysis, it is to define that social entrepreneurship aims at addressing social problems which are largely neglected or mishandled by the existing systems. The adoptive measures as part of the process include, but are not limited to, the earned income strategies, adopting innovative and inclusive strategies in order to ensure sustainability of the organizations. The current research adopts this definition of social entrepreneurship to guide the research and emphasizes on how various organizational structures influence social settings to attain social impact.

The review so far emphaized that social innovations occupy significant proportion in the practice of social entrepreneurship. However, Mulgan et al. (2007) argue that while social entrepreneurship is certainly one of the institutional forms to adopt or promote social innovations, there are many other contexts where social innovations takes place such as design, technology, public policy, cities and urban development, social movements and community development, etc. It is argued that most of the path-breaking social innovations that address basic human needs come from developing countries where the need for such innovations long exist (Seelos and Mair 2005). On the other hand, Boschee (2007) emphasizes that social innovation and social entrepreneurship are siblings and the intersection of these two powerful instruments result in genuine sustainability and self-sufficiency. When we refer to social innovation, it is significant to discuss about the work done by Murray, Caulier-Grice and Mulgan (2010) who have developed six stages that take ideas in the social innovation space from inception to impact creation.

The six stages of social innovation from 'prompts' to 'systemic change' as illustrated in Figure 1.1 are driven by a systematic process. Though the process classified is contextual, it is not necessary for all social innovations to follow it as presented. This is to

Figure 1.1

The six stages of social innovation

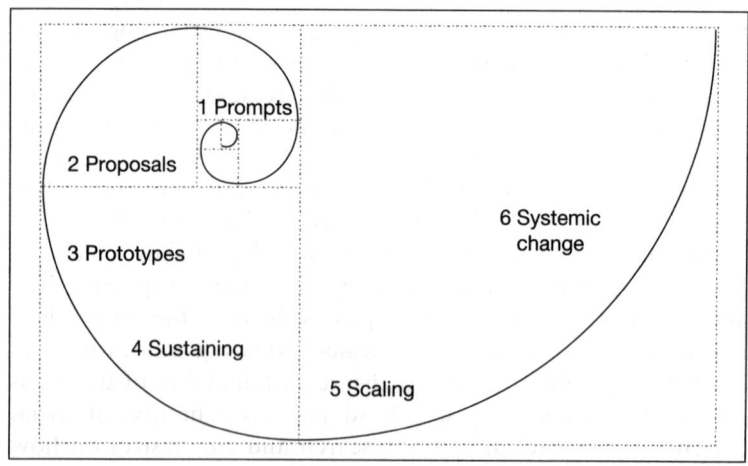

Source: Murray, Caulier-Grice and Mulgan (2010).

emphasize that some social innovations may just shift their gear to reach superior stages by suppressing the immediate stage. For example, some innovations may just jump straight into 'scaling' from 'proposal' or 'prototypes'. However, in a general scenario, social innovations take inspiration from 'prompts', which highlights the need for innovation that includes crisis, poor performance or a new strategy. It is highlighted that this stage understands or analyses in-depth root causes rather than simple symptoms of the problem. Framing the right question at this stage is the key to find the right solution. In the second stage, ideas are generated based on the problem identified and questions raised. The third stage deals with testing the ideas generated in the previous stage. There are several methods available to test these ideas ranging from traditional pilot testing to the randomized controlled trails. This stage may also be accountable for adopting trial and error based experimentation. The successful innovations from this stage moves to the next stage where the sustainability-related issues emerge. A sustaining social innovation is the one which is able to sustain on its own through a variety of means ranging from adopting market-based approaches or charity or grant-based approaches. The next stage typically involves scaling and diffusion of the sustainable social innovations in order to enhance the impact. The final stage of social innovation deals with systematic change. This stage requires various elements, sectors and innovations to come together in order to participate in the movement of value creation. In fact, the process of social entrepreneurship gets boosted by adopting social innovation in different stages.

Thus, social entrepreneurship can be a catalyst to promote social innovation and vice-versa. There are synergies between these two processes. However, how far each utilizes the other depends upon the need and the context. A social entrepreneur who understands the background of the problem sufficiently employs social innovations in the right context. The same happens when a social innovator employs social entrepreneurial approach.

Though social entrepreneurship has been projected to have larger implications for social transformation, it has ample resemblance to the practice of entrepreneurship, a business theory (Meyskens et al., 2010). It is conceived by a number of researchers that social entrepreneurship is an advanced stage of business where business is done with social relevance (Bornstein 2004; Bishop 2006). However, it is also believed that the entrepreneurship element in social entrepreneurship is an adverse situation to understand the complex and significant issues involved in the process (Parkinson and Howorth 2008). At this juncture, it is crucial to understand the basic contribution of entrepreneurship in social transformation and what kind of role it plays in the social entrepreneurship practice.

Business Entrepreneurship and Its Credibility in Social Entrepreneurship

The idea of social enterprise neither comes from capitalism nor from corporate business models. Social enterprise is a term designed to replace the capitalist form of business, that is, pursuit of profits for personal gain. In certain cases, social enterprises generate revenue in excess to costs of production, but the main intention of income generation is not profit making. Its fundamental organizational objective is to benefit collective good (Trexler 2008). However, so far, social entrepreneurship academic research has been driven by scholars from business management and economics who demonstrate that social entrepreneurship constitutes an important subset of entrepreneurship (Drayton 2002; Hill, Kothari and Shea 2010; Mueller et al., 2011). In addition, national governments have started to recognize social enterprises as businesses with social relevance. For example, the United Kingdom, Finland and Ireland have enacted special laws to consider social enterprises as businesses (Defourny and Nyssens 2010). Parkinson and Howorth (2008) argue that overemphasis on entrepreneurship in social entrepreneurship is an inadequate situation in order to understand it thoroughly, whereas Mort, Weerawardena and Carnegie (2003) and Nicholls (2006b) emphasize that there is a cross sectional acceptability to focus on the 'social' in social entrepreneurship which is key for its success. Further, it is argued that social entrepreneurship adds the missing part in traditional entrepreneurship with a mission to change society (Mair, Robinson and Hockerts 2006), which is rooted in community culture (Peredo and Chrisman 2006).

Kirzner advances a step and attributes that entrepreneurship is not a distinct feature of any particular person, instead he emphasizes that it is a human characteristic. That means, as a human character, it can be found in any individual, but only those who use such character to nurture their behaviours become an entrepreneur.

When entrepreneurship is not unique among certain individuals, then it is not relevant to relate it to a particular kind of activity. In a way, it is to argue that such behaviour demonstrates both economic and social action. Such arguments allow to demonstrate that social entrepreneurship falls under the umbrella of entrepreneurship (Koppl 2006; Shockley and Frank 2011). Shockley and Frank (2011) opine that social entrepreneurship theories neglect or ignore the entrepreneurship process which is crucial for the very basic existence of the former. However, Urbano, Toledano and Soriano (2010) argue that social entrepreneurship constitutes a separate field of scholarship, which is a distinct form of entrepreneurship. They argue that it is certain due to the diverse contexts that promote its existence. This is all about replacing the profit maximization with the stakeholder–management approach (Perrini 2006). The different views expressed in support of social entrepreneurship is the result of management and economic theorists on one hand and social scientists on the other who deliberately ignore the impact created by the processes of both 'social' and 'entrepreneurship', respectively.

Starting from its inception and practice, personal profit motive has been the central engine that motivated private enterprises (Schumpeter 1934). In spite of the private motives behind, its role in building social order is quite evident. In the process of marketing their ideas and win over selfish ends, entrepreneurs attribute for social wealth by inventive new technologies, establishing new institutional forms and creating new jobs, which all result in real-time production. For example, the 'invisible hand' debate proposed by Smith (1776) describes that the private value created by enterprises offers value for different social communities by offering goods, generating employment and achieving growth (Auerswald 2009). In other words, entrepreneurship as it stands is useful because of its productivity, which ensures well-being of the human beings through its products, and sustenance of the needy through generated employment. In addition, there are cases to prove that the commercial enterprises do abide by their ethical values, thus restricting profit maximization as their sole objective. For example, The Tata Group in India acts socially responsible by prioritizing the needs of employees and communities. Hence, it is clear that both business and social entrepreneurship are needed in order to mainstream individuals from various social problems from different perspectives. However, social enterprises demonstrate a

strong commitment for social change, unlike their economic counterparts. Social entrepreneurship, like entrepreneurship in the
business sector, cannot be understood in a purely economic sense,
and that needs to be sustained with a social context, particularly
with reference to local environment (Jack and Anderson 2002).

Ironically, many commercial businesses consider themselves to
have social objectives, but social enterprises are distinctive because
their social or environmental purpose is central to what they do.
Rather than maximizing shareholder value, their main aim is to
generate profits to maximize social and environmental impact. The
major difference between social and economic entrepreneurs lies
in their ideologies which guide their choice of mission, means and
ends (Prabhu 1999). Traditional entrepreneurs frequently act in a
socially responsible manner under their ambitious CSR mission;
they donate a part of surplus to the non-profit organizations that
are already established to cater the needs of deprived. Though CSR
is a business strategy and a legal obligation in certain territories,
it is found that a variety of scholars refer CSR initiatives of for-
profits to social entrepreneurship (Austin 2000; Boschee 1995).
There is a risk that such attribution may dilute the actual existence
and contribution of social enterprise. Moreover, the philanthropic
activities or initiatives taken up as part of the CSR do not have any
direct link with the organizational primary mission. On the contrary, social entrepreneurs are mission-driven and are well aware
about what they intend to do for society through their entrepreneurial activity and mission-driven approach. While the efforts of
the entrepreneurs in business can be measured by financial returns,
the social value context enforces social enterprises to achieve social
returns. For example, more profits to the owners or shareholders
indicate greater success of an entrepreneur as a business leader,
whereas unless the living conditions of the selected stakeholders
are not improved, the social entrepreneurs are considered as not
successful.

While entrepreneurs equilibrate supply and demand in an
economy (Cantillon 1755/1964), social entrepreneurs equilibrate
supply and demand in social economy (Nicholls 2006c). Commercial
entrepreneurs differ with their social counterparts in relatively four
basic contexts including people, context in which an enterprise is
located, their deals and opportunity exploitation. While entrepreneurs aim at profitable markets, social enterprises aim at covering BoP markets alone or both BoP and high-end markets with

cross subsidized models. As the target population differs in both the cases, their target geographical contexts also differ. In addition, the deals and opportunity exploitation in social context moves in normative structures, whereas in case of entrepreneurial orientation it is driven by pure market dynamism. As a whole, social entrepreneurs usually consider growth on a different scale from commercial entrepreneurs (Austin, Stevenson and Wei-Skillern 2003). In addition, several authors believe that social entrepreneurship is distinguished from entrepreneurship by the increased interaction with all stakeholders and its accountability levels to a larger society involved in business, its impact and governance (Haugh 2007; Spear 2006; Thompson and Doherty 2006).

The core of enterprises is to operate in a profitable manner in terms of maximizing private gains, whereas a social entrepreneur strives to create social value through their innovative strategies. For example, let us take a major social issue—lack of sanitation and sewage. Now, let us see how these two types of entrepreneurs behave to address the problem. An entrepreneur views what is the market that would pay for solution? What is the highest amount he can charge for it? How low can his production and running costs be? On the other hand, a social entrepreneur sees: How can he solve the issue in a sustainable way? Who are the neediest people he can employ? How can he empower individuals in the given area and educate them about the need for sanitation? How can he recycle the waste? How can he achieve maximum social impact? (Austin et al. 2006). The behaviour which is constructed and restricted by organizational mission decides the activities and the orientation of enterprises. For example, once David Bornstein asked a leading Ashoka fellow why he did what he did. In response, Fabio Rosso who developed an innovative system for delivering electricity to people in rural Brazil said, 'I am trying to build a little part of the world in which I would like to live' (Bornstein 2004; Kummitha and Majumdar 2015). His intention to create a fulfilled world is to guarantee social integrity and social inclusion.

As discussed, social entrepreneurs provide services to the disadvantaged communities, whose development and inclusion has been bypassed by existing institutions. Numerous risks involved in such markets make it difficult for private enterprises to enter. They see it as a risky proposition. Though social entrepreneurs have limited experience of the markets during the initial days and find it difficult to build the ventures due to the limited financial and human resources, their mission to create social value inspires their action. However, regardless of the sector that they are involved in, business or social, one thing strikes as significant across entrepreneurs—the passion. When you ask entrepreneurs how they did what they did, you may not get immediate logical justification as their intuition and vision to see things are different. Schumpeter (1934/2002, 85) denotes about this intuitive behaviour:

> The success of everything depends upon the intuition and the capacity of seeing things in a way which afterwards proves to be true, even though it cannot be established at the movement, and of grasping the essential fact, discarding the unessential, even though one can give no account of the principle by which it is done.

The other notable difference between entrepreneurship and social entrepreneurship lies in the fact which Schumpeter (1934/2002) believes that an entrepreneur's role has nothing to do with running an organization. The role of an entrepreneur only occurs during the "very beginning of the organizational lifecycle of a business. Once the business is operational, the entrepreneur ceases to be an entrepreneur and at that point he/she becomes a manager, using his or her instrumental rationality to run the business". Further, Schumpeter explains, "Everyone is an entrepreneur only when he actually carries out new combinations and loses that character as soon as he has built up his business, when he settles down to running it as other people run their businesses" (Schumpeter 1934/2002, 78). In other words, the entrepreneur seizes entrepreneurial opportunity to 'carry out new combinations', while the manager takes over once the opportunity has been institutionalized. In social enterprises, especially when they are at nascent stage, a social entrepreneur simultaneously acts as a manager due to the lack of middle-level managers in the sector (Thomas and Kummitha 2013). Further, research by Christopoulos and Vogl (2015) articulates that social entrepreneurs typically undertake managerial roles while running the organization. This is to say that social entrepreneurship is a continuous process of building organizations by employing innovation and entrepreneurial methods throughout the process. However, effectuation theory raises a question whether any entrepreneur seizes his entrepreneurial quality despite the business is built, as he/she continues to innovate and the process of entrepreneurship evolves over a period of time with the basis of trial and error (Sarasvathy 2008).

Recent trends employed in social entrepreneurship also demonstrate that there is a high possibility that the practice of social entrepreneurship may also lead to negative externalities. For example, it is evident as part of the women entrepreneurship encouraged by micro credit that the borrowers are unable to cope up with the burden of debts as a result of which they experience destruction in the social and community ties. In addition, it is believed that social entrepreneurship bears the risk of commodifying social problems leading to privatization of all services where social enterprises, instead of the State deal with the service delivery (Curtis 2008). This may reduce the role of the State from welfare or socialist state to a neoliberal state where social entrepreneurship could widen the economic sphere and thus expedite the neoliberal agenda.

It is understood that when social and commercial entrepreneurs fundamentally differ in their mission and objectives, it may be meaningless to argue that at certain point of time, all entrepreneurship will emerge as social. Even if we consider the business carried out by social enterprises as part of cross subsidized methods, its objective is to create superior social value for its clients (Dees 2001; Leadbeater 2007; Nicholls 2007; Townsend and Hart 2008; Weerawardena and Sullivan Mort 2006). A number of scholars argue that the distinction between economic and social value may generate a rift between these two sectors (Santos 2009). So, we should get away with this distinction and rather understand the economic and social wealth generated by these two models as unique since both kinds of wealth creation may result in social well-being within their own limits (Zahra et al., 2008).

Social entrepreneurship, as a concept, stands in a critical juncture where it continues to gain recognition despite the fact that its meanings, intentions and definition are unclear. In order to foster the field further, Center for the Advancement of Social Entrepreneurship (CASE) at Duke University argues that proponents need to build a strong community of practice and knowledge and strengthen the ecosystem that helps practitioners. The concept continues to gain recognition, even though it is not well understood. If it is to have lasting, positive social impact, proponents will have to be strategic in building a strong community of practice and knowledge, and in strengthening the ecosystem that supports practitioners. Though there is a growing interest in the subject and empirical contributions to academic inquiry, it is found that the depth of social impact created by the sector is largely not measured (Austin et al., 2006).

It is demonstrated that the measuring impact is very important which not many organizations carry out in systematic and scientific ways (Floyd 2014). Further, such impact measurement with a research strategy offers critical understanding of the field. A variety of methods have been so far used to measure the impact created by social ventures such as social return on investment (SROI),[4] local multiplier 3 (LM 3), Gamma Model, three Es framework (economy, efficiency and effectiveness), which is based on input, output and outcome model and social impact assessment etc. (Irena et al. 2016). The effort of these methods focus on the outputs and outcomes rather than the processes and approaches adopted to achieve them (Ormiston and Seymour 2011). These approaches have so far dominated the field as it has been important to showcase impact achieved to the impact investors. The quantitative measurable frameworks are key to demonstrate the impact and capable social value being generated by ventures in order to impress the investors, who are primarily interested in seeing the projected achievements in numbers. However, in order to understand the social transformation, it would be ideal to adopt qualitative methods.

So far we have discussed the different meanings, processes and differences in the entrepreneurial processes. The discussion promises that social entrepreneurship is set to play a crucial role in transforming societies. Thus, it is quite imperative to understand ground realities that fuel the practices of social enterprises. In addition, there is a need to draw a framework from such understanding that dictates the functioning of social enterprises. It is relevant, especially in India, as it has seen plenty of innovations and social enterprises grounded in order to address the huge population who live in deprivation and exclusion. Ashoka also shows its interest in India by recognizing a majority of its fellows from there. The social exclusion and deprivation on the one hand and social innovations used for promoting the participation of the deprived and excluded in the mainstream by many of the social enterprises on the other is a challenging and yet interesting process. It becomes

---

[4] SROI facilitates a systematic approach to incorporate social, environmental, economic and other forms of value creation into decision making of the ventures. It offers a numeric understanding and impact of a project or activity initiated by a social business. While measuring the impact or return on investment, it takes all possible domains into consideration where social entrepreneurial value creation is plausible. For more details about SROI, please refer to Millar and Hall (2012).

quite important to document such realities and draw the areas from where social enterprises gain their strength. Hence, this study attempts to understand the processes and practices involved in attaining social transformation by selected social enterprises in India. The study aims to contribute to the existing literature on social entrepreneurship in terms of analyzing the transformation created by social enterprises. Based on the review of relevant literature, the study aims to achieve the following objectives: (a) to understand the social entrepreneurship landscape in India, (b) to analyse social transformation achieved by selected social entrepreneurs, (c) to understand community participation in the process and to draw common understanding for strengthening the field and (d) to draw a social entrepreneurial framework which can help us to understand its practice. In order to achieve these objectives, the book addresses the following research questions: (a) what is the social entrepreneurship ecosystem in India and how is it supportive to the growth of the sector? (b) what framework do social enterprises adopt for achieving their mission? (c) how do we understand the micro level processes involved in social value creation by social enterprises? and (d) what do we learn from the successful social enterprises? The research adopts an in-depth case study approach for addressing these research questions. A detailed discussion about the methodology adopted and processes followed as part of the data collection follows.

Research Methodology

Based on the insights derived from the literature, it is decided to select four social enterprises in India to understand the ways in which complex social problems are addressed. As part of the sample selection, social enterprises that have been started not earlier than 15 years are considered. Sufficient emphasis has been given to consider only such social enterprises which have shown strong commitment to become sustainable on their own in near future. It is to understand that all the ventures must have already initiated or are in the process of initiating mission-centric business ventures to support their social value creation principle. In addition, diversity in region and sector where social enterprises are located is given due consideration. That means, all four social enterprises selected for this research come from diversified regional backgrounds in India. The research adopts qualitative case study methods as the research attempts to build theory rather than testing the existing theory. Thus, the qualitative research results in comprehensive descriptions as well as explanations of processes and allows preserving the chronological flow, assessing contexts and delivering rich explanations (Miles et al. 2013). The research is further enriched by several approaches within the broader qualitative methodology context, which includes case study analysis, narratives and discourse analysis (Hammersley 1992).

In addition to qualitative interviews with various respondents within social enterprises and communities, group discussions were carried out among the communities in order to deliberate their views and participation in the social entrepreneurial process. For qualitative interviews, an unstructured interview pattern was adopted. All interviews were held at work places in the case of employees of social enterprise, and in residence in case of community members. During the interview with each respondent, a detailed note was prepared. All the interviews were recorded and then noted in the field notebook. In this study, cases were selected based on the working definition proposed in the review of the literature. The study, while addressing the objectives and research questions as discussed, built upon focusing to (a) study the alternative realities the cases have fostered, (b) understand the efforts of social enterprises to enhance the financial and innovative capabilities of the organizations and (c) analyze the strategies adopted by the selected cases to attain their vision.

Case Selection

Before selecting the cases for this research, a sector-specific search for social enterprises was carried out on the Google search engine. In addition, the researcher also carried out a thorough review of the literature on social entrepreneurship landscape in India. India, as it is a large country with a variety of geographical, social and cultural differences, the cases were selected with proper representation from different geographical locations. The main intention was to understand the process of problem solving from different geographical and cultural contexts. Accordingly, it was decided to select four cases, each representing the north, south, east and the west regions of India. As discussed in the review of literature, proper care was taken to represent both area- and issue-based social enterprises within the sample selection. Accordingly, two cases each represented both the categories. The cases were selected using purposeful sampling as the unique case selection offer maximum variation and ample evidence to contextualize experience from varied backgrounds. While selecting the cases using purposeful sampling, the research gained from the cases selected as they offered 'rich information' (Patton 1990). Scholars such as Armato and Caren (2002), and Dul and Hak (2008) opined that in qualitative case selection, the heterogeneity of cases offer effective context for the phenomenon under scrutiny. Based on such principle, Barefoot College in Rajasthan and Gram Vikas in Orissa were selected as area-based social enterprises, while Goonj from Delhi and Enable India from Bangalore were selected as issue-based social enterprises. All selected cases are well-recognized in the field in the global context. Thus, it is to understand that all cases are successfully operational in terms of the social impact generation. The major condition taken into consideration while selecting the cases included (a) success of organization, (b) transformation of societies in which they exist, (c) presence of a strong leader, (d) existence of the organization for at least 15 years, (e) level of their cooperation and willingness to participate in this research and (f) accessibility to their location.

Research Instrument and Data Collection

Social entrepreneurs and their organizations were contacted through the networks of the researcher. The researcher was accompanied by an employee of each organization while approaching the other employees. Other community-based respondents were approached with the help of key informants. Due to the variety of respondents involved in the research, a total of four sets of unstructured questionnaires were used for different stakeholders including (a) community members, (b) employees of the organizations, (c) heads of various sections that are referred to as second-level social entrepreneurs in this research and (d) heads of the organizations or social entrepreneurs. Respondents from various backgrounds and expertise provided sufficient data for triangulation (Feagin, Orum and Shoberg 1991). Triangulation offered significant scope to understand multiple perspectives from both inside and outside the organizational structures. A total of 208 personal in-depth interviews were collected from four social enterprises. In addition, eight group discussions with community members and employees of the social enterprises added value to understanding the local contexts.

Field Research

Before collecting the data for this research, a preliminary survey was carried out in Barefoot College in Rajasthan. Gaps in the questionnaire were filled from preliminary study and strategies needed to be adopted for data collection were identified. The social entrepreneurs were contacted by email in which the background information about the study was communicated and the support of the social enterprises was solicited to facilitate an appropriate environment to conduct the study. Initially, three social enterprises responded positively, whereas one organization did not show up. However, the researcher used his extended networks to get access to the fourth social enterprise and successfully convinced the social entrepreneur. Once the permission was sought from all the four social enterprises, the researcher approached the key persons assigned for the purpose by social entrepreneur in each field area. The next step of study involved undertaking extensive field work in the four field sites. All the interviewees were aware about the research and its implications. The key informants took active role in the field research. The researcher believed that taking help from informants would be highly useful as they come up with better knowledge about local areas and were capable of understanding the settings better for reflection (Eisenhardt 2007). Key informants came from the organizations concerned in case of issue-based social enterprises and in the case of area-based social enterprises, the researcher employed villagers as key informants. The language used for the interviews and interaction was English, and Hindi in the case of three organizations such as Barefoot College, Goonj and Gram Vikas, whereas for Enable India, English was instrumented.

Data Collection

Data collection was carried out in a period of four years in different phases. For Barefoot College, the data was collected during April—November, 2009, whereas in case of Enable India it was from February to April, 2012; for Goonj from May to August, 2012 and for Gram Vikas from July to September, 2013. As discussed earlier, the researcher visited and interviewed the founder members, various sections of employees and communities. Questions to the heads of social enterprises were largely related to the decisions to create their social enterprise or decisions to transform a conventional organization into a social enterprise. In addition, information was sought to understand how resources are managed and the ways in which communities were educated to join the initiative. On a broader context, the questions also aimed to understand how the social enterprises have been transformed from small grassroots level institutions to well-known social enterprises that benefited the lives of several thousands. Questions to the members of the community included, but were not limited to, how their lives have improved, how they saw the social enterprise or the social entrepreneur and how they engaged in activities initiated by the social enterprise. Further, employees of the organizations were also questioned about the working of the organization, various innovations employed from time to time, accountability, transparency and how their lives have improved after being employed by the social enterprises. The average interview lasted for an hour with the shortest one taking about 40 minutes and the longest one for about 1 hour 30 minutes. All semi-structured interviews and group discussions were initially tape-recorded and later transcribed. The data was then analyzed and the content was used to describe the social contexts and the impact created by the selected social enterprises.

Data Analysis

The current research represents an embedded analysis which highlights a specific aspect of the case. While analyzing the data, the researcher first adopted within-case analysis where codes in each case were identified and later extended to cross-case analysis where common themes were located that transcended the cases (Yin 2003). Initially, lean coding was developed with a few codes and then expanded based on the author's re-review of the data (Creswell 2007). Several codes, developed over the period of initial analysis, were later reduced and combined with each other based on their compatibility. The researcher did not show keen interest in counting the number of codes as it was assumed that unless the codes contributed to addressing research questions, they did not make any difference. In addition, counting the code frequency could lead to unequal preference to some of them due to their larger representation (Miles et al. 2013). The research further avoided to adopt prefigured coding based on the literature as it could limit the research to the codes predetermined (Crabtree and Miller, 1992).

After the codes were classified, they were converted into categories or themes. Then, the data was further explored from multiple perspectives to support each category (Stake 1995). Some data was discarded which did not pertain to the research questions of this study (Wolcott 1994). The analysis under each theme was interpreted beyond the data based on interviews collected. The interpretations included variable references to the data collected, hunches, lessons learned and observations made in the field (Lincoln and Guba 1985, Hammersley 1992). The data was analyzed against the research questions framed earlier.

This chapter has broadly discussed about three major contexts: (a) theoretical understanding of social entrepreneurship, (b) background and objectives set for the study and (c) methodology including procedure followed for data collection and analysis. The chapter also made certain focus on the need for ecosystem building in the context of social entrepreneurship. Accordingly, the next chapter discusses in detail about the social entrepreneurship landscape in India that includes the existing ecosystem which supports growth of social entrepreneurship practice in India.

2

Social Entrepreneurship Landscape in India

We have traversed a path that few have dared to. We are continuing on the path that still fewer have courage to follow. We must pursue a path that even fewer can dream to pursue.

—Verghese Kurien[1]

The previous chapter discussed about the theoretical and normative issues related to the concept of social entrepreneurship. This chapter aims to understand landscape of the sector in addition to analyzing how various perspectives in the given paradigm support growth of the sector in the Indian context. When it comes to practice, it is evident that the field of social entrepreneurship needs a supportive political, economic, social and institutional environment in order to excel (Poon 2011). Accordingly, the chapter focuses broadly on the roles various actors play in ecosystem building to promote social entrepreneurship.

Third sector in India represents a strong and vibrant civil society (Baviskar 2001). A significant proportion of poor and excluded in the country provide ample opportunities for social enterprises to thrive. India has a spectacular history of successful social entrepreneurs. Though their presence dates back to a few centuries, the post-independent period has proffered a friendly environment for their growth. The growth of the sector has always been tempted by a

[1] Dr Verghese Kurien was a well-known social entrepreneur in post-independent India who transformed the milk industry and was often known as the 'Father of Milk Revolution in India'.

strong civic participation to address local problems. In fact, several grass-root innovations and successful interventions emerged due to the failure of existing institutions to address the concerns of the poor and excluded. Initial efforts from a socialist-turned-neoliberal State and the strong presence of third sector have been in vain as the exclusion space dominated the social order (Kummitha 2015). This resulted in a new class of people joining the pool of exclusion to extend the trauma, which is a direct result of the neoliberal developmental trends adopted by the State and market mechanism (Jazairy, Alamgir and Panuccio 1992; Rajasekhar and Satpathy 2007). In fact, the State and its institutions responsible for addressing the social problems themselves emerged as social problems on their own. For example, Pritchett argues that public sector in India is one of the world's top 10 biggest problems besides AIDS and climate change. He further emphasizes that India has been credited with the most awful record of serving the poor (*The Economist* 2008). Frank (2010) believes that many challenging social problems including daunting social issues such as poverty and many other problems associated with it can be addressed by creating enterprises, industry and promotion of various activities that bring more jobs. Accordingly, one of the reasons that necessitates the existence of social enterprises is to recruit, train and employ people from excluded sections whose lives often get included in the mainstream with their efforts. For example, the Work Integration Social Enterprises (WISE) aim to facilitate the excluded communities to get into mainstream by integrating them in the job markets (Borzaga and Loss 2002; Davister, Defourny and Gregoire 2004). Their participation in market activities gets enhanced by their employment provision and at the same time they become a part of the service or product delivery that enlarges the scope for larger social inclusion. Such interventions not only enhance their employment and market participation but also create an environment where they become a part of product/service delivery processes in social enterprises. While doing so, they take larger pride in promotion of inclusive societies.

In India, the continual withdrawal of State due to its neoliberal negotiations and the subsequent increased role of corporate and third sector to serve markets and excluded sections, respectively, have been on rise since the 1980s. However, State in its socialist form, especially during the 1950–80s, initiated several programmes to promote participation of people in development activities. For example, the creation of Central Social Welfare Board in 1953 for the purpose of promoting people's participation in development through local voluntary agencies was a critical step for enhancing the participation of third sector in developmental activities. Later, the National Community Development Program and National Extension Services widened the role of NGOs (ADB 2012). The third sector gained further attention in the seventh five year plan,[2] which formally acknowledged the importance of popular participation of the third sector in State-run programmes that aimed at poverty reduction and addressing social problems. This attracted the NGOs to extend their reach and be active partners in the developmental discourse. The active liberal penetration of the State with markets from the 1990s resulted in mounting criticism from pressure groups. Such stand of the State further widened the scope for NGOs to experiment on different social problems. Accordingly, by the next decade, NGOs appear to be closer to people in need and have promised to fill the gap and be accountable (Das 2001).

In addition, the continuous exclusion space has opened new avenues for social sector to experiment and contribute to the growth of excluded sections. In fact, the exclusion space occupied in the current social context in India is much larger than the population of Europe and North America put together. For example, according to CIA World Factbook, 54 per cent of the population in India live under the poverty line of $1.25 a day as of 2005 which is equal to 650 million people (Garia 2011). India is the 10th largest economy in terms of GDP; however, it is placed in the 129th position when it comes to per capita income. Though 53 per cent of its population depend on agriculture, its share in GDP is limited to 17.5 per cent in 2011–12, which was reduced from its early figures 17.8 per cent in 2010–11 and 18.2 per cent in 2009–10.[3] Agriculture, being a predominant source of livelihood for more than half of the population, receives significantly low attention from the State policy. A

---

[2] Government of India, starting from 1951, introduced the Five Year Plans which envisage national planning and the developmental issues requiring attention for a period of five years with proper budget allocations. Currently the 12th plan is in operation (Kummitha 2015).

[3] http://data.worldbank.org/indicator/NV.AGR.TOTL.ZS (accessed 4 December 2015).

plethora of social problems in India restrict participation of significant number of population in civic activities, leaving their voices unheard. In fact, there are several sections of people who barely represent planning and execution of developmental interventions. This has resulted in growing dissatisfaction within the civil society and pressure groups which later initiated various crisis management activities. For example, it is argued that a strong civil society fills the gap by offering innovative solutions and entrepreneurial market orientation for the unaddressed social problems. This opened space for social entrepreneurship to undertake level playing role. In India, sectors such as agriculture, education, energy, financial services, health care, housing, sanitation, etc., have been attracted by the growth of social entrepreneurship. Accordingly, a growing body of social entrepreneurs have started to appear in these areas which have the potential for developing sustainable business models (ADB 2012). The target potential for growth of the sector is located in providing services or products for low-margin, high-volume products to the 450–600 million people who are stuck up in the exclusion trap.

This trend has opened up optimum space for the third sector to experiment, innovate and dictate fate of the large proportion of the excluded while addressing its own SO.[4] It has resulted in the emergence and steady growth of the social enterprise sector. The innovative practices adopted from time to time helped the sector to grow with creating and nurturing a variety of resources to strengthen their initiatives. For example, it is argued that during 1999–2000 alone, 80 per cent of the total funds raised by social enterprises came from local activities, fees, charges for services and community contribution, whereas the support from government and foreign agencies was restricted to 13 per cent and 7 per cent, respectively (Srivastava and Tandon 2002). There is a growing evidence to prove that the presence of social entrepreneurship is fast scaling to new areas, leading to robust social innovations and incremental improvements in the human evaluation. However, it is to state that growth of social entrepreneurship sector is not promised in isolation. The ecosystem that supports, nurtures and promotes growth of social entrepreneurship in the country is fast growing.

---

[4] In the late 1980s and early 1990s, there had been a strong debate for attaining sustainable development in view of the report 'Our Common Future' released by the Brundtland Commission.

Such ecosystem comprises of state, markets, global civil society and academia. Recently, it has been found that the growth of ecosystem has not only provided sufficient resources for social entrepreneurship industry within the country but has also spread the innovations to other parts of the globe. In addition, social enterprises in the Global South have been benefiting from the strong and active ecosystem in India.

Klaus, who heads Schwab Foundation for social entrepreneurship that supports social entrepreneurs through various resources at the global level, believes that:

> India has some of the most advanced and innovative social entrepreneurs. We believe and already see that many of the models developed in India, for instance rainwater harvesting for schools pioneered by Barefoot College, are exported around the world. India is therefore a key country to look for leading social entrepreneurs. (Krishnan 2006, 2)

Clinton (2010) highlights four reasons for the strong presence of social enterprises in India, which include (a) the presence of long existing non-profit organizations, (b) significant portion of social problems and allied opportunities available due to the large portion of people living in the country under extreme poverty and deprivation, (c) the tight family and community ties existing in India which offer an array of resources to take up social activities and (d) certain ethos that are prevalent among Indians including confidence, perseverance and *jugaad,* which is an Indian way of getting things done despite lack of supportive environment. India has been the testing ground for innovative social experiments by various agencies including academic pioneers such as MIT's Poverty Action Lab or the Social Enterprise think tank–Ashoka.

The first notable social entrepreneur after independence in India was identified as Vinobha Bhave, followed by Kuriyan of Amul cooperate, who brought significant transformation in the societies in which they institutionalized their activities, whereas first known recognition for social entrepreneurship in India came from Ashoka which selected its first fellow from India in 1982. Ashoka demonstrated the significance of its connection with India by proclaiming that:

India is home to Ashoka's first fellow, elected in 1982. For the past 25 years, India has served as a testing ground for most of Ashoka's international Fellowship building programmes and other key initiatives. Today, there are over 400 fellows working throughout India making significant contributions to a wide range of field, from appropriate technology to gender equity, from health care delivery system to income generation.[5]

By involving in India, the experience that Ashoka gained is also quite significant, which helped it to demonstrate its global presence and articulate its capacity.

In general, the number of people showing interest to take active part in socially relevant activities across the globe has sharply risen in the recent past. For example, a recent study conducted by GEM[6] (2009, 9) in 49 countries reveals that "the percentage of the working-age adult population that is explicit about its involvement in social activities (total social entrepreneurial activity) varies considerably around the world, from 0.2% in Malaysia to 7.6% in Argentina, with an average of 2.8%." In India, the scenario appears to be further encouraging. Though there is no constructive data available about the participation of people in social activities, the presence of a huge number of non-profit organizations in India and the people associated with these organizations speak about the larger social interest in action.

Srivastava and Tandon (2002) believe that there are about 20 million people working in the non-profit sector in India as paid workers or on voluntary basis. Out of them, a total of 26.5 per cent work in religion-based entities, while rest of them work in a secular environment. The growth of the third sector in a typical NGO mode has been critically attributed to the availability of funds from aid budgets, philanthropy and charity-based initiatives. Due to the easy flow of financial resources into the sector, the poor accountability of the organizations is often criticized. Accordingly, Fowler (2000b) believes that the greater challenge for non-government developmental organizations is related to the transformation

---

[5] https://www.ashoka.org/country/india (accessed 4 December 2015).

[6] GEM or Global Entrepreneurship Monitor conducts world's foremost study on entrepreneurship every year and releases the findings in the form of a global report. GEM is a joint project between Babson College, USA, and London Business School, UK, which was initiated in 1999. The aim of the study is to consider why some countries advance in entrepreneurship while others lag behind.

of its own industry due to various non-professional developmental activities it has embarked on.
Especially, the growth of the social entrepreneurship sector is attributed to the active youth participation. However, the field in India faces a variety of constraints. A study undertaken by GIZ[7] (2012) reveals that there is

> a lack of an investment pipeline for investors; limited investment readiness of enterprises due basic management skills gaps; a lack of seed funding for start-ups; a lack of local capital including debt; high transaction costs for investors to identify and undertake investment due diligence on enterprises, particularly outside the metros; a low scalability of enterprises due to finance, human resource shortages and enabling environment constraints; and defining impact and performance of investments in enterprises. (p. 9)

The constraints, as specified in GIZ study, come from all levels; however, especially the growth is limited due to financial matters which form a basis for other constraints to emerge. For example, the financial constraints disable social enterprises to recruit skilful employees. In several cases, even if the social enterprises succeed to recruit, they fail to retain them for longer periods. The skilful employees consider their involvement in the social enterprises sector as a transition period to move to better places. Intellecap, a leading social enterprise think tank points out that the top three challenges that social enterprise industry in India faces include (a) hiring and retaining qualified staff, (b) rising capital and (c) building value chain (Intellecap 2012). This exemplifies how social enterprises struggle to maintain their sustenance and growth despite disadvantaged resource availability.

When it comes to philosophical orientation, Leveau-Vallier (2011) believes that there are two sections of social entrepreneurs in India–Gandhian social entrepreneurs and global Indians-turned-social entrepreneurs. Gandhian social entrepreneurs are those who are locally embedded and inspired by the Gandhian philosophy of social change. The Gandhian model is an inclusive model based on village development and self-administration, whereas global

---

[7] GIZ or Deutsche Gesellschaft für Internationale (German Agency for International Cooperation) is a German federal institute which enriches its international cooperation by offering financial support to education and sustainable development initiates across the world.

Indians-turned-social entrepreneurs are foreign-returned individuals who are interested in addressing social problems in India. They include a contingent of youth who have earlier studied or were employed abroad, largely in the United States of America (USA) with finance and information technology (IT) background. Both the sections of social entrepreneurs believe in market-based interventions for achieving social value. While the advancement of social sector in the form of social entrepreneurship is quite encouraging, the marketization of social services is daunting (Elkinton and Hartigan 2008). On the other hand, it is found that the social enterprises have been so far initiated in two contexts (a) by those who have shown empathy towards problems faced by others, and (b) by the victims themselves who come forward to initiate a social enterprise. For example, Pukkar, a social enterprise in Mumbai is initiated by street kids to provide an array of services to young street kids, which includes providing food, shelter and training on other livelihood development activities, whereas a significant number of social enterprises generally emerge out of empathy.

Social entrepreneurs in India rise across the age groups. The author spoke to many aspiring young social entrepreneurs at different occasions; the reason for most of them to start a social enterprise is related to the distressed social realities they witness, which constrain several sections of the society from accessing basic facilities. The young social entrepreneurs believe that availability of funding should not form a basis for addressing social problems, rather they argue that identifying a social problem should take the lead. The former approach is what the NGO sector has been adopting. They further have an opinion that any relationship or partnership with State is synonymous to corruption, delaying in approvals and literally difficult to handle, so they believe that it is better to avoid intervention of State in their activities. However, as they grow, it is found that a majority of them tie up with the governments at different levels to fulfil their goals. For instance, Ramana Babu Killi, the co-founder of Green Basics, associated with the Government of Goa, works to transform agriculture into an organized industry. Despite various constraints that may come up during the interactions with the government, it actually offers a level playing supportive environment, where the social enterprises get an opportunity to access several resources that are otherwise impossible to acquire.

Though youth take lead in building the sector, change leaders from other age groups have also been keen to initiate social ventures to address social problems in their own community or other communities which are in need. For instance, Mukundan, a 60-year-old social entrepreneur, invented a stove burner in 2002. The innovative burner he created was 30 per cent more efficient than the existing ones. Aavishkar, a social investor, invested INR 8 lakh (approximately $13,000) and bought 49 per cent stacks in the venture. Aavishkar not only invested in the venture but also mentored and offered other necessary resources. Though initially the venture had to undergo critical financial setbacks, today it turned out to be a million dollar social enterprise. The initial success encourages the social entrepreneur to innovate and introduce several other products for the development of deprived and excluded.

It is to understand that entrepreneurs do not negotiate or compromise with existing systems. If they find that something is inappropriate in the existing systems, then they develop new ones to serve in better ways and change the market equilibrium, for instance, the cases of FedEx and eBay are classic examples. Social entrepreneurs also create new systems that offer improved services or products to question the status quo. I interacted with Amit Saurabh, the founder of Prayas Bharat which is a not-for-profit venture that aims at addressing school dropout issue in Jhabua.[8] I asked him why he would not be interested in convincing the existing school systems sponsored by the government to address the issue and instead create parallel institutions which may not be a feasible option in a resource-constrained environment. However, Saurabh, an inspiring young guy like many others in their early 20s, propelled, 'I strive to create additional systems, if required, until my desire to achieve universal education in the district is fulfilled'.

There are social enterprises that improve both demand and production patterns and revolutionize the entire industry in which they operate. For example, RugMark, a campaign venture initiated by noble laureate Kailash Satyarathi, aims to abolish child labour in India's rug-weaving industry. His institution has pioneered in creating RugMark certification programme and a campaign to educate consumers. Carpets with RugMark label assure customers that the carpet is manufactured without any child slavery. This experiment has transformed the entire carpet industry where child labour has been

---

[8] Jhabua is a tribal district in western Madhya Pradesh, which has a literacy rate of 44.45 per cent according to the 2011 census. It is recorded as the fourth lowest literacy district in India.

abolished on one hand and the buyer gets satisfaction by encouraging ethical businesses on the other hand. This venture has consequently helped in creating adult employment. Satyarthi's idea has left him as a social entrepreneur and as an activist, who in turn adopted and practised several innovations as part of promoting RugMark. This proves a point that the established social entrepreneurs could also take up activism and advocacy as a method to promote social transformation. Thus, a successful social entrepreneur who has carried out an innovative experiment may persuade the government to adopt it into the policy mechanism with his/her activism (Martin and Osberg 2007). When social enterprises add up to advocacy, then there are larger possibilities for creating change at system levels.

The other significant method to achieve larger social transformation is to build successful collaboration and networking. For example, Pratham, a non-profit organization based in Delhi and Mumbai, addresses illiteracy and malnutrition issues among children from the poorest neighbourhoods. Its strategy is to partner with community organizations, governments at grass-root level and various corporations. The intention for such partnership building is to share the existing resources. In fact, this experiment has worked well in terms of minimizing its costs. Though it recruits and trains teachers from the communities concerned, its strategy for using existing physical infrastructure helps to work within the limited resources it possesses. Excluded persons from the concerned communities such as, unmarried women, persons with disability (PwDs) and youth from the underprivileged groups, get a chance to serve as teachers. These strategies helped Pratham to get rid of several costs associated with accessing infrastructure. Taking inspiration from Pratham's activity, many such initiatives have grown across the country. For example, Bharat Calling, a budding social enterprise in rural Madhya Pradesh, aims at providing training to graduates from tribal habitats. The aim of such training is to enable the graduates in acquiring necessary skills and exposure to get admission in well-known higher educational institution. From the first year of its inception, the impact has been quite encouraging where a large number of graduates, who undergo training, successfully secure merit-based free seats in various higher education institutions. Bharat Calling uses volunteers, interns and government infrastructure to run its activities.

The professional approach embodied within the philosophical boundaries of social enterprises attracts more appreciation in the process. For example, Aravind Eye Hospitals, established in 1976 by

Dr Govindappa Venkataswamy and Thulasiraj has been a successful social enterprise which has shown significant professionalism and community upliftment by delivering social impact. The hospital offers health care for a cross-section of population. The cross-subsidized model adopted and various innovative steps it opted for have benefited more than 3 million patients, often free of charge. As part of the subsidized method, the poor and the deprived avail the treatment without or with a nominal fee, while the rich and affordable pay the market-based fee. The financial capacity of the patients plays no role in the quality of treatment.

In India, social businesses are often classified under micro, small and medium enterprises (MSME) and are being monitored by the Ministry of MSME. These industries are typically expected to be either manufacture or service delivery enterprises. At the policy level, the federal government in India understood the need for promoting business skills among the deprived and downtrodden, especially among women, as a significant move in order to address the basic social problems of the excluded and their market participation. Accordingly, the Government of India (GoI) has declared the current decade as the 'Decade of Innovation' that aims to nurture innovations and enterprising across the country. The recent 12th five year plan asks for greater role of social enterprises and emphasizes on innovations to take lead in promoting inclusive growth (Planning Commission 2011). Especially after the success of Grameen Bank in Bangladesh, the federal as well as state governments in India started to focus their policies on micro finance and self-help groups (SHGs) to promote small and medium scale enterprises, which are operated by women. With several such policies in operation, women across communities organise themselves into groups in order to avail interest-free loans from various nationalized banks to nurture entrepreneurial skills and promote their social and market participation. The initial findings report that the SHGs led by women not only enhance their income but also promote their participation in family, panchayati raj institutions[9] and village developmental activities. In addition to the government support in microfinance institutions,

---

[9] Panchayati raj institutions are local self-governing institutions which came out of the Gandhian vision. These local political institutions are expected to look after village level planning and developmental activities. Further the idea of such institutions aim at demonstrating the capacities of the villages who are expected to enrich their own development.

private players also play crucial role. For example, the Bharatiya Samruddhi Investments and Consulting Services (BASIX) founded by Vijay Mahajan was the first microfinance project to lend money to the poor. Vikram Akula is another founder of a successful Indian microfinance project. His organization, SKS Microfinance, offers microloans and insurance to poor women in impoverished areas.

The social enterprise sector in India, as it appears today, is shaped due to the active contribution from key players in the ecosystem. As described by GIZ (2012) in its report, ecosystem building is crucial for nurturing the field of social entrepreneurship. The ecosystem as noted in Figure 2.1 typically comprises of (a) government and policy mechanism, (b) impact investing industry, (c) incubation, (d) academia, (e) legal systems, (f) institutional and non-institutional actors and (g) international collaborations and partnerships. The role of each sector is discussed in detail further.

Figure 2.1

Social entrepreneurship ecosystem

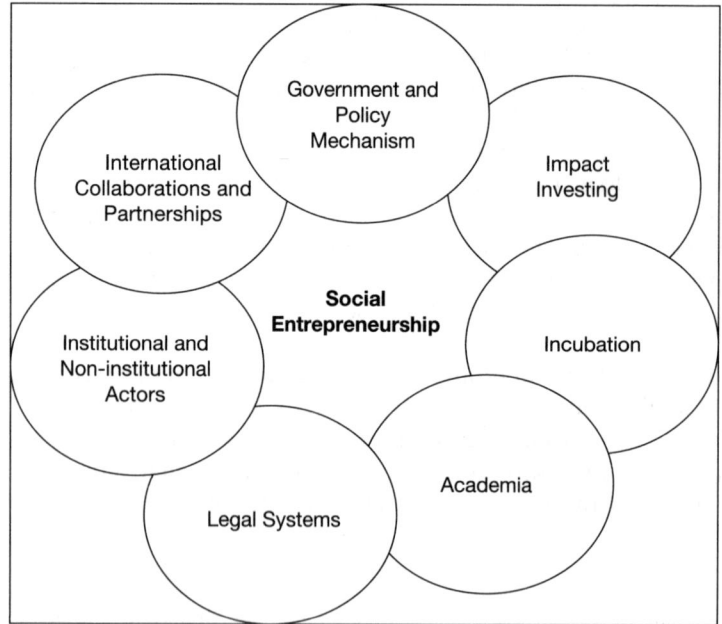

Source: Author's own.

Government and Policy Mechanism

Social entrepreneurs in India struggle to identify ways in which they can partner with government. The government is slowly opening itself to the sector. Recently, it has introduced India Inclusive Innovation Fund (IIIF) to promote socially relevant businesses. The fund aims to invest in innovative and sustainable ventures that have exemplary ideas to run scalable and profitable ventures. The prime focus of IIIF is to address social needs in key areas such as "health care, food, nutrition, agriculture, education/skill development, energy, financial inclusion, water sanitation, employment generation, etc."[10] The fund is deposited with the Security and Exchange Board of India's (SEBI) alternative investment fund with an initial corpus of INR500 crores (approximately 80 million USD). A total of 20 per cent fund is committed by MSME and the balance is attributed by other stakeholders such as banks, insurance companies and overseas financial and developmental institutions.

The fund, first of its kind in the subcontinent, will continue to expand its corpus. It aims to offer modest financial returns to keep the momentum going while not compromising on the social impact. While the scale at which the sector is growing and the substance of this fund may not tally, it shows a growing indication that the government began to address the most pressing problem of capital supply to the innovative ventures that have large social impact, but yet struggle to sustain. The fund largely ensures to promote enterprises which fall under micro, small and medium category. In addition to filling the capital needs of the industry, the fund also partners with other stakeholders in the space such as incubators, angel investors and research agencies in order to mobilize the ecosystem building. In addition, the recent Startup India plan—as proposed by the Prime Minister of India, Mr Narendra Modi—is expected to promote startups by relaxing legal constraints, providing financial support and offering tax exemptions.

State policy sometimes enables the process of social entrepreneurship; it also acts as an impediment for the growth due to its failure to understand the potential of the field. While in general, social enterprises would want their experiments/initiatives to be taken up by the State policy in order to multiply or maximize the successful impact creation, there are several social enterprises which adopt government programmes and enhance social impact. For example,

---

[10] http://www.innovationcouncil.gov.in (accessed 4 December 2015).

the mid-day meal scheme initiated by the Tamil Nadu Government has been scaled throughout the country by Akshaya Patra, a social enterprise (Raina 2013). The State also enables several legal mechanisms in support of the growing social entrepreneurship innovation space. For example, the Companies Act enacted in 2013 enforces that any company which has a net worth of INR500 crores ($7.6 million), a turnover of INR1,000 crore ($15 million) or a net profit of INR5 crores ($0.7 million) should incur at least 2 per cent of the last three years average net profits on socially responsible activities as part of their CSR (Ray 2013). The CSR could form as a significant financial contribution which social enterprises with their innovative approaches can grab to initiate their activities. In addition, the support from government influences other players in ecosystem and enhances prospects for the growth of the sector. Spear et al. (2013) argue that government should take active part in the growth of the social entrepreneurship industry, including to facilitate pre-conditions, infrastructure development, governance-related support, support in terms of finance, skills and access to market; however, the actual scenario in India is far away from institutionalizing structures required to facilitate such processes.

Impact Investing

Impact investing industry in India is one of the worlds advanced industries (Huppé 2014). In addition to the support from various government programmes in terms of offering finances and additional resources for nurturing the field, private investment takes the lead. Financing innovation in social sector is relatively complex due to lack of tolerance for failure which may be one of the possible outcomes when innovations are employed. It is found that conventional sources of investments in social sector such as grants and donations etc. have not significantly shown keen interest so far in supporting entrepreneurial approaches in social sector, whereas, venture capitalists and social investors focus on social innovations (Rajan and Hari 2013). Thus, most inspiring and challenging innovations attract attention of investors. In the recent past, several social investing initiatives have been started to support the social entrepreneurship sector. The impact investing industry aims at investing in impact markets. The aim is not to maximize profits but to advance social value. The financial returns on investment principle is always tied with the social value creation principle. Accordingly, various funding and supporting organizations from different parts of the globe have been actively involved in building the sector in India.

A survey conducted by Beyond Profit[11] opines that the growth of the sector and a large proportion of social enterprises present in the country are the result of recent developments in third sector in India. The survey concludes that in 2009 about 68 per cent of social enterprises studied were in operation for five years or less. In addition, about 90 per cent of the organizations in the sector run on revenue less than USD500,000 a year. Due to its early stage existence, it is found that more than one-third of them are forced into financial losses. However, the positive aspect is that about one-third of the social enterprises have grown significantly between 2009 and 2010 with more than 50 per cent growth (Intellecap 2010). Most encouraging part of the finding is that a significant proportion of social enterprises which were part of the study have shown tremendous commitment towards their market penetration which aims at building their SO. About three-fifths of all SEs have adopted innovative business models to sustain their ventures. Such market-driven approaches attract impact investors in their support and address one of the most significant constraints for the growth of the sector—access to financial resources.

The other significant, yet desirable, development that the study has noticed is that a plenty of for-profit models that evolved in the last five years have originally had their inception from not-for-profit models. In other words, many of the non-profit models which existed earlier are now transforming to become for-profit entities. For example, microfinance institutions have successfully become for-profits which were initially started as not-for-profit models. Access to institutional debt for social enterprises has always been a distant dream in India as there is no single set of rules that dictate the game. Hence, largely social entrepreneurs depend on bootstrapping and non-institutional finance provision to acquire financial support. However, the growth in the impact investment is considered to be a vital part to transform the scenario into a desirable environment.

---

[11] Beyond Profit is a social enterprise magazine which is published by Intellecap, a key player in social enterprise ecosystem.

Nevertheless, the impact investing industry is yet to evolve in its fullest form. In fact, in India it is relatively in the nascent stage. It comprises of organizations with both domestic and international repute. A large part of the industries has no relation with philanthropy. Though all social enterprises as such face severe financial constraints which hamper their existence and growth, those which are located in rural areas are subjected to further vulnerability. In spite of the efforts from both government and investment agencies, there is a strong need for a better financial provision for a range of social enterprises working in rural areas. The rural-based social enterprises face severe constraints due to their geographical disadvantage. That is the reason most of the successful social enterprises exist in cities despite the fact that most excluded and downtrodden live in rural areas. However, the growth in the impact investing industry offers hope for many such social enterprises to get access to institutional finance. Thus, its growth is a well appreciated momentum that has potential to encourage citizens to come up with path-breaking ideas that could bring light in the lives of the excluded. Some of the largest actors in the field of impact investment include the Omidyar Network, Aavishkaar, Acumen Fund and Elevar Equity, etc. Further, there are a set of global actors that support selective segment of social enterprises. For example, Central Square Foundation supports ventures on education and Ankur Capital supports early stage social entrepreneurs. All efforts put together, the ecosystem from the financial perspective is fast emerging to contribute for the growth of the field.

Among the major funds to invest in social enterprises in India, the Acumen Fund was established in 2001 with seed capital from Rockfeller Foundation, Cisco Systems Foundation and three other individual philanthropists. The fund focuses on service delivery fields such as health care, water and housing. Its aim is to realize a world beyond poverty through social enterprise investing. The fund offers grants or equity investment through philanthropic capital it receives from different global organizations. On an ideal level, the fund's concentration is on the families which earn below USD4 a day. The Grassroots Business Fund is another equity investor in social enterprises that works for BoP population. This fund specially operates on agribusiness, artisans and innovations in finance-related social enterprises.

Aavishkaar Venture Capital is an equity investment fund that is located in Mumbai. It aims at investing in social enterprises that work for the people coming from BoP. Aavishkar has, for example, invested in Vaatsalya hospitals which provide affordable health care facilities for semi-urban and rural population. These hospitals operate as a chain with multiple branches. While most of the advanced facilities in health care are centred around metropolitan and capital cities, Vaatsalya aims to provide quality health care with advanced facilities in two-and-three-tier cities. Various global players which comprise of international developmental agencies such as Development Finance Institution (DFI), banks that include Deutsche Bank, the Entrepreneurial and International Development Bank of Netherlands and the World Bank have invested in Aavishkaar fund.

Dasra is a Mumbai-based organization that coordinates with philanthropists and social entrepreneurs. It operates Dasra Social Impact Programme along with Village Capital, another investment fund. Those recruited as part of the programme undergo an intensive training programme that enables them to stretch their ideas into venture form. In addition, city- or region-based impact investing organizations have come into light in the recent past such as, Mumbai Angels, Hyderabad Angels and Venture Nursery in Mumbai. For example, Sushanto Mitra, who heads Lead Angels, assists ventures in early stage to grow effectively by addressing their concerns related to funding, incubation and mentoring.

Though investors are expected to play a crucial role in nurturing the field, so far their participation is constrained to the for-profit businesses within the social enterprise sector where they expect relatively high returns on their investment. While their social commitment is of no doubt, it is found that their investments are dominated to extract significant returns on their investment. The impact investment itself is in its nascent stage, where the indicators for measuring impact investment are in the process of thorough research. Hence, the role that these investors opt needs to be directed by such indicators, in order to make sure that the social value creation is not compromised at any stage of social venture creation and its growth.

Incubation

Incubation system in the country is growing actively. Incubation systems hosted by academic houses, to name a few such as the Indian Institute of Management (IIM) Ahmedabad, IIM Bangalore, Indian

Institute of Technology (IIT) Chennai and IIT Mumbai, have played pioneering roles in developing several business ideas into profitable ventures. With adopting the blended value approach, these incubators are now hosting a plethora of social ventures. In addition, several non-profit incubators such as Villgro, Dasra, UnLtd India and Waste Ventures host innovative ideas and dictate their success path with a variety of supporting systems they created. National Science and Technology Entrepreneurship Development Board (NSTEDB) of the Department of Science and Technology, Ministry of Science and Technology, GoI, sponsors the Technology Business Incubators (TBIs) in order to nurture knowledge-driven and technology-intensive enterprises. There are about a total of 52 TBIs located in various universities across the country. In addition, the University Grants Commission (UGC) has also started promoting the incubation system by supporting incubation centres in social sciences institutions such as Center for Social Entrepreneurship at Tata Institute of Social Sciences (TISS) to nurture student-run ventures.

The incubators play a guiding role and accompany the ventures in each stage of their success. They support the venture with a package of resources and services ranging from conducting workshops for idea generation to providing them continuous support for several years of their successful existence. Incubators facilitate various meetings with investors, provide office space for the ventures for a stipulated time, offer technical assistance and other shared business services. They also provide a modest financial support to the ventures as grants, loans, etc., for instance, the Incubation Center at TISS has partnered with the DBS Bank to offer stipends and support grants for students who opt to become social entrepreneurs. While stipends help students to look after their living, support grant assists the growth of the ventures. The incubator also provides virtual incubation where many ventures which are remotely located in different rural segments secure benefits. These ventures are provided with all the facilities and resources, except physical space. For example, ventures such as Bharat Calling in Madhya Pradesh or Krishi Naturals in Gujarat receive virtual incubation support from the TISS incubator located in Mumbai.

Among various social incubators in India, UnLtd India's incubator has been accredited as one of the five best incubators across the globe besides Echoing Green and Unreasonable Institute. Villgro Innovations Foundation is a Chennai-based incubator which recruits enthusiastic and ambitious social entrepreneurs with an inspiring plan. In addition to the in-house mentoring and training, Villgro also provides seed capital and other allowances required for the sustenance of budding social entrepreneurs.

The facilities that the incubators provide differ slightly from each other. However, typically incubators provide facilities such as office space including desk space, Internet, telephone facility, access to printer or coping machines, conference rooms for organizing meetings and providing mentor services by various experts from a variety of domains as required by the social ventures. Especially, all the incubators offer one-stop mentoring facility which is crucial for the success of ventures. For the services, a few incubators charge nominal fees whereas the other incubators offer all services free of cost. In such cases, the running and maintaining costs are sponsored by the host institutions in some cases where the incubators are located in academic institutions or with funding from external sources in case of incubators based in and outside academic environment.

Altogether, the incubation system in India accounts for large portion of social enterprises initiated by the young population of the country. The incubation centres at various academic institutions and social incubators from elsewhere have been in the forefront in terms of nurturing social enterprises by offering different set of resources and skills required for their growth. Some incubators are engaged in nurturing social ventures from the very beginning such as, idea generation itself, whereas the other incubators assist at some point of time, preferably in the first three to five years of venture growth. Hence, it is to state that the role of incubators in nurturing and promoting social enterprises is quite evident and crucial.

Academia

Global action to include social entrepreneurship in academic programmes has influenced academics in India as well. Though the practice of social entrepreneurship in India dates back to a few decades, academic institutions have joined them in the recent past to initiate social entrepreneurship education in India. Hence, it is expected that graduated students have the potential to launch socially relevant ventures that address social problems and generate employment. In total, there are about 26 academic programmes in India directly linked to social entrepreneurship education in which (a) three institutions run full-time masters programmes including the TISS in Mumbai, Deshpande Foundation in Hubli and Ambedkar University in Delhi, (b) 14 institutions run a minor/an elective or a foundation course including reputed institutions such as IIM Ahmedabad, IIM Bangalore and IIT Madras, (c) three institutions run part-time or distance education including the Entrepreneurship Development Institute (EDI) in Ahmedabad and Indira Gandhi National Open University (IGNOU), Delhi, and (d) non-accredited programmes run by Villgro, Chennai; Center for Social Initiative and Management (CSIM) in multiple places and Dasra in Mumbai (Thomas and Kummitha 2013).

The successful amplification of social entrepreneurship as an academic field has been so far endorsed by change leaders from practice. The academic environment has advanced from both academic and social perspective. For instance, until recently, parents were mostly unhappy about their children opting to become social workers or social entrepreneurs; however, now parents are encouraging them to join social entrepreneurship academic programmes. Hundreds of students graduate with social entrepreneurship academic background every year in India alone. Many of these academic institutions have developed dedicated ecosystem to promote the social ventures created by students. For example, TISS which recruits about 30 students every year for its masters programme in social entrepreneurship so far institutionalized about 30 social ventures that address multiple social problems in sectors such include agriculture, waste management, education, water and skill development. The incubation system created for the purpose facilitates necessary infrastructure including monetary support as grant through their partnership with DBS Bank (Kummitha and Majumdar 2015). Though starting a venture is integrated into the curriculum of TISS, initial results proclaim that all those who graduate with social entrepreneurship education background may not initiate social enterprises immediately after their graduation as most of them may need additional exposure and experience. Thus, they may initially need to get hands on experience by undertaking different roles that range from helping other social entrepreneurs to initiate their ventures and scale the proven ventures. In fact, it takes a team of visionaries to achieve social impact. Interestingly, well-known entrepreneurs in the contemporary era such as Bill Gates, Steve Jobs and many other great entrepreneurs did not come out of MBA or entrepreneurship programmes or some even did not finish their colleges. The profiles of social entrepreneurs will also be the same where a few of them may come with social entrepreneurship academic background initiating ventures and the remaining would have graduates from social entrepreneurship background in their teams. In addition to the formal education systems offering social entrepreneurship education, non-profit organizations have also joined the movement. For example, the masters programme offered by Deshpande Foundation represents this category. However, the social entrepreneurship education is expanding to newer academic institutions and the participation of non-profit organizations in the momentum is worth encouraging.

Legal Systems

The legal systems present in the country appear to be quite rigid for the growth of the industry. A social enterprise in India may be created under different provisions such as Societies Registration Act 1860, Indian Trusts Act 1882 and Companies Act 1956. Since there is no special mention to the term 'social entrepreneurship' in the legal proceedings, social enterprises in India can be registered under two methods: (a) third sector or (b) business sector. The organizations registered under third sector are not allowed to undertake business activities, whereas the organizations registered under business sector are expected to spill high rate of taxes and are not liable to contribute for social causes. There is a lack of credible legal structure that enables to create social enterprises as they are associated with blended value creation. Hence, largely lack of a legal base for the registration of organizations is claimed to be a setback, which has to be overcome by existing social enterprises, using various innovative mechanisms. For example, Clinton (2010) argues that despite the lack of special legal status unlike L3C in USA or CiC in UK, social enterprises often thrive in India. There are many laws in various countries such as the Social Entrepreneurship Act 2011 in Republic of Slovenia, Social Value Act 2013 in UK or Italian Law on Social Enterprises, which have offered support for the growth of social entrepreneurship in their respective countries.

The growth of social enterprisers in these countries have strong link with the national policy and legal mechanisms, whereas the social enterprises in India have succeeded in spite of having no supporting policy.

The time it takes for creation of an enterprise remains a hurdle in India for those who would like to venture into creating an enterprise. It is estimated that on an average, 34 days are required to start a business in India (World Bank 2011). Due to several legal and bureaucratic obstacles involved, in practice it would take more time than 34 days. There is a terrible burden of restrictions to start an enterprise. Especially, for non-profits to undertake mission-related ventures, profits of which will be utilized for the prime cause of social value creation, is altogether a difficult task due to the legal structures operating in the country. Thus, the government should take up necessary measures to support the third sector and civil society in building a successful social entrepreneurship movement. The Startup India plan which is initiated in 2016 in this regard is expected to relax legal barriers in order to initiate startups quickly by adopting single window clearance with the help of a mobile application.

Institutional and Non-institutional Actors

Since 1982, Ashoka has elected over 2,200 leading social entrepreneurs as Ashoka Fellows in which India alone represents with about 400 fellows. This recognition provides venture with living stipends, professional support and access to a global network of peers in more than 60 countries to all the fellows. As discussed earlier, India is home to Ashoka's first fellow and for the past 30 years, India has become a testing ground for most of Ashoka's international fellowship building programmes and other key initiatives. Since 2003, Ashoka and American India Foundation (AIF) have partnered to co-invest in social enterprises in India. In addition, other well-known support is offered by Skoll Foundation and Schwab Foundation. The support offered as part of international recognition is quite significant. For example, Arbind Singh from Nidan,[12] who

---

[12] Nidan is an organization that works on issues ranging from advocacy to education, including skill development, health, social security, financial services and micro-finance, etc.

secured the Social Entrepreneurship Award by Schwab Foundation, felt that Schwab Foundation offers recognition to path-breaking innovations at appropriate time in the venture growth stage. The recognition helps to build networks and connections and to strengthen the work. He claims that being a social entrepreneur in India is challenging as the norms are not established. As a result, the process of social entrepreneurship becomes an extremely tiresome activity as it requires establishing public good behind every action. In addition, the challenges increase when the market penetration becomes the centre of focus for the venture. The international supporting organizations largely deal with the proven social enterprises to scale or replicate their ideas in other regions. Their recognition brings visibility for social entrepreneurs both in domestic and global scale. AIF is another leading international development organization charged with the mission of accelerating social and economic change in India. Since 2001, it has raised over USD30 million and offered grants for education, livelihood and public health projects in India with an emphasis on elementary education, women's empowerment and HIV/AIDS. In addition, United Nations institutions and other aid agencies also started to support the field. For example, UNICEF has been actively involved in capacity building of the Butterflies, a social enterprise in India, in addition to its engagement with many other social enterprises across the globe.

Apart from the institutional arrangements, informal networks, for example, Caring Friends, a Mumbai-based voluntary likeminded group, facilitates donor–social entrepreneur interaction in order to create synergy between the innovator and potential investors/ philanthropists. Nimesh and Ramesh, well-known stock brokers in Mumbai, have started this initiative which has been supported by enthusiasts coming from diversified backgrounds such as bankers, doctors, journalists and academicians. The group facilitates monthly meetings in which potential social entrepreneurs are given space to present their venture and the need for the philanthropic or investment partner. This results in immense response from the group of enthusiasts who attend the meeting. However, getting a chance to speak to this group is subjected to a rigorous selection process adopted by the moderators. This group not only exposes the social enterprises in need to a larger group of potential donors or investors, but also helps in various ways through their network. So far, the group has supported an array of social enterprises from different social spectrums and regional backgrounds. For example, Caring Friends supported Bhagini Nivedita Gramin Vigyan Niketan (BNGVN) which has been founded by Nileema Mishra, a Ramon Magsaysay Award winner. BNGVN works to empowers villagers in terms of providing opportunities to live with dignity through their enhanced market and social participation.

In addition, another very important portion of resources received by social enterprises are in the form of volunteers. Volunteers offer instrumental support to the sector by filling the gap of skilled professionals. Several social enterprises including Goonj and Aravind Eye care, which have their reach spread across multiple states, have benefited from volunteers. Volunteers play a crucial role in the functioning of these organizations. Many social enterprises always attract a range of volunteers from abroad and India. Rahul, the founder of iVolunteer, a non-profit organization which aims to connect social enterprises with volunteers, opines that the non-profit sector can never afford professionals. On the contrary, people who want to volunteer are not aware about the platforms where to seek opportunities. So, iVolunteer offers the necessary platform that links these two environments. Social entrepreneurship has been so far effectively supported by both institutional and non-institutional mechanisms. The global organizations including Ashoka and other institutional and non-institutional volunteers are actively engaging in resource facilitation.

International Collaboration and Partnerships

As discussed earlier, a large section of social entrepreneurs in India emerge with their international exposure and accordingly tend to get robust collaborations. Especially since the introduction of MDGs, international collaborations have received greater attention, as eight MDG spoke about developing global partnership and knowledge sharing for development. The global supporting mechanisms, on which this research has constantly emphasized, offer crucial support for the growth of the sector in India. In addition, the Indian diaspora plays a well-noted role in terms of offering financial support to the field. For example, the diaspora contributed a sum of USD49.3 billion in 2009 alone for various social causes. The GoI recognizes contribution rendered by diaspora and recognizes it by celebrating Pravasi Bharatiya Divas on 9 January, every year (Bakshi and Baron 2011).

India is regarded as a social entrepreneurship superpower which needs to strengthen its base so that it would contribute for eliminating poverty not only in India but also in other developing countries. A handful of successful social entrepreneurs in India such as Barefoot College and Nuru Energy Group, have been tremendously contributing for benefiting the excluded in African countries. Several other social entrepreneurs in India who are succeeded in creating certain impact are looking forward to spread their impact on a global scale. The global think tanks such as Ashoka, Schwab Foundation and Skoll Foundation fellowships are highly useful in realizing their goals to spread the impact. In addition, the federal government in India as part of its bilateral relations, especially with African countries, encourages institutional support from Indian social enterprises to experiment their proven ideas in other African countries.

This chapter emphasized that thorough ecosystem promises streamline growth for social entrepreneurship. Thus, there is a larger need to strengthen or give ample space for ecosystem to excel. In India especially, where the existence of government itself has emerged as a notable social problem, the role social entrepreneurs need to play is crucial in order to address various social problems. The presence and success of social enterprises which have been active in achieving social transformation since decades offer hope as their growth has been prospered despite the absence of an active ecosystem. Thus, an active ecosystem with ample resources to support the social entrepreneurship industry would enhance the strength of the industry and offer scope for larger social transformation. The following chapters will focus on analyzing several such social transformations achieved by renowned social enterprises in India in different social contexts.

3

Enable India: Inclusion of Persons with Disabilities

Enable India is registered as a non-profit organization in Bangalore, Karnataka, a southwest Indian state. The prime objective of the organization is to achieve economic independence and dignity of PwDs. Its philosophy is embedded within its structural boundaries which emphasizes on the philosophy proposed by Baba Amte,[1] who demonstrated that the excluded and downtrodden require a chance not charity. Enable India offers supportive environment for PwDs to grow and accomplish their goals in addition to earning a dignified life. While addressing the capability concerns of the PwDs, Enable India attempts to explore ways in which the sustainable solutions can be achieved.

When we talk about disability in India, it is largely understood as a curse. If a person is disabled, it is ironically believed to be a result of his/her sin in an earlier birth, for which the person is being penalized now. Accordingly, family and society judge that PwDs are incapable and are constrained by several difficulties to live on their own, unless supported by a well-wisher or a family. In a family where one of two children is disabled, the family offers prompt encouragement to the normal person but not to the disabled because of lack of confidence or excessive care towards the PwDs. For example, if someone has to go to market, the boy without disability is expected to go. This expectation is not just restricted to any particular activity or situation. In addition in most cases, the PwDs are considered

---

[1] Baba Amte was an Indian social worker and activist who had shown enormous commitment for the upliftment of poor and deprived affected by leprosy.

as burden and most of the families would not want to invest in them due to lack of faith in their capabilities.

Background of the Social Problem

Enable India falls under the employment generation model within a set of broader social enterprises. Though the employment is not directly offered by the organization itself, the efforts thus far intended are to create employment where it never existed for the selected deprived sections. The exercise first started as a home-based remedy and expanded over a period of time to become one of the most successful social enterprises in India. When Hari (15 years), brother of Shanti Raghavan, visited her while she was working along with her husband Dipesh Suthariya as a software engineer in the USA, he was diagnosed with Retinitis Pigmentosa which resulted in deteriorating his eyesight. Both the sister and brother-in-law, moved by the sudden disaster in their family, decided to assist in his rehabilitation as he was under a sad state of mind. As part of the rehabilitation process, they introduced him to advanced mobility and computer training in which they had expertise. This intervention and support made him confident and he started to realize that he could still achieve his ambitions, stand on his own and gain his full participation in society.

Later, when he returned to India to restart his life after a few years of training in the USA, both Shanti and Dipesh also joined him to pursue their professional career in Bangalore. After Hari became the topper in MBA at Narsee Monjee Institute of Management Studies (NMIMS), Mumbai, he attended several interviews for securing a suitable job. While the interviewers appreciated him for his talent, none of them were able to offer a suitable job for him in their companies due to multiple reasons ranging from lack of belief in his capabilities to lack of proper infrastructure in the work place to accommodate him. As a result, Hari was totally disappointed because he was unable to get a job, despite performing well in about 60 interviews. Shanti, who was a sole witness to the entire process, perceived the problem from a larger perspective. It has helped her to understand the plight of disabled in a society like India. She further felt that the PwDs, in spite of their academic ranks, are unable to earn confidence from the markets. A survey conducted by National Center for Promotion of Employment for PwDs in 1999 revealed that public sector in India employs 0.54 per cent PwDs among their total workforce, whereas the private sector stands at a total of 0.28 per cent and corporate sector at the bottom with a mere 0.05 per cent disabled persons. It is also estimated that 74 per cent with physical disabilities and 94 per cent of persons with mental retardation are unemployed and left without any source of survival (International Disability Rights Monitor 2005). A report from the World Bank (2009) claims that there is a sharp decline in employment rates among the PwDs in the country, ranging from 42 per cent in 1991 to 37 per cent in 2002. The situation has not seen any constant improvements until the date.

According to Census of India, 2011, there are about 27 millions of PwDs living in India in which 15 million are men and 12 million are women. These figures are equal to 2.21 per cent of the total population of the country. This should be considered as a conservative figure when we compare it with data available from other sources. For example, the World Bank (2009) suggests that about 4–9 per cent of the people in India are disabled which is much higher than what the Census has portrayed. In order to promote their work participation, the GoI reserves 3 per cent of jobs in public sector for PwDs. On the contrary, in several cases, public sector organizations do not opt to fill the mandatory reserved jobs. In addition, several private enterprises restrict the participation of PwDs for backend jobs, not allowing them to climb the ladder in the work promotion structure (Dawn 2012). People with disabilities continue to be exploited or underserved as far as their capabilities are concerned. They are well short of receiving services and facilities due to their poor performance in the mainstream social activities. They are mostly restricted with the least preference by various social policy measures, leaving them at the bottom in all major social indicators such as health, education and employment, etc. (Mishra and Gupta 2006).

PwDs, about whom the State policy has spoken fairly well, are unable to receive proper treatment from families, societies, markets and the government-led institutions. Further, their capabilities have mostly been underestimated and are seen as dependents. Shanti who had witnessed the scenario from a close proximity considered the need for adopting various rigorous and innovative ways in order to demonstrate the capabilities of PwDs. Hence, she decided to use her hands-on experience[2] in rehabilitation of visually challenged for making a larger social change. Instantly, she started teaching a few visually challenged students on computer techniques at her house in 1999.

Thus, Enable India is a result of her vision to achieve economic independence and dignity for the PwDs. With a mere and simple vision 'to empower PwD', the organization strives to get into the core issue related to empowerment and employability. The empowerment objective largely deals with creating a supportive environment which is expected to fulfil their needs. The services offered by Enable India to achieve its objectives include, but are not limited to, pre-employment services such as counselling and training, supplemental education, placements and then subsequent work place solutions (WPS). In addition, Enable India undertakes various consulting and other technological services to (a) promote disabled friendly work environment in work places and (b) achieve its own sustainability through incomes earned in the process. Though there are other players operating in the field, the activities undertaken at Enable India differ with them in a number of ways. The major difference comes in the form of its orientation towards balancing capabilities of the trainees and their job roles. As part of this initiative, Enable India, while negotiating with employers, matches the skills of the PWDs with job roles. In addition, the WPS is another significant activity that keeps Enable India as a superior entity in the field. Thus, Enable India fills the gap that has been largely ignored by both state and developmental organizations.

Upon successful completion of training, PwDs are placed in various job roles in the market. The typical target ranges from predominantly dominating software companies to sales persons in retail market. Negotiating jobs for PwDs require a lot of momentum where all stakeholders, especially the employers who recruit the trainees, have to be persuaded. This requires a combination of articulation, dedication and innovative approaches to adopt, which we will discuss in detail as the discussion moves further. Enable India does not only aim at placing the disabled in a dignified job, but it envisages continuous employment for them where the employment redeems dignity and self-esteem.

---

[2] Shanti gained experience while rehabilitating Hari and considered that such experience is valuable to help other disabled people to come out of the exclusion trap.

The Idea of Enable India and Growth of the Social Enterprise

Initially, Shanti worked on a part-time basis, spending about couple of hours in early morning and late nights in her small room, while also attending her full-time IT job in Bangalore. She soon realized that training the disabled and getting jobs for them is a toughest task in the entire process of their empowerment, especially in countries like India the process is rigid where sensitization towards skills of the disabled is minimal. The software training and allied placements in various software companies in Bangalore was a blue moon as companies were thriven to get high-skilled employees. When referring to high skills, all the doors for PwDs are shut due to the strong misconception prevailing among the employers that the disabled are low-skilled. Social taboos negate the capabilities of the deprived, which degenerates the attempts made to include the excluded in the mainstream. However, not compromising on her aim in spite of the social construct of reality, she had decided to work full time for Enable India from 2004. The passion that Shanti had attributed to see a better world where the most excluded gets a dignified and acceptable social life was commendable.

After Shanti became an Ashoka Fellow in 2005, the office was moved to a bigger place. As Shanti took it further as a full-time engagement, Dipesh, her husband, also joined her in fulfilling the dream. They initiated dynamic curriculum for teaching, training and skill development of the visually challenged; the knowledge and talent pool produced hitherto was appreciated by the software companies who in turn offered jobs for the trainees. This success resulted into spreading wings of the social enterprise through offering services to other deprived sections other than visually challenged, such as physical disabled starting from 2005 and hearing impaired from 2007. However, given their expertise, the organization continues to deal largely with persons with visual disability. Overall, the social enterprise has grown; it trains about 500 differently abled every year that come from various sections of disability. On an average, more than 60 per cent of those trained get placements through a dedicated placement cell established in 2008. The remaining candidates generally go for either higher education or continue to receive training until they secure a job. In the course of time, Enable India has been working with 290 companies from all over the country in terms of undertaking collaborative practices to enhance the potential of the disabled to get a job in places like Bangalore, Bhubaneswar, Chennai, Delhi, Hyderabad and Pune.

Various Activities Initiated by Enable India

Training, Placements and Follow-up Activities

In India, especially in Bangalore, software is a thriving industry. Thus, Enable India focuses on training the PWDs in computer and capacity building. The other reason for entering into the software industry is that the founding team members come with similar expertise. Apart from training in computers, it also emphasizes on life skill development. It includes: (a) necessary skills for decent living such as imparting English language proficiency and communication, (b) disability specific basic skills such as mobility, note taking, process discipline, life skills and (c) general employability fundamentals such as analytical skills, attention, real-world exposure and work shadowing which make the candidate employable. As the employers' reach expand over a period of time, the trained candidates are placed in sectors including, but not limited to, IT, IT business processing units, hospitality industry, telecom, garments, health care, etc.

The profiles of the candidate are generally a mix of both rural and urban. However, since last few years, candidates from rural areas have outnumbered the urban candidates. "Since our training has a significant proposition of English language component, we would appreciate if many people from rural areas join as they generally come without any exposure of English language" says Dinaker, a person with visual disability who is currently employed at Enable India. This platform works as an enabler for them to get English language skills as well. Urban-based students generally tend to learn language skills during their schooling. In order to facilitate smooth functioning of the classroom environment, which has trainees from heterogeneous linguistic background, the trainers are capable of speaking multiple languages. The advanced environment is a result of transition from its initial set-up where English was the only language taught in the class. However, with more trainees joining from rural backgrounds, the language usage has been interchanged in order to accommodate several needs from the heterogeneous groups.

Each candidate has to undergo a registration and profiling process before actually getting into training. The profiling is based on the skill sets and qualifications of the candidates. Such profiling helps Enable India to classify the specific kind of training required and employment that may be suitable for the candidate, upon completion of their training. Profiling is an important task as each candidate has to be scrutinized and, based on the skills and capabilities, he/she has to be placed in categories which describe the necessary skill requirement to match the market needs. Candidates are categorized based on their interests and skill sets into one of the many training programmes conducted at Enable India. The programmes are further customized to enable the skills of the participants that will help them to be efficient in their real-time job experiments.

Nagaraju, another visually challenged employee in the organization narrates how the computer training has been imparted among the visually challenged candidates.

> Without looking at the computer we listen to the audio and complete the task. The output remains same in case of both sighted and visually challenged, you write a mail and so I, you might browse internet and I also do that. The output is same and the process is same. We use various software such as Jaws and screen reader in order to understand the content and applications in the screen and computer respectively.

Such explanation/view narrates that there is enough sensitization among the PWDs as well. It is not simply about placing them in the real world or maximizing empathy in society, but also PWDs realizing their own capacities and comparing themselves with abled persons. Innovations employed at different levels in the organization facilitate the process.

In several cases, mere small solutions would solve the problems. For example, persons with hearing disability are employed in shell petrol filling stations as pump agents. The work profile of a pump agent has a strong link with dialogue, both hearing and speaking. The persons with hearing impaired are neither able to speak nor hear. In the approach adopted by Enable India, the pump agent approaches customer and asks about his requirements among the different services available and inquire how they would want to pay and select between cash or card. For facilitating the inquiry, a signboard is designed with different titles including services available and mode of payment. So, the customer looks at the signboard and selects according to his/her need and choices offered. The small sign board becomes a solution. Solution could be anything from a drawing board to a technology. The innovative ways adopted and processes involved facilitate the social functioning of PwDs.

The persons with hearing impairments are carefully placed in back-end jobs, which require semi-skilled profiles. Largely, they get into the jobs related to data entry as their strength is vision. When it comes to persons who are visually impaired and with whom the organization has strong interaction since its establishment, they have developed Career Centric Computer Training Programme (CCCTP). In order to get enrolled into the programme, the candidates must have completed at least 12th standard which is a basic qualification to get placed in the corporate industry. In order to reach the unreached, candidates are recruited on the first-come-first-serve basis for the training programmes. Earlier, the recruitment was based on merit, later due to the internal deliberation and discussion, the criteria has been reduced to the current method. The training is generally for nine months. Basic skills in computer are taught as part of the training. In addition, the curriculum includes a strong life skills approach which emphasizes on how to negotiate, how to overcome the consciousness of being disabled and how to integrate themselves in social living. Enable India has inspired various players in the ecosystem to understand the larger picture of inclusive development and participate in the process. For example, as a result of its inspiring work, Cisco systems, a hardware company started to promote the cause and recognized Enable India as its partner to achieve the objectives of later. In addition, it also identified Enable India as Cisco academy for visually challenged. As part of the association, Enable India provides job training and WPS to all the PWDs in Cisco systems. In addition to jobs in software companies, the visually challenged also receive training for semi-technical jobs. These job profiles may need technical expertise but not the core issues related to technology.

It is found that 76 per cent of the total employers are either happy or very happy with the performance of employees recruited from Enable India. Initially, employers seem to have several reservations to employ persons with visual disability, especially due to issues related to their vision or issues that arise while following the instructions from a team lead without any verification, among many other, which are considered as notable constraints. However, after working with them for some time, their colleagues and employers are quite happy. Prasad narrates his experience that:

> I work with Wipro, a product based company. My job role looks after consolidating deliveries and interacting with customers, if the product is not scheduled to be delivered in the given time. So, basically I undertake a key activity where direct interaction with end customers is required. So far, the management is very happy about my work. The feedback has been extremely good. There are two other employees in my section along with me who are also alumni of Enable India. Initially the sighted employees had a different opinion about us, however, within a short time, they have changed their perspective. We all now work as a team.

It proves that the PwDs who are assisted with relevant skills and training are capable of earning their lost dignity. In fact, when the employees first see PWDs in their teams, they develop misconception about their capabilities. It is the skills and capabilities of the PWDs that speak for their merit. Accordingly, they impress and inspire other team members.

The capacity building at Enable India starts from mapping the skills of candidates to preparing them for becoming suitable candidates for the corporate profiles. The entire process revolves around the candidate's development cycle. If someone is fairly employable already and comes with good skills, then the gaps are fixed, if any exist, with customized training and then a job is searched for the candidate. Moses explains how they map skills and employment. "During the profiling, we estimate current stage of the candidate with a variety of tests and see the current requirements within the given set up. We have three major categories—skilled, semi-skilled and unskilled." As discussed in Figure 3.1, if someone has not completed 10th class and wants to get a job, then he will be classified as unskilled and assisted in getting a job, preferably in the manufacturing sector. The skilled category comprises of jobs in development, human resources, support-related or operation-related positions. The next step involves analyzing whether the candidate is readily skilful to take up a job or needs certain training. If they

Figure 3.1

Job roles and the relevant education required

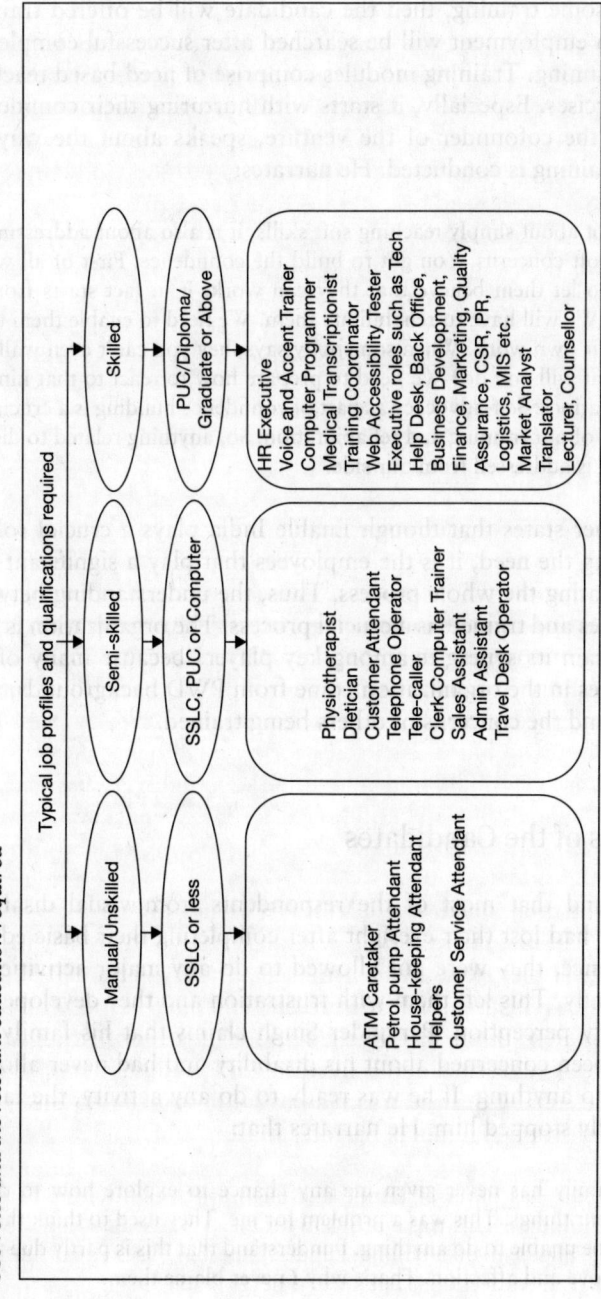

Typical job profiles and qualifications required

Skilled — PUC/Diploma/Graduate or Above

HR Executive
Voice and Accent Trainer
Computer Programmer
Medical Transcriptionist
Training Coordinator
Web Accessibility Tester
Executive roles such as Tech
Help Desk, Back Office,
Business Development,
Finance, Marketing, Quality
Assurance, CSR, PR,
Logistics, MIS etc.
Market Analyst
Translator
Lecturer, Counsellor

Semi-skilled — SSLC, PUC or Computer

Physiotherapist
Dietician
Customer Attendant
Telephone Operator
Tele-caller
Clerk Computer Trainer
Sales Assistant
Admin Assistant
Travel Desk Operator

Manual/Unskilled — SSLC or less

ATM Caretaker
Petrol pump Attendant
House-keeping Attendant
Helpers
Customer Service Attendant

Source: Author's own.

Notes: SSLC—Secondary School Leaving Certificate equivalent to 10th pass from the school.
PUC—Pre-university Certificate equivalent to 12th pass from the school.

require some training, then the candidate will be offered training and then employment will be searched after successful completion of the training. Training modules comprise of need-based teaching and exercises. Especially, it starts with nurturing their confidence. Dipesh, the cofounder of the venture, speaks about the ways in which training is conducted. He narrates:

> It is not about simply teaching soft skills, it is also about addressing their soft concerns. You got to build the confidence. First of all we need to let them believe that they can work. It in fact starts from there. We will have to rehabilitate them. We need to enable them to do their own work. When somebody says, hey you can't even walk, so what will you do? We need to prepare how to react to that kind of situations. Self-advocacy as part of confidence building is a crucial aspect of our training and rehabilitation. So, anything related to disability is addressed from our side.

He further states that though Enable India plays a crucial role in catalyzing the need, it is the employees that play a significant role in facilitating the whole process. Thus, the understanding between employees and trainees is a crucial process. The organization is able to maintain its synergies among key players because many of the employees in the organization come from PWD backgrounds, who understand the concerns of others being trained.

Profiles of the Candidates

It is found that most of the respondents from visual disability category had lost their eyesight after completing their basic education. Hence, they were not allowed to do any major activities by their family. This left them with frustration and they developed an inferiority perception. Parvinder Singh claims that his family has always been concerned about his disability and had never allowed him to do anything. If he was ready to do any activity, the family reportedly stopped him. He narrates that:

> My family has never given me any chance to explore how to do different things. This was a problem for me. They used to think that I will be unable to do anything. I understand that this is partly due to their love and affection. That's why I never blame them.

Though it comes out of emotional bonding as the parents are possessive about their children, finally, this situation leaves them without performing any role in building their careers. In several cases, parents are not even ready to send their children to Enable India, especially from other places in the country. A respondent proclaims that she had to convince her parents using a variety of tactics. Initially, her parents bluntly rejected her proposal. Since Enable India provides training at no fee basis, the candidate told her parents that she has been offered a scholarship towards the training costs. As a result, she was not required to pay any fee. Then the parents felt proud that their daughter stood in the competition and succeeded in getting a scholarship. That is how the parents were convinced to send her for the training. She further narrates, "That was the excuse for me to come out, otherwise being a low vision girl, my parents would have never sent me out. They always used to say, 'no need of going out. We will take care of you.'" So, the transformation is basically required from the family itself. For transforming prevalent cultural constraints, both candidates and Enable India take up a variety of trajectories.

When it comes to educational backgrounds, majority of the candidates who enrol for computer training come with non-computer-based education background. All the candidates come from the social sciences and humanities education background. However, they believe that their training in computer is a firm move to get a dignified life. They further feel that as social sciences and humanities do not require lab-based experiments, they were encouraged to get enrolled in those subjects. However, after attaining computer training at Enable India they strongly consider that computer training is far easy for them. The candidates are quite eager to learn new techniques, programmes and enhance their skills for delivering their tasks. Due to lack of basic understanding in the computer training on the part of the candidate, it is turned to be a quite difficult task for Enable India to get the training done in nine months, which is a standard training period. Shanti described about their training model:

> Some candidates finish their course in time whereas several others need more time than the typical nine months. It is partly due to their lack of proper background in the computers. Hence, we have adopted customized training programmes for all the candidates based on their profiling.

Transforming one's own belief about his/her capabilities is a far difficult task, especially because of the established mind set which was created by families. Those who undergo training sometimes find it far difficult and leave before completing the programme. In such cases, Enable India and the other peer groups counsel the candidate to come back and get trained. For example, a trainee from Indore who joined the medical transcription course found that the course was highly difficult and had left for home, after which he had informed the organization over phone that he had quit the training. However, the team at Enable India, through counselling, brought him back and today after completion of training, he has acquired placement in Lake Systems, a Bangalore-based multinational conglomerate working in software industry. Had he not been persuaded to come back, his condition back home would have been constantly impoverished. Leaving the training and going back to earlier situation could be linked with self-exclusion principle within the broader exclusion theories. According to the theory, the deprived and downtrodden fail to absorb opportunities available due to their misconception. This is one of the many forms of exclusion which are prevalent. Proper mentoring and counselling would avoid conditions that enable self-exclusion to take place.

Enable India provides a life-transforming experience. As discussed earlier, PwDs who first visit the organization come with a lot of distress and lack of exposure. It needs first to build their confidence. Ramgopal believes that:

> After joining Enable India I have got some kind of confidence. I should admit that I did not have such confidence before joining here. I always had doubts about my survival. I didn't know what to do in 2009 when I became visually challenged. Though National Institute of Visually Handicapped (NIVH) where I had an earlier association has committed to find a job, it couldn't succeed in realizing their promise. I have learned few skills in NIVH; however, the skills and confidence levels I have got in Enable India have no comparison to NIVH. Shanti madam and the staff of Enable India have given excellent support.

Typically, after completion of the formal training, the candidates are offered pre-employment training courses that give them an understanding about the industry in which they are expected to get a job, in addition to life skills and communication skills. In case, if some of them are found to be unemployable even after the training or need exposure of working environment before being placed in a workplace, they are strategically placed as interns in various start-ups. Once they acquire relevant exposure and confidence by working in the start-ups, they are expected to be ready to get into the corporate sector.

Strategy and Operations

Working Culture

I have interacted with several PWDs before selecting Enable India as a case study for the research. Most of them have expressed that they are well aware about the social enterprise and its activities. Though it is well known among the PWDs across different parts of the country, due to its physical presence in the state of Karnataka[3], more than 80 per cent of the people who register with the organization for training come from the state of Karnataka, followed by two other states that share borders namely, Maharashtra and Andhra Pradesh. When it comes to gender proposition, women constitute about 33 per cent of the total candidates reregistered for the programmes.

While recruiting staff in Enable India as a policy priority, only differently abled persons are recruited in various jobs. However, failing to get a person with such background, the persons without disability are considered. This move is justified to create a strong synergy among the employees and trainees of the organization. The entire organization including staff, administration, core committee and trainees largely come from disability background, hence, they can easily understand the problems of others within the organization. It helps them to take collective actions. The researcher has also found that there is a bonding built among the PWDs in the organizational context which enhances their social capital and achieves well-being beyond market penetration alone.

Lingdow, one of the trainee amplifies that "I found that Enable India is very encouraging. It is different at least for me because it highlights the need for employment as a way of social integration;

---

[3] India is a federal republic with several states. There are at present 29 states and 7 union territories in India.

it appears as if empowerment comes as part of the package." Both employees and trainees are inspired by the philosophy and working culture of the organization. Especially, employee integration in the organization is crucial for its existence and growth in a sector where lack of professionals is one of the major problems.

Institutional Partnerships to Promote Credibility

Since Enable India does not offer an outcome on its own—in this case employment—its mandate is realized through structural partnerships with institutions capable of enhancing the prospects. Both Shanti and Dipesh have had an earlier work experience in the software industry and the relevant networks they initiated in the process have been useful for them to strengthen their prospects in the market. Such networks are helpful in building partnerships. During partnership building, their expertise in the field and networks have been useful for them to relate themselves to the way how employers work in the market and to the prospects of their trainees as potential employees.

Enable India, as a business case, resembles the social innovation school of thought which highlights the use of innovative solutions for addressing social problems. However, Enable India attempts to create a mission-centric and market-based initiative to emerge as a hybrid venture through strengthening its sister organization, that is, Enable India Solutions Private Limited (EISPL). Innovation in the organization starts from the very entry level of the training and placement followed by WPS. WPS is a crucial activity initiated by Enable India in order to provide additional services once the PwDs are placed in job roles. As part of the post placement retention service, Enable India offers WPS package to all those who are placed in various companies. As part of the WPS, problems faced while performing duties, which include technical, personal and psychological, are addressed by a dedicated expertise team. This helps the candidates to stick to employment with confidence. The solutions may sometimes involve technology, aids, change in process, change in behaviour, different training methodology or any specific help related to a particular project.

While adopting several learning methods, Enable India has grown strong in empowering PWDs. As they evolved from an initial charity-based organization, they now speak the entrepreneurial language. Praneesh, a key employee in the organization, narrates that:

Our concern for disability should be considered as a business case by the employers. This approach helped us in reaching out to a win-win situation for both the employer and candidate. Since inception we never approached any employer for job oppurtunites just because we are helping the PwDs. We are aware that a charity-based approach would not appreciate overall development in a long run. As part of our current approach, we strongly advise the employer to recruit only when they get best out of the candidates. If our candidates are not best, then there is no negotiation for recruiting them with the same set of skills.

The usage of entrepreneurial language helped them to negotiate with companies in market terms, which both the parties thoroughly enjoyed. The market-based dynamism is also essential because retaining PWDs without sufficient skill sets is most likely not possible in the job market. Thus, convincing them in the market language is essential. He further narrates that:

Here we are also talking about retention. So, without meeting the skills of the employer it is impossible to run the show. The other prominent issue we ask the employers to do is to take the best and pay the best. Our larger approach is to achieve overall development related to families of the PwDs. So far, our experience is that most of the disabled whom we train come from deprived economic and social backgrounds where their earnings would alone bring their families into mainstream. Hence, we expect our candidates are paid best par with other employees. The experience has been so far positive that most of the employers pay good salaries. As a result, we see a lot of happiness among the families.

Thus, the efforts do not revolve around training and employing alone but they highlight the overall development of the candidate and the families concerned. It reveals that unlike conventional institutions which aim at mere project-based output, social enterprises aim to achieve larger social goals such as enhancing happiness among families and communities and striving for their well-being.

The success of this initiative is centred on various organizational strategies. One of such strategies includes maintaining long-term collaboration with companies or employers, which is called as

Employer Outreach Programme(EOP). As part of the EOP, Enable India adopts a variety of strategies to associate with employers for a long term. This helps them to identify various roles that the differently abled can perform with each employer and further negotiate terms for them. In the process, several times Enable India catalyzes sensitization workshops for employers in which a business case for employing disabled is made. Such presentation sensitizes employees towards the essence of inclusive organization building and the empathy that they would need to have in order to encourage their colleagues who are disabled.

As Nicholls (2006b) described that social entrepreneurs stick to the supply and demand principle, Enable India is committed to create both demand and supply in the market. Demand creation starts with approaching employers with a business case to enhance their understanding about the essence of having PwDs in the teams. In addition, the employers who are most likely sensitized about the PwDs and their needs get to know about their skills, capabilities and concerns. This sensitization process helps the employees to offer few jobs in their organization to the PwD. Well-established employers such as Wipro and Cisco respond quite positively as they have well-established systems in place and they have already established sufficient infrastructure. They are willing to neutralize risks, if any exist, by employing PWDs. Though risk-taking may be an extreme wording, but given the horrific reception PWDs receive in a society like India, these employers are in advanced position and encourage them to fulfil their dreams. About 60 per cent of companies accept to recruit PWDs in the first go after sensitization presentation. Krishna, one of the employee of the organization who himself is a person with visual disability, describes that "Basically opportunities are available and we do the advocacy part and demonstrate that the PwDs are on par with others in terms of skills and capabilities." The demand creation is one of the crucial steps in the process, whereas the supply side is yet another complicated and most challenging task. This requires a fundamental focus on empowering the candidates which takes a lot of time and most energies from the organization.

As discussed, not all the employers are ready to accept the proposition expressed by Enable India to recruit PWDs. Though some organizations may immediately accept, a few employers do not see it as a feasible option due to their misconception about the capabilities of the PwDs. Devi points out that:

We all have certain inabilities; how we overcome them is what matters. Similarly, disability may have some permanent inabilities. In your case, when there is no light, you need torch light, whereas for a person with visually impairment, a cane is a solution. Accordingly, we use various strategies to impress companies.

There are four models largely adopted by Enable India to motivate employers to recruit their trainees: (a) collaborative training, (b) peer competition, (d) testing and probing, and (d) opening up. Collaborative training helps to persuade some employers who may not be ready for employing PWDs. This is where Enable India asks them for collaborative trainings. As part of it, Enable India and concerned companies organize collaborative training where the employers are sensitized by their direct participation in the event. Over a period of time when the employers invest their time and money, they get confidence in employing PwDs. They also see the potential of candidates and further train them to absorb. Peer competition is another strategy for approaching the employers by showing peer competition. The peer competition has so far worked well. By showing or marketing peer competition, confidence among employers is enhanced. For example, when Wipro knows that International Business Machines Corporation (IBM) has recruited PwDs in their core operations, then it also feels comfortable to recruit PwDs because the roles of the employees in Wipro and IBM are almost the same. If it works out well in IBM, it should also work in Wipro. Thus, the peer competition strategy works well with well-established companies as they are aware about the pros and cons from engaging in such activity. Especially, the peer competition manages to impress employers. As part of testing and probing, Enable India requests the employers to take Enable India candidates on a contract basis and understand whether the candidates are able to meet the requirement. If the candidate is able to meet the requirements, then they may be offered a permanent role. For instance, Enable India asked a nascent start-up called 'Thick silver', which is into the distribution market, to take up a candidate as an intern. After recruiting him, a pilot project was taken up and his work skills were assessed. The pilot project was successful and the candidate was offered a full-time job. The fourth strategy called 'opening up' is involved when the employers are not willing to accept any of the three models mentioned above; Enable India asks them to join as observers in the employment forum it conducts.

This allows them to understand various dimensions involved in the training. This deeper interaction would sensitize the employer who will later open up for employing the trainees. Adopting strategies as part of convincing employers has been a challenging task and it is unveiled through continuous adoption of innovations.

In addition to persuading the external organizations to offer job roles, Enable India also deals with capacity building among the trainees. As discussed, a large section of persons trained at Enable India come from deprived backgrounds. They not only come from deprivation and poverty but also have several misconceptions about technological developments. Shashikala, a visually challenged candidate who is currently employed as HR trainee at Aditi Technologies, claimed that:

> The quality of the training helped me to gain perfection not only in computer training but also in several other issues. Initially I was afraid to handle a computer or experiment with it but in course of the training I gained confidence and today my work demands a lot of computer usage in which I have grown my expertise.

It is to say that the PwDs come without having any expertise or understanding about computer training. Thus, Enable India has to literally nurture their potential to enhance their understanding about computer training and build confidence which is crucial for the overall development.

Adoption of Social Innovation

It is the commitment to achieve SO, and adoption of innovations in every aspect that make Enable India unique, otherwise most of the activities that are taken up at Enable India are generally carried out by several other organizations in the field. Since the inception, innovation has become a prime engine for the organization for its survival. Let us say it has been induced from primary training to employment, pre-employment services, supplemental education, consulting and enabling other institutions working for the PwDs. Though the innovations are not path-breaking in the field of PwDs, it certainly takes care of necessary requirements related to the needs in the sector. WPS has been an important and key activity that is relatively innovative. Generally, it is believed that due to various market dynamics, employee retention rates are significantly low in market. Especially, for persons with visual disability, it becomes most difficult. However, with the WPS, 90 per cent of the PWDs are not only able to retain their jobs but also get pay hikes and promotions. Richi narrates that:

> Whenever I am unable to work due to the software issues, I always get support from Enable India. The very next day I receive someone from Enable India to help me in performing my duties properly. So the support I am getting from here [Enable India] is quite encouraging.

Adaptation of WPS not only helped them to retain their jobs but also held them from experiencing humiliation and disintegration from mainstream.

The success that the social enterprise enjoys today has not resulted in training alone. It has also got to do with the persuasion that Enable India has carried out throughout its inception with various employers. Especially, it goes with a belief that having PWDs in teams and in organizations will boost capabilities of other employees. Such persuasion has helped employers several times to realize and to understand the need for having people from diversified backgrounds in groups. However, Dipesh narrates that:

> Enable India never asked any company to recruit someone because the candidate comes from deprived background. We always emphasized on the skills and talent of the candidate and having such candidate in the organization or group creates positive synergy and improves the production. We always want employers to see us as a business case.

As part of the advocacy, Enable India also claims that apart from the talent that these trainees accomplish, their presence also helps in the growth of the organizations because it promotes motivation levels of other employees in the organization.

Social Value Creation

Rewriting social realities or creating alternative social reality with regard to Enable India is surrounded around how the lives have been transformed. I spoke to several of those who have been trained at Enable India and employed by different employers. The respondents proclaim and see the transformation in different ways. As transformation or creation of social value is quite subjective, the author has attempted to project it from the respondents' perspectives. For them, it is about the actual change in the incomes, lifestyle and community recognition or gaining self-esteem. This section aims to emphasize on understanding the social value created. Data from field research is extracted to analyze views expressed by the respondents.

All the respondents reported that there is no relation between their educational background, their interest or passion and their current profession. However, they claimed that they are comfortable in their current jobs. A study conducted by CSIM (2010) found that 76 per cent of the visually impaired trained at Enable India believe that the training has helped them to address several issues related to their future, including self-confidence and their professional life. When we talk about the transformation, the conditions in which they were put up earlier and the way they are now empowered is quite inspiring. Though they all are employed in the best of the companies, they may continue to face exclusion and exploitation in one or other way. However, there are significant improvements in the actual and relative well-being. One of the respondents, Karonolis Lingdow, who comes from a poor family in Meghalaya, a north-east state in India, narrated his story. Back at home, he was brought up along with six other sisters and five brothers. After being trained at Enable India, he was placed in Rediffmail as a spam operation executive. He expresses how his association with Enable India and later his job with Rediff helped him to gain respect in his own community. As Lingdow puts it forward:

> Ten years back whenever I used to walk on road, people used to look at me and call me 'Hey blind fellow'. That is the only thing I used to hear from the community. However, it did not take much time for them to realize my talent. I always had an excellent academic record. I never failed in any examination. When I passed class 10, the community was impressed as I could finish it in the first attempt itself, which was rare in my locality even for sighted kids. After that I completed my Intermediate [+2] immediately and that's how my name was featured in local newspapers. Since then everyone started recognizing my potential. I later completed my graduation. Then I moved to Bangalore to join Enable India. Now whenever I go home, the way villagers talk to me is potentially changed. There is a drastic change since the last 10–15 years. In fact, recently, last December, when I was travelling in a shared cab from my local railway station

to home, one of my friends from Bangalore called me up on my mobile phone. The only way of communication with him was in English as both our local languages are different. My fellow passengers in the cab were silent when I was on phone. They were surprised by the fact that I could converse in English. Later they asked my sister about my whereabouts. My sister told them that I am working in a well-known company in Bangalore, which was received by them very positively.

Largely, such reactions from communities are experienced by most of the respondents. For example, as Parvinder Singh confirms:

Now the orientation of the community has entirely changed. I am placed with a job in 2009 and since then I go home once a year for 10 days. I see a lot of positive sense in the way the community, relatives and family see me. Everyone say they are proud about me.

The difference that Enable India brings includes trust in the employers and confidence in the candidates. Neelima, who has earned a job before completing the basic training at Enable India, proclaims that:

I have earlier completed my computer training in some other institute. However, no employer was willing to recruit me due to their misconception about my capabilities and skills. I tried a lot and tired instantly. Someone told me about Enable India. I got registered myself in Enable India for one of the training programmes. However, I secured a job in the IBM, much before I could complete the training. I can confirm with confidence that my skills were recognized by IBM because I was associated with Enable India. Had I attended the interview on my own without any affiliation from Enable India, then they would have never believed my talent. In fact, I have experienced enough, they do not believe that we are capable of doing things.

The profiling helps Enable India to understand the candidates better and offer them necessary service. Neelima's case is a classic example of understanding the range of prejudice that exists in job market about the capabilities of the deprived.

In a few cases, family members who never supported their differently abled children to move out of the home feel proud about the success of children. Richi narrates: "Now my parents are proud that I am earning with dignity. They are very happy. They inform all relatives that I am grown and grown enough to take care not only myself but also my parents well-being." The success stories negate social realities and prove the abilities of disabled in order to cross family and social boundaries for their own inclusion. Raghavendra, who works as an HR Executive in People Equity, claims that the independence he got with the help from Enable India's training is immense, where earlier he was never allowed by his family members to at least use electricity switches, now he is confident enough that he can travel alone across the globe. He had lost his eyesight when he was 25 years old because of an accident. Since then his family and friends were overprotective of him and never let him do anything. When he wanted to attend a conference in Mumbai, his family did not allow him to travel. That was when he realized how important it was to be independent. Thus, he decided to learn mobility and started to use the cane with the help of the training received from Enable India.

The training, employment and further follow-up activities by Enable India help candidates to be included in mainstream society where their participation is assured. Parbind Singh who works as a Sales Support Executive at Ascent India claims himself as an 'Enable Indian'. He never knew how to speak English before taking his training at Enable India, though he had completed his Bachelors in History. However, with a lot of struggle he could manage to get training from Enable India which changed his future course of planning and execution. Now, as he claims, he has nurtured the skill of being curious and critical because of which he has attained skills that help him to be included in the society. In fact, his job role requires fluent English as he is expected to talk to different companies over phone to inquire about their products/services. So, Singh, who never knew how to speak English, now only speaks English as part of his job. Further, the experience also brings self-respect within the society in which the differently abled persons live. Neha Agarwal, who was trained earlier and is now placed in IBM, expressed that the biggest change that she witnesses is the enhanced self-respect in the family which she had lost along with her eyesight. Now, she has started to move alone in the places where she used to go when she was sighted. She claims that she lost all hopes and never thought that she would be able to be independent in her life. She considers this phase as a birth into a new life of hope and success. It proves to highlight how minor issues such as walking independently or being able to speak in English are far more important for PwDs. Hence, it is not simply about training and employment that we must be concerned about when we talk about social inclusion in this context. Enable India constructively helps the PwDs to regain the respect, freedom and independence that they once had and which they lost in the process.

One of the respondents, Prasad, puts it in a simple way, "Before I came here [Enable India], I was depressed and always questioning the God, why am I given this punishment. But today I am happy about the way how I live. I am independent and extend support to my family." Yet not all the cases are ideal which result in a successful ending. Some of the respondents felt that their skills are continued to be underestimated even after the training and they are not allowed to work according to their capabilities. Siva Shankar felt that he is unable to find a job that suits his skills. He narrates, "As I did not have any other job, I had to compromise and join a low profile job where I get much less than what other fellows with my skills are paid." Parvinder Singh claims that he has been exploited by paying a different salary structure compared to his fellow employees. In his own words:

> My manager says you should thank the consultancy as they gave you this job. People like you should not demand anything. Though I am happy about the employment, still I am always worried that the job is not suitable for my qualification. When I ask for a suitable job or salary, then my employer doesn't cooperate.

There are even other problems related to usage of technology, for example, Ramgopal was appointed in Synthia Technology Pvt. Ltd, a medical transcription company, based on his remarkable performance in a written test. However, later he was ousted from his job as his employer updated the software which would require a different set of skills than the one in which he was trained.

The updated software transcription comes out as an image which Jaws, the computer software for PwDs, could not read. Though Enable India tried to resolve the issue through WPS, it did not work out. As a result, he had to search for some other job. In a few places people do not have the basic courtesy about PwDs and their issues. Ramgopal puts it forward that in a company where he earlier worked, his colleagues never used to talk to him. Even if he wished them by saying "good morning", they never responded. He recalls how he was respected when he was sighted. However, in that company since he became completely blind, he claims that he has lost his respect as well. He wants to mingle with people but the response has always been depressing.

On the other hand, most of the respondents felt that they were not discriminated by their employers in any other ways except salaries. Prasad responded that, "Obviously, once you join a company, especially in a corporate world, there is no variation. If you are visually challenged, physically challenged or a sighted person, it doesn't matter. Their work has to be completed." Though few respondents said that initially they were not provided the necessary facilities to initiate their duties, with the intervention of Enable India through their infrastucture auditing, these facilities were later made available. PwDs fail to have peer interaction due to the lack of network among the peers. Hence, many of them never had any chance to interact with others. Richi narrates that:

> Earlier I thought I am the only alien who got this problem. Everyone was normal around me. I have studied in sighted school and college, because of which I didn't get to see persons with visually challenged. But after coming here [Enable India], I found that many are similar to me and I get a lot of strength while interacting with them. I was so excited to know that many people exist similar to me and all of them are earning on their own. This enhanced my confidence levels.

Further, the new bonding and social relations are enhanced by the usage of social media. This not only helps them to get access to an array of peers and friends but also to know the various opportunities that exist in the market.

Murali narrates how the transformation amounted to his reintegration into the society.

> I completed my bachelor as a sighted person. All my studies have been through when I was sighted. I lost my vision after my graduation. Though I have undergone a surgery, it did not result in any betterment. The problem has been noted as retina pragmatism, which does not have any cure in medical history. I used to spend my entire time at home. I was psychologically distressed as well. With the distress, I never thought about my career opportunities. Later I came to know about Enable India and joined there in 2010. It has paved way for an unexpected journey. As a result, my entire life has been

changed. What I was earlier and what I am now is completely different today. Those who have seen me throughout my life know what
that transformation is all about. I am currently employed in Cisco, a
major software company in Bangalore.

The individual case studies offer rich knowledge about the life transformation which is the major objective of the social entrepreneurship
process. Parimala's case offers very enriching experience. Parimala
is a visually challenged female (28 years) who comes from a poor
family. Her father works as a fourth-grade employee at a private
firm. One of her sister is intellectually disabled[4]. Parimala is visually
challenged by birth. However, her family has been supportive and
the family members have found that she has got good skills. She has
completed her Masters in Economics. She was trained in Enable India
in 2003–04; it was when Shanti had embarked into Enable India
as a full-time employee. Since, Parimala was one of its first trainee,
it was certainly a tough call for the organization to find a job for
her. Shanti had to take her to various companies for several days in
order to attend interviews. Finally, they could place her in IBM India
as a third-party contract worker. She has completed her training at
Enable India besides her Masters in Economics. The training was for
about 11 months. Though she was placed in one of the pioneering
IT companies, she claims that the problems that she faced continu-
ously taught her various lessons. This whole practice has helped her
to understand several dimensions of social structures and the ways
in which these social settings/structures respond to the excluded sections. According to her, IBM had been a different kind of experience altogether. Since she was working as an employee of the third
party, IBM was not willing to accept her inclusion in its mainstream
employment. However, once she was included after some struggle,
she was never promoted to the next level, that is, full-time employee,
in spite of her commendable adoption of job profile, whereas the
other teammates were easily promoted. Parimala had to struggle a
lot in order to get to the next level; it took her more than two and
a half years, whereas for others it was just about one year. Even
at the next level, that is, from a full-time employee to a permanent
employee, it took her more than three and a half years. Though both
the attempts were tough, she had to exhaust all energies to succeed in

---

[4] Intellectual disability refers to the significant limitation in intellectual functioning and adaptive behaviour of those who have been affected. It is also known as
mental retardation.

her second attempt to become a permanent employee. Finally, during the transition period, she realized that she was losing her capabilities/ skills and concentration on work. Several times she committed a lot of errors/mistakes while performing her roles as a full-time employee because of the psychological depression which resulted due to the discrimination. Generally, it would take enormous time for managers to realize her potentiality and build confidence about her capabilities. The managers, during the initial stage, were reluctant to give any role to Parimala, anticipating that she may not perform well. She claims that it was one of her team leads who helped her to get permanent employment. The team lead holds an LLB degree and took her case very seriously to the top-level management.

The cases discussed in this study narrate a simple process and ways through which social transformation is achieved. Once the concerns and existing social realities that hampered social participation are understood, they are tackled by employing various processes. Such transformation has been possible with continuous innovation and strategies adopted to offer structural inclusion for the excluded sections.

Replication and Scaling the Impact

Over a period of time, Enable India realized that as an organization it may not be able to address the needs of the PwDs or empower them as a whole in a country where on an average, about 3 per cent of the people are PwDs. With a motto, 'your vision cannot be limited because of your limitation', they have started training other organizations which are engaged in the empowerment of PwDs to undertake the entire process within their organizations. In other words, Enable India believes that it is impossible for it to address the problems of PwDs across the country. Thus, in order to transform the systems, the idea has to be reached to several places. Accordingly, they started to train various grass-root organizations which are working in the PwD sector. As Shanti elaborates:

> We don't want to expand as a big organization, but, we want to build other organizations who can take this training forward. You can't simply get into a village in Maharashtra having your office in Bangalore, or it will take a few years or decades to build trust among stakeholders

if you start one on your own elsewhere. So we want to avoid this delay and rather we will enable local organizations or NGOs, so that they can carry forward our work in their respectable regions. This approach gages a significant impact. Down the line, we further want to empower persons with disability to take up such initiatives in different areas.

The bottom-line intention of employing such approach is to benefit the maximum PwDs in relatively quick times. The resources, such as training, content making and other expertise, which Enable India acquired over a period of time are shared with other organizations free of cost. The content has been developed by Enable India investing the resources they have acquired.

In addition to sharing the content, the trainers of other organizations are trained by Enable India in order to maintain rigour and quality in training. Public sector organizations which recruit PwDs as part of the 3 per cent disability quota also approach Enable India for training their employees. Instead, Enable India trains their trainers in order to decentralize the process wherein each organization will be capable of handling their own employees who come from the disability background. This certainly leaves the organizations to be confident while recruiting the PwDs. For example, the State Bank of India (SBI)—the largest public sector bank in India—approached Enable India to train their employees with visual disability, who are by and large considered as unwanted human assets with the bank. However, Enable India has encouraged the bank to have their own dedicated team to train their employees as the recruitment of PWDs is a continuous process in the bank. Accordingly, Enable India has trained the trainers of the SBI who in turn are expected to empower the PwDs. However, towards the end, Enable India monitors the quality of the training conducted by other organizations through its monitoring mechanisms.

The existence of Enable India for over one-and-a-half decade has faded out deprivation and exclusion of a number of PwDs in a significant way. The inclusion achieved has not only facilitated confidence but also offered necessary skills for their existence. The PwDs who were always seen as a burden in the families are now being considered as an asset. With this initiative, communities have realized the potential of the PwDs. The success of the social enterprise lies in a broader mechanisms it has created in the field of its operation. For example, Enable India generally approaches various potential employers requesting to consider recruiting PwDs in selective roles;

now the condition has reversed with positive approach from companies where they also show interest in recruiting PwDs.

In several cases, Enable India became a brand for PwDs upon which they make an ideal deal with the employers. For example, Roshan Rajan who had excellent computer training through his course in NIIT could not get a desired job in the IT sector. However, with the help of Enable India, he was contacted by various companies and finally he acquired a job. Further, it is found that several candidates who are trained at Enable India are now charged up to start a social enterprise on their own or replicate the Enable India model in their respective locations and serve the needy and excluded. If this trend continues, then Enable India might even get into hosting an incubator in support of the ventures initiated by the trainees.

Sustainability Orientation

In spite of many innovative methods adopted in reaching the unreached, Enable India currently works with various fund raising models which are significantly dominated by the grant seeking mechanism. It approaches various funders to run the programmes. Due to its young team and lack of institutional reforms, as of now, the organization runs with funding from external funding agencies such as Sir Dorabji Tata Trust, American Indian Foundation, Charity Aid Foundation and institutional funds like Accenture, Axis Bank, etc. For example, based on the intake of every year for various training programmes, funding is received from funding agencies. All funds are based on the projects. When the project ends, the funding also ends simultaneously. However, the outside support is unable to cater to all the needs of the organization. For example, several employees in the organization expressed their distress over salaries. One of the biggest problems with social enterprises in India which depend on the non-profit operation mode is that they are unable to cater to the employees' financial needs, especially the salaries. Accordingly, they are unable to retain most of the recruited staff. While Enable India does not face any issues related to retention of employees, there is a need for the organization to look into this aspect. In fact, this situation talks about the venture's weak financial status. When non-profit organizations depend upon donor-based funding, they do not encourage overheads beyond a certain basic amount, which is largely around 15–20 per cent. This limitation influences the salary/remuneration conditions of the employees in the organization. Thus, this financial constraint encourages non-profits to look for market integration methods which help them to act independently on the internal organizational issues. In addition, the organization has not developed any corpus to sustain the activities as it believes that it is not fair to seek more funds from the donor than what a training programme really requires.

As discussed, the innovative approaches that the organization carries out places it under the social innovation school of thought. When it comes to social value creation, it is imparting incremental developments in the lives of PWDs; however, the sustainability issues from financial independence perspective need special attention. In order to transit from social innovation school to social entrepreneurship school of thought, it needs further attention and strategic operations.

It is recognized within the organization that the brand value needs to be cultivated from which it emancipates the potential for making finances within broader social value outlook. They believe that the organization, as it stands, aim at a specific target group; thus, it may be disastrous for them to generate incomes from the activities undertaken. Accordingly, they are not of the view of charging fee from the beneficiaries/trainees. However, the aspiration to attain own incomes are proposed to fulfil by creating EISPL, a private limited company which aims at marketing the content such as videos, audios and written documents developed by Enable India in viable markets. EISPL is a mission-centric social enterprise which aims to supplement its profits to Enable India in order to enhance its social value creation. The plan is that EISPL will become a sustainable venture on its own over a period of time and then help Enable India to sustain its activities. Praneesh explains regarding the content developed which will be marketed under Enable India Solutions.

> We have developed certain e-learning software and books, which are part of our commitment to promote self-learning. It enables a student to get trained without a teacher or a guide. As part of the efforts to scale the impact and to become sustainable, we would like to reach out to as many as possible. However, it does not mean that we want to take a step back with regard to our primary objective. We are committed to achieve better quality life for PwDs in the country; hence, the gap gets filled by e-learning tools.

The specialized content in the field developed to empower people with disability by Enable India has got a lot of value not only in domestic markets but also visible internationally. So, the attempt by EISPL is expected to become a strong focal point. The overall intention is not to market the products among PwDs but to target other agencies such as government organizations, NGOs and corporations which have sufficient funds to buy these products. However, "If any disabled as an individual requires the content, we provide her/him at free of cost. Our entrepreneurial process only aims at organizations or government," he further concluded.

In addition, Enable India undertakes various allied activities in order to expand its financial strength. It includes various consultancy services such as disability audit and organizing the disability awareness programmes in various companies. These activities, in turn, help the newly placed PwD staff in the companies to avail relevant facilities which they may require during their course of work; further, the other employees become aware about disability issues and finally, Enable India makes some money. So far the EISPL has just evolved. It requires a strategic planning and a strong team to initiate activities and achieve its objectives.

However, Enable India misses out to adopt various ways of acquiring SO as it stands today. A cross-subsidized model is the best available option which Enable India continues to ignore. As part of the cross-subsidized model, the trainees can potentially be asked to cover their training costs. This does not mean that the social enterprise takes a narrow focus on social value creation. Empathy and organizational vision continue to focus on attaining larger value creation as its prior focus. Few respondents have mentioned that they would have happily paid, if they were asked to pay a fee. Richi responded that when there is some value that she is getting out of the training, she believes that nothing should stop her from paying the necessary fee. Since she comes from a well-to-do family, she would have paid without any reservation. However, most of the candidates could not pay. In fact some of them do not have any resources to look after their living in Bangalore. In such cases, Enable India looks after their living by offering scholarships. Hence, given the presence of both varieties of respondents, a cross-subsidized model is a much appreciated method. Another respondent Prasad narrates that, he had in fact asked Suresh, his trainer at Enable India, how much he should pay, but it was later confirmed that the training was for free. The other option probably Enable India could explore is that once the candidates get into jobs after completion of training, they could pay back to the organization, potentially ranging from 10 per cent of their incomes. One more option they could explore is to charge for the services offered under WPS. However, the management of the organization hesitates to collect any fee from the candidates as it believes that being disabled itself is a condition to be in poverty. With such generalization of view, Enable India misses several ways of attaining SO. Though they are serving the larger interests, the potential ways of becoming sustainable are missed out in the process.

In summary, Enable India addresses a very important social issue which requires urgent attention. The investigation from this research informs that Enable India has been successfully employing innovations in different space in order to maximize social value. However, their financial side is less explored. This is to understand that the availability of financial resources in the form of grants do not inspire them to operate on entrepreneurial methods. While they continue to ignore several possible aspects to achieve SO, there is much more Enable India could possibly do in order to enhance its SO through adoption of market-based approaches. While EISPL could potentially open up their SO, it is a long way to go before any profits from it may be used to maximize social value creation. In fact, it requires a dedicated team of experts to run the latter. Thus, the success of the latter and its potential contribution for the former is a matter of time and efforts that would go into its operations.

Despite the financial matters, Enable India has the potential to keep the society engaged in protecting the rights of one of the excluded sections to achieve their market and social participation. Its success and inspiring stories motivate several donors to contribute to its success. The more entrepreneurial strategies the organization adopts, the more social value Enable India could possibly create. With this inspirational discussion, the next chapter aims to understand how another social enterprise, which is located in rural India, helped communities to attain their basic rights and dignity through its continuous innovation.

4

Gram Vikas: Revitalizing the Rural Living

'Gram vikas', when translated, means 'village development'. Gram Vikas is a social enterprise that works with rural and tribal communities in Odisha, an east coast state which is considered as one of the backward states in India. Gram Vikas is an area-based social enterprise which undertakes works related to multiple social issues including education, health, safe drinking water, sanitation, livelihoods and alternate energy, which are sustainable, socially inclusive, gender equitable and empowering for the deprived. In order to achieve its mission and reach out to the maximum people, Gram Vikas partners with villagers through local governance institutions, which are established for this purpose. These local organizations offer space for Gram Vikas to explore ways in which both development and empowerment are achieved within the philosophical boundaries of democracy and good governance.

Background of the Social Problem

Odisha is considered as one of the poorest states in India. While growth of the country on the one hand is impressive in the recent past, the growth rate of the state of Odisha has lagged behind the national average since 1970s. Agriculture which accounts for 64 per cent of the total workforce in the state has failed to occupy a crucial role in the economic growth with its mere representation of 32 per cent. According to the 2011 census, the population of Odisha is about 42 million, out of which 37 per cent people live below the poverty line (BPL). Scheduled Caste (SC) or Scheduled Tribe[1] (ST) represents about 79 per cent of the total poor. Though there is a steady decline of poverty from 57 per cent to 37 per cent in the state between 2005 and 2010, the quality of the life for those who have been lifted from the BPL is still in traumatic conditions. About mere 42 per cent of rural households have access to basic sanitation facilities and 74 per cent of the rural households do not have access to piped water. However, a small number of people who have access to water get it in unhygienic quality. A whopping 80 per cent of the morbidity and mortality cases in rural areas are due to infections by water-borne diseases (Government of Orissa 2004). Poverty is significantly traumatic in western and southern districts of the state where a large proportion of adivasi and Dalit population reside. Various facilities including health, education, transportation and communication are poorly maintained in the sub region. The brief discussion about the contextualization of the problems narrates that a majority of the population in the state, especially in rural areas, face multiple deprivations and lead an inhuman life. Thus, several of these problems became base for Gram Vikas to locate itself there and address these problems.

The Idea of Gram Vikas and Growth of the Social Enterprise

The primary evidence about the state of Odisha reveals a shocking state of people and lack of proper provision to promote their participation in the mainstream. Four decades back, the situation was much disastrous. It was then that Gram Vikas as a movement emerged in the backward region of the state. The idea of Gram Vikas was originally derived from a student movement, the Young Students Movement for Development (YSMD) which was formed by a group of students from Madras University to assist in organizing various developmental activities for the poor and the marginalized.

---

[1] Scheduled Tribe and Scheduled Caste are historically underdeveloped, subjected to exploitation and poor social, economic, political and cultural participation. These communities are also familiar as adivasis and Dalits, respectively. In this book, the words such as Scheduled Castes and Dalits and Scheduled Tribes and adivasis are used interchangeably.

Initially its prime task was to respond to social problems and assist the affected to regain confidence in various ways. One of the first well-known responses from the group was offered to the victims of war of independence in Bangladesh in 1971. YSMD under the leadership of Joe Madiath set up various relief camps to resettle people affected during the war. Later within the short spam of six months, the State of Orissa[2] was affected by a disastrous cyclone, which resulted in affecting millions. This touched the YSMD and about 40 people from the group travelled to Odisha to extend their help. Though the intention of the visit was to help the flood-affected people, their stay in the area for a year while constructing roads and repairing agriculture lands had led them to understand various critical social problems persistent in the area, which included poverty and underdevelopment among many other.

The group after settling from the distress resulted by the cyclone felt that their efforts could only result in immediate relief, but the larger aspects of dignity and development for the rural population was far beyond imagination. Hence, the group decided to stay back and assist villagers in the developmental discourse to solve their own social problems. Initially, the activities undertaken were based on trial and error basis in consultation with the villagers. The experiments started dealing with problems related to agriculture as a large proportion of people in rural areas depend on it. It was found that the area surrounding Mohuda, where the group was located, had abundant source of water. However, the natural conditions were daunting for agriculture as there was no water management system in place which would strengthen agriculture production. The group with deliberate discussion with villagers united different communities and emphasized the need for collective farming. As part of the collective farming, it was agreed that farmers would allocate some land for the landless poor for the purpose of cultivation as part of the norms prescribed under collective farming. In order to get better yielding, lift irrigation system was introduced. But unfortunately, the greedy landed class, after seeing the improved production, did not allow the landless to claim stake. Several attempts of the group to reunite these two classes had not produced any result. This taught a lesson to the young group about

---

[2] The state of Orissa has been renamed as Odisha in 2011.

the need for a strategic move to work beyond social realities for the achievement of social equity. The lesson later dictated the working of the organization.

Then the next move of the group was to initiate a dairy activity that was believed to generate incomes for the tribal population. It did not take them much time to realize that the cow milk based dairy was neither feasible nor operational. The local customs of the tribals manifested that the milk from cow was not meant for human consumption. In spite of repeated demonstrations by the group explaining the benefits from milk consumption, the community was not convinced. So, the second failure in a row critically opened space to self-evaluate the weakness and strength of the team, their selection of problems and approaches adopted.

Hence, it was felt that before initiating any activity, examining and understanding the local culture and aspirations of the people was key to advance in the search for a better developmental agenda. As part of the process, winning the trust from communities was the most desired need for them to sustain their initiatives and get communities on board. However, the communities which comprised of tribals were sceptical about encouraging outsiders. In addition, two failures in a row had further widened the gap between the young team and communities. Tribals were basically fed up with the then existing structures and the people from mainstream society who often approached them with a lot of promises including lucrative loans, animals, houses and wells, etc., which were never materialized. The outsiders often enjoyed local hospitality and ran away after collecting some money from the tribals. Hence, tribals were suspicious about outsiders. In fact, due to the exploitation that they had experienced by outsiders, the same fear prevailed while considering to entertain Gram Vikas. Due to this belief, it became way tougher for the group to gain acceptance, in spite of their cyclone relief efforts. After thorough understanding of local cultures and rapport building, Gram Vikas had been institutionalized on 22 January 1979 under the Societies Registration Act. However, in spite of its establishment, Gram Vikas continued to lack a specific vision to dictate its objectives except developmental orientation because of which it has ended up undertaking an array of developmental activities which the organization has failed to sustain for a long time.

While exploring to establish trust with the communities, addressing concerns related to their health was found to be a prominent method. Health as a mean to restart the entire approach was partly reasoned by a fact that it was the most prevailing problems which led to several other social problems. Malaria was quite prevalent in the area, whereas the medical facilities were at minimal. People were not aware about the relevance of safe drinking water, quality health and hygienic food. This had led to start offering rudimentary health care systems. In addition, health as a focal point of entry into the communities was a good strategy as it was expected to strengthen the bondage. As part of the programme, initially village health workers were identified from the community and were trained to cater the health needs. This initiative helped Gram Vikas to gain trust from communities of which they were in desperate need. In the process of trust building, Gram Vikas was later involved in supporting tribals to take up various agitations against exploitation related to land, which is quite common in tribal vicinities. In addition, the following few years were invested in further understanding of local contexts, tribal cultures and helping them to fight against money lenders, which turned out to be a real trust winning episode. The organizational initial efforts to win the trust revived the damage that has been already done by the so-called developmental agents who negated the interests of the most excluded in the given context.

However, initially, the philosophy of the organization just revolved around development. Thus, the social enterprise strived to work on all the issues that were believed to hamper social functioning. Accordingly, an array of activities was undertaken by the organization, which included water and sanitation, education initiative and self-help groups to encourage women to undertake small-scale enterprises. Other activities also included construction of a brick factory which continues to operate till date. In addition, a bamboo factory was also initiated. Bamboo and bricks were used for construction of Gram Vikas campus and sanitation-related constructions initiated by the organization. A biogas initiative was launched in 1989, which took a momentum due to its presence in the national policy priority. In addition, Gram Vikas initiated from time to time different set of activities which have larger social implications, and accordingly it stood out as an area-based social enterprise.

Various Activities Initiated by Gram Vikas

Gram Vikas at present works in 24 districts[3] of Odisha. In addition, it is also operational in Chatrapur district of Madhya Pradesh, Srikakulam in Andhra Pradesh and Sairekela Karsawan in Jharkhand. Altogether, it is operational in 1,090 villages as of March 2014. Gram Vikas has embodied within tribal agitation to fight against the exploitation from different backgrounds. Joe, the Director of Gram Vikas, explains that:

> Though Gram Vikas aims at holistic development of the areas where it works, the social enterprise emphasizes on tribals because government does not show any inclination to work for their benefit. The excuses government opts may vary from time to time for ignoring these sections which includes sometimes claims such as that the tribal villages are too small to develop.

Throughout its reach, Gram Vikas undertakes a set of activities pertaining to improve living conditions of the poor and excluded communities. As discussed, in order to undertake the activities it envisages, Gram Vikas advises the villagers to come together and form into different committees in order to coordinate, discuss and deliberate among the villagers.

Community participation is a crucial aspect in the activities undertaken by Gram Vikas. As described in Figure 4.1, community participation, enterprises initiated and innovation practised are key aspects in the structure building process to address social problems which prevail in rural areas. Gram Vikas has initiated various activities and moved beyond conventional ways to achieve social transformation and promote alternative realities which they believed are useful for communities. The detailed list of activities undertaken so far are discussed below.

Community Health

Gram Vikas was initially touched by the poor sanitation facilities in the villages. In addition, lack of access to safe drinking water further degraded the situation. Lack of safe drinking water and

---

[3] A district is an administrative division within a state or territory.

Figure 4.1

The overview of Gram Vikas

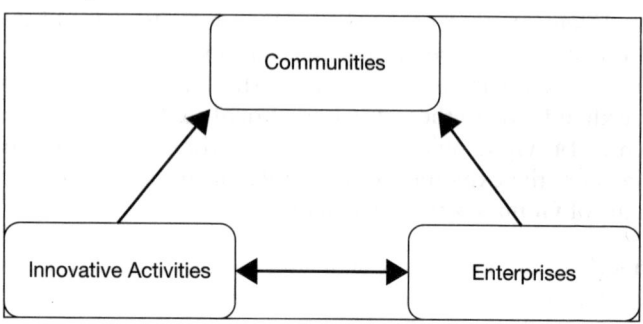

Source: Author's own.

poor sanitation are hazardous for a healthy living environment. In order to address this basic concern, Gram Vikas health development programme came into existence. As part of the programme, Gram Vikas follows a threefold approach that includes preventive, promotive and curative services to promote healthy living conditions among the communities.

As part of the preventive measurement, Gram Vikas established sanitation infrastructure facilities in various schools. This brings in where students pressurize families and communities to undertake hygienic sanitation-related activities in their respective houses and communities. Children who are familiar about usage of toilets in school influence communities to adopt the practice of hygienic sanitation. The second level of the activities are promotive in nature. As part of the promotive measurements, Gram Vikas organizes various health camps with partnership from government programmes and agencies. Among many other aims, the major role that these camps focus on is to end malaria which was quite prevalent in the tribal areas. Health committees in villages pressurize government agencies to provide basic health facilities, while the curative measures include training and capacity building on various health-related issues among the communities. Local health workers are recruited and trained as part of this initiative in order to diagnose illness, provide treatment and refer them to necessary hospital.

Education

Education programmes at Gram Vikas aim at providing basic education to all children in the areas of its operation. In the first phase, it strengthens government-run schools. In the areas where a government-facilitated schooling system does not exist, Gram Vikas establishes its own education structures. Such establishments are operational in remote and hill areas where government finds it difficult to operate. Initially, Gram Vikas established village-based schooling systems. The schools aimed at teaching children about essential social and cultural skills that are relevant for participation in social life. In addition, primary schools provided elementary education to residents in primitive locations. However, later with unveiling government crèche programmes, Gram Vikas shifted its focus to cluster-based schooling systems with an emphasis on tribal children. Today, there are about five residential schools being run in different regions to promote the secondary education of both boy and girl children with special attention to the latter. These schools are operated on residential basis where children from tribal communities live and learn. The schools provide free education and accommodation to girls which has enhanced participation of girl children in education programmes, whereas boys are asked to enrol with nominal fees. In addition, Khel Vikas of Gram Vikas trains school-going children in various sports including weightlifting, badminton, football and volleyball. So far, many of those who have been trained in Khel Vikas have won several prizes in state and national level competitions.

Natural Resource Management and Food Security

Gram Vikas promotes communities to undertake land and water conservation, community forestry and horticulture through sustainable management of natural resources. Tribal-dominated and poverty-affected areas such as Ganjam, Gajapati and Kalahandi districts are being operated by Gram Vikas to run these programmes. In order to enhance food security measures, several options have been made available to increase community incomes through various alternative livelihoods such as fisheries, horticulture and livestock. Social forestry is promoted with a view to utilize the unutilized waste land for the purpose of growing trees for fuel, fruit, fodder and timber.

Integrated Watershed Development

Integrated watershed development programme of Gram Vikas aims to (a) build watersheds in specific regions, (b) protect land from soil erosion, (c) improve soil's ability to absorb rain water and (d) enhance vegetative growth and agricultural productivity. Several ponds have been revamped to harvest rainwater that will be useful for cultivation. Government has recognized Gram Vikas as one of the project implementing agencies in the Bolangir, a drought-affected district. As far as the coverage of the project is concerned, villages are motivated to construct, manage and maintain community-based integrated watershed development programmes. Initially, watershed committees and local community groups are created to manage watershed activities. These committees also look after issues related to community involvement in the entire process.

Horticulture, Agriculture and Livestock Development

Gram Vikas also assists tribal communities in developing agricultural land resources. The cultivation of cashew, pineapple, mango, jackfruits and vegetables are promoted and supported through field training, credit support and seed distribution. Horticulture has increased earning capabilities of the families which resulted in better livelihoods for the deprived. In addition, the villagers are motivated to nurture a variety of livestock to substance their livelihoods. Training in five key areas, namely masonry, plumbing, bar-bending, stone dressing and painting, are key for families categorized under BPL. Young men and women are especially encouraged under this training, who in turn are expected to earn respective jobs in industries or start enterprises on their own.

Renewable Energy

Gram Vikas demonstrated that rural areas require disaster-proof shelters, clean water, sanitation and electricity like any other urban area. Especially, Gram Vikas built confidence among the rural poor and deprived who never thought of having privileged basic facilities. Gram Vikas assumes that habitat development is a crucial tool in poverty reduction. This offers a pleasure of dignity and upholds confidence to lead a better life. Accordingly, various community-based energy programmes such as bio diesel, micro, hydro, smokeless *chulhas* (stoves) and solar photovoltaic applications to provide rural households with renewable energy have been initiated. In addition, solar lightening system is promoted in areas where grid-based electricity supply does not exist. The solar systems have replaced kerosene-based lamps which have social, economic and environmental implications. The rural youth are trained to take up any minor repairs that may come up in the process of maintaining the solar lighting systems. The significant part of the activities undertaken gets manifested by a fact that they not only benefit the communities with the provision of basic facilities but also earn dignified jobs for them within their reach.

This further gets intensified by Gram Vikas venturing into micro-hydro projects. Micro-hydro power is a cost-effective option for decentralized rural electrification by training village youths and technicians to design, create and manage community-based micro-hydro projects. The community plays a crucial role in undertaking the projects. In addition to the continuous innovation and learning, Gram Vikas is also tied up with Practical Action South Asia (formerly known as Intermediate Technology Development Group) and Engineers without Borders, a US-based firm, to scale up the micro-hydro projects. Further, Gram Vikas is also engaged in generating biodiesel from the local available resources. Like diesel, the use of biodiesel is multifold. Though the quantity produced is limited, it is largely used for the local use. Biodiesel produced is used in different activities including ploughing, irrigation and threshing through a multipurpose tiller.

The biogas programme of Gram Vikas was one of its first kinds initiated in Odisha. The federal government headed by

Indira Gandhi had given significant priority for the biogas initiative in its 20-point programme in 1985–86. Hence, the government of Odisha had also shown keen interest in the industry due to the enormous funding available from the federal government. Accordingly, it was understood that Gram Vikas was the only organization to work on the biogas initiative in the State. Thus, it was approached by the government to scale the initiative. Within 10 years, it established about 54,000 biogas units with about 1,000–1,200 employees working for the entire units sanctioned. This was equal to 80 per cent of the total bio diesel initiatives in Odisha. However, it was found that the project was just contributing to those who were already placed top in the economic ladder, leaving the poorest of the poor aside. Though there was no specific objective set for the organization, it did not take much time to realize that they were moving away from their intentions. The biogas initiative which was started as a community-supporting initiative, in turn, emerged as one of the strong programmes which spread across the State. With government's intervention, this has opened up earning strategies for Gram Vikas which resulted in gaining enormous financial benefits for the organization.

Water and Sanitation

The water and sanitation programme of Gram Vikas is one of their key activities. This was created to unite all villagers or the entire community in the village. It is believed that the lack of proper drinking water and sanitation facility in rural areas of Odisha was one of the major reasons for prevalent diseases. Hence, Gram Vikas has taken a steady commitment to improve water and sanitation facilities in the areas of its operation. In addition, the sanitation issues in rural areas have direct implication for the health and dignity of communities, especially for women. It adopts an innovative cycle which includes mobilizing communities to realize the need for proper sanitation facilities and construction and usage of proper sanitation systems. As part of this endeavour, Gram Vikas mobilizes, educates and trains communities on various issues involved, such as how to construct, maintain and manage the sanitation system within communities. As part of the process, communities come together and take active role in constructing toilets and bathrooms for all the households with a 24-hours water supply system from a tank constructed in the village as part of the approach. Initially, a sum of INR1,000 (about USD17) is contributed by each household towards corpus that is utilized for the future sustenance of the activity.

Creation of inclusive societies was one of the major aims of the water and sanitation programme. However, there was a need to adopt innovative methods and approaches in order to address the rigid caste system persisting in the social context. Due to the prevalent caste system, people from different castes had different water systems. Several meetings within the organization resulted in a sole declaration that the water and sanitation programme, which aimed at 100 per cent sanitation coverage, could be a way out in order to address the caste system. For this, all social groups had to be brought together. In fact, it was to bring consensus among the communities. Caste is a prominent factor in the social hierarchy that divides different sections in India. Further, in order to achieve 100 per cent coverage, round-the-clock water supply was necessary. These two issues seemed to be overambitious as it requires innovative strategies and capacities for persuasion. Most of the villages where Gram Vikas initiated to work were not electrified. Hence, water supply for 24 hours as part of the 100 per cent sanitation programme was a mere impossible task. That is where innovation of gravity grasping of water from about 4–5 kilometres has worked well. Principles of gravity of flow and siphoning were introduced, so that water traverse over small hills to ultimately reach a tank constructed in the village and then to reach houses from there. As Joe mentions:

> Our desperate need for water which is centre to the entire sanitation project has resulted in exploring new ways to unleash the problem. That was when we have introduced a gravity-based system to supply water to the areas where there is no provision of ground water plates. The process is very simple. We identify an area which could be within 4–5 kilometre radius where water sources are available. Through gravity, we link water to the nearby villages in order to provide water to all households in the village.

This programme also takes inspiration from the philosophy of the organization that aims to bring together all households in a community. It means, the programme does not isolate any individual or family in spite of the social hierarchies that exist in rural settings. As part of achieving total sanitation, construction of 100 per cent toilets and running water are essential. This was never believed to be realistic by many of its own staff, funding agencies and also the government. In fact, communities also had reservations about the possibility of construction of toilets and their usage. Such arrangements in a plenty of cases tended to clash with the existing social structures that do not allow certain sections to access equal rights or facilities along with the advanced sections in the same locality. However, Gram Vikas had taken it on communities and made it mandatory that unless all households without any bias participate in the activity, it would be impossible for it to implement the programme in any given context. Such strong stand facilitated various sections within rural settings to unite for a cause. Initially, in order to prove what they believed in, a pilot project was carried out covering 337 families in five villages. The programme later was extended to another 40 villages covering 3,000 families. As a total, by end of 2013, there are about 61,000 families that benefited from the programme spreading across 1,050 villages.

In spite of the strong arrangements by Gram Vikas to achieve 100 per cent coverage under the water and sanitation programme, initially 5–10 per cent people in the villages did not show their support. However, it is considered that without 100 per cent coverage, the ambitious project would just become a grant seeking and toilet construction work for those who are in need, rather than realizing the intention of transforming rural settings. The notion deployed was 'either all or none'. The central focus on the mission and ambition further persuaded the remaining villagers to act according to the wishes of organization and be part in the social transformation. The policy of 100 per cent inclusion is the first step to crush the barriers of caste and class that are much prevalent in rural Odisha.

Housing

The housing project of Gram Vikas is quite ambitious. Gram Vikas has designed houses which have an area of 41 square metres each. They are much larger than the typical dwellings of 10 square metres where generally the tribals or other deprived people live. The houses developed by Gram Vikas include two multi-use rooms, a kitchen and veranda. The cost of this dwelling is INR51,163 (approximately USD850) with the family contributing 30 per cent of the cost through their labour and local materials. The remaining 70 per cent is facilitated by Gram Vikas as a soft loan from the Housing Development and Finance Corporation, a private financial institution. The loan is repayable by the household over 15 years at 9 per cent interest. The financing of this programme has changed since it began in 1991 from a full grant to a full loan, with the entire cost of the house now being met by the family. Total grant to a total loan is an incremental step to promote communities to live with dignity and to achieve sustainable intervention, for the services they use. In fact, communities gain dignity, confidence and self-respect as the houses are bought by their own finances.

Small-Scale Enterprises

Gram Vikas has been one of the first organizations to undertake business in support of the non-profit work the organization undertakes. Accordingly, it has anchored a brick industry which is a cost effective, energy efficient and environment-friendly brick production unit. Gram Vikas has adopted Chinese technology for making bricks which it bought from China with the assistance extended by Swiss Agency for Development Corporation and Development Alternative. The brick industry was a viable rural industry which has supplied bricks to all Gram Vikas constructions and also created small employment for masses, who otherwise would have ended as migrated labourers. This project was financially attractive and easy to maintain. The bricks are stronger and are produced from pollution-free technology. In addition, bamboo and Cane industries have also been initiated to support the organization. The usage of these industries has been twofold: (a) they are expected to contribute to the material needs of Gram Vikas for construction purpose as a lot of work the organization has carried out requires material produced by these three industries, and (b) they are further expected to contribute for the SO of Gram Vikas.

After extensive research carried out in collaboration with the Massachusetts Institute of Technology, Boston, and Center for Micro Finance, Chennai, Gram Vikas came out with the smokeless *chulha* programme. The programme adopts Gram Vikas innovative *chulha* design that includes double-pot, and mud stove design. This is prepared with local made mud pipes. In the process, local employment was created for the potters. The implementation of the programme adopted a local entrepreneurial approach through training women and youth in order to manufacture the stoves and promote their usage. This offers employment and steady incomes to the families involved.

Gram Vikas undertakes these activities in villages which are in need. Due to its backwardness, major portion of the villages in the state require such activities. However, Gram Vikas undertakes these activities selectively where communities come together and demonstrate their active participation in the entire process to attain better living conditions and promise scope to sustain the initiative for longer duration.

Strategy and Operations

Gram Vikas' major strategy and operations are associated with community participation and their contribution. The identification of villages or communities where the presence of Gram Vikas is required has been done in two ways. Primarily, Gram Vikas on its own identifies the villages. Social networks that the organization has developed over a period of time with the communities facilitate such selection. For example, some employees or the volunteers of the organization identify such villages or communities through their social connections, or understanding social contexts through random visits. For example, when Gram Vikas comes to know about a particular village with a problem, an employee from Gram Vikas goes to a local tea shop and since people have never seen him, they are curious to know about him. The interaction results in villagers wanting to implement the activities in their villages. In this approach, initially the success rate was not more than a mere 10 per cent of the villages which were motivated. But as the organization gained popularity in local contexts, there has been a high percentage of success registered. Second, communities affected by social problems approach the organization to implement the activities. For instance, very often villagers come forward and ask Gram Vikas to visit their village to initiate development activities. For instance, if there is a nearby village where the work has already been implemented, relatives from other villages approach Gram Vikas to implement the activities in their villages as well. In response, Gram Vikas will have a small group meeting among employees before meeting the entire community.

Community Participation

In the problem context, the residents of the poor communities where Gram Vikas works have limited say in the decisions which influence their lives. It is at this level that they require developmental institutions that account for their real development. Gram Vikas creates such platform wherein the development of these deprived becomes a reality. Gram Vikas fosters such reality through bringing communities together. Accordingly, communities are asked to form self-governing people's institutions which act as focal points for all developmental activities being undertaken in any given community or village. The reason for establishing such institutions is to enable communities to utilize its fullest potential where they can address the problems that are prevalent in their vicinity. Each family in a community is asked to join the general body in order to elect representatives in the institutions.

The formation of a Village General Body (VGB) is necessary and a key step to embark on SO. The VGB consists of every headman and headwoman of all households in a given village. As the initial step, based on the consensus, the VGB signs a Memorandum of Understanding (MoU) with Gram Vikas. Members who show up leadership skills in the VGB are made up to form a 10 member led village executive committee (VEC) that is responsible for day-to-day activities in the village. The VECs are registered under the Societies Registration Act of 1860 which enables them to undertake financial transactions that are related to the developmental activities.

The creation of the VEC also helps the community to take up their representation to the government with a strong voice. Ashish, an employee at Gram Vikas, narrates that the activities undertaken by Gram Vikas are routed through the communities. First of all, the village committees are formed where a member from each family becomes part of the general body committee. Then they discuss about how to implement the activity and how to collect the corpus from the community. Each family is expected to contribute a one-time investment of INR1,000 (USD17) towards the maintenance fund. Village committee looks after this fund. In addition, the committees also collect about INR 20–50 (approximately 50 cents to USD1) per month from each family for the usage of electricity and water, which also becomes part of the maintenance fund.

Communities take active role in each and every activity. It was not the case initially during the 1980s. People used to fight with difference of views on whether to trust Gram Vikas or not. For example, a relatively small group had expressed its willingness to construct a water tank in one of the villages. With the support from the small group which formed a committee, a water tank was constructed. As the structure was visible, people started trusting the organization. Meanwhile, the local committee became strong. They also met all other villages and convinced them to be part of the developmental design. The committee informed the remaining people that there is a water source at about half kilometre from the village, and requested their cooperation in tapping the water using the gravity system. Five more households came forward and installed water supply for the tank from the water source. Then someone stole the water pipe. But the committee sorted it out. They found that the pipe was stolen by the other group, which was against the creation of the water system. Within two days, water supply was materialized. Finally in next few months, after understanding the benefit, everyone accepted to be part of the committee structures and took part in the later developmental plan.

For undertaking any activity, the resource mobilization aspect is vested among the stakeholders. For example, communities represented by committees offer sand, labour, etc., whereas Gram Vikas offers cement, concrete, etc. According to a government policy, where 100 per cent sanitation is guaranteed, government is supposed to provide water facility. So, wherever it is possible, Gram Vikas submits proposals to the government and makes sure that the funds are sanctioned to the water supply. In addition, a provision under

Mahatma Gandhi National Rural Employment Guarantee Scheme (MGNREGS)[4] also has been used to complete the developmental activities undertaken. Joe narrates that, "Though government sanitation programmes aim at BPL families, it is with our intention we aim at total coverage. We take care of remaining funds required." As part of the operations, several VECs within a cluster of few villages form an area committee. In addition, various sub committees are formed within a village to look after different activities and support the VEC at large. The sub committees may individually look after issues such as gender sensitization, education, health and sanitation. The division of labour among each community and different sections of the people had led to their active participation, transparency and accountability within the social enterprise.

Participation of Women

From the very beginning of the creation of VDCs, women are encouraged to take part in the developmental activities. Women are basically deprived of social participation. It becomes much relevant in Odisha due to its backwardness. Participation of women in both economic and social activities means increased visibility and development for entire families and communities. In order to ensure their participation on the social front, their participation in economic activities has been encouraged. The concept of SHGs has been introduced to these tribal and Dalit families where women are made part of the groups through which they have started earning respectable incomes. Further, this allowed them to access credit from banks. It has opened space for women to explore social settings outside their communities for the first time. The advanced groups have leveraged income-generating activities including livestock rearing, processing of minor forest-based products, whereas few other groups started investing in cultivation of cashew, tamarind, paddy, etc. Gram Vikas played a crucial role in building women-led enterprises.

---

[4] MGNREGS is a State-sponsored scheme which guarantees a 100 day work for each and every household from BPL. The work provided under the scheme will be utilized by the local level governing bodies for various rural developmental activities.

During a group discussion at Mohuda, it was elaborated by a group of participants that:

> Whenever we require loans as part of our business, Gram Vikas stood for us. When we approach banks as a Gram Vikas representative, there are always ways in which we are facilitated with a loan. Meanwhile, our business became quite well known. For example, everyone came to know about the pineapple production here. Every day about 8–10 loads of raw pineapple is transported to the markets in Bhubaneswar, Cuttack and Berhampur.

In addition, various government programmes are being introduced in the ill-fated areas with active presence of Gram Vikas. The group further narrates that:

> All of us have received Kisan credit cards. Kisan credit card is a scheme based on which we are provided a loan on just 7 per cent interest for agriculture. If we could return the entire money in the time stipulated, the interest rate comes down to 4 per cent, where both beneficiary and government pay 2 per cent each. Though it is a government scheme, we would have never been able to acquire it on our own, given our social backwardness. Gram Vikas demonstrated with the bankers and motivated us to avail the facility.

Thus, while innovatively operating on ventures and activities initiated by the organization, Gram Vikas has steadily encouraged and educated communities to participate in government-led developmental programmes in order to achieve rapid transformation.

In addition, women are brought together with the spirit acquired from SHGs to discuss about various developmental activities in their villages and become part of the discussions on the social dais. This allowed them to speak publicly and question the status of various developmental activities undertaken, stand of the State and local administration in several cases. Various government programmes such as education, sanitation, childcare programmes and midday meal programmes have been assessed by women from SHGs. Gram Vikas provides training to the SHGs on basic record keeping and financial literacy, and encourages them to generate income through their group activities. When it is believed that the groups are equipped enough to handle larger amounts, then they are introduced to the banks through various bank linkage programmes which enable them to get loans from banks to extend their businesses.

Social Value Creation

Employment Generation

Gram Vikas with its 300 employees stands as one of the largest social enterprises in rural India. Like other typical social enterprises, Gram Vikas also empowers the deprived and excluded from communities to undertake various job roles in the organization. Such move not only highlights yet another role a social enterprise undertakes in the form of WISE, but also provides livelihood to the selected employees and their families. Badri, an employee who joined the organization 20 years ago, narrates that he had just studied class 6 and came from a deprived background where the entire family of seven members used to depend on one-and-a-half acre land that they had. As he explained, it was really tough to have three square meals a day for his family members. In fact, his wife and a daughter used to work as daily labourers and he used to take care of farming. However, due to the low wage payments and poor farming, family maintenance was turned as a way tougher. In fact, he had to ask other two children who were eight and seven years of age, respectively, to start working with their mother. Within the passage of time, he came to know about an opportunity in Gram Vikas and approached the team members. Though he was neither qualified nor skilled enough, after listening to his plight, they offered him a job and proper training to take care of the records in the office. Due to the job, within a short time, his family living improved. He was able to get his daughter married to an employed groom. His other two children are well-educated and currently employed in Bhubaneswar. He claims that he had never expected such a changeover in his life. The employment resulted in better living standards. In case of the social entrepreneurship discourse, it is expected that social enterprises employ most excluded and discriminated in the various job roles. In fact, the whole intention of WISE is to integrate the excluded into job markets. Life transformation in case of Badri is a clear indication of such orientation. In fact, it was found that such case narrations are quite common as the researcher interacted with several other employees. For example, another employee Viswas claims that he comes from a local tribal community. He joined the organization just six months ago. He was also a school dropout and Gram Vikas has employed him after his community recommended him to be taken on board as he came from the most deprived background.

Gram Vikas, on the one hand, facilitates employment for the marginalized and deprived at the assistant level and manages senior positions with well-qualified candidates. However, it is found that those who come with better qualifications would never want to continue with the organization for long time as their aspirations and requirements are in most of the cases higher than what a social enterprise can generally offer. Off late, it is found that in spite of its strong pro employee welfare measurements including housing, health insurance and competitive salary packages, Gram Vikas is unable to attract motivated and qualified people on board. In addition, the organization is unable to retain those who have been induced after thorough training. This has been demonstrated as a strong reason for the lack of focus to scale the initiatives beyond or creating new organizations to support the existing ones. For example, as it is stated by Anil, a senior employee:

> People do not care whether they work to create social transformation or for a for-profit entity; their intentions of high salaries have to be fulfilled. We have lost the best of our trained people to UNDP, UNICEF, WHO and many other multilateral donor funds, etc.

Though Gram Vikas provides better facilities than several other social enterprises, still it continues to face human resources related constraints. Joe elaborates that, "The biggest problem we see in order to move forward is to handle the human resources. Being in multiple activities to ensure development in rural areas, Gram Vikas has so far failed to attract or retain qualified and motivated employees." Even it restricts the growth plans to scale the organization. Further, he emphasized that, "Before jumping into various other forms of institutional building, it would be far better to sort out the issues that arise in the institution. Especially employees leave us due to their high expectations in terms of salaries and other facilities." It is found that this is where the morale of those who stay with the organization is distracted. However, there is always a reason to be joyful about the number of employees that continue to stay with the organization for decades.

Gram Vikas is also inspirational in promoting entrepreneurship through encouraging its employees to take up several entrepreneurial opportunities that exist in the process. For example, those who worked as supervisors in the biogas plants were helped to start their own enterprises and they started biogas plants in various parts of the state. To encourage and boost their morale, it was told that those who failed in their efforts may return back to Gram Vikas to their existing job roles. This has led to 500 supervisors becoming entrepreneurs from which only six people have returned due to their failure. Gram Vikas has offered technical support to all those who have started biogas plants on their own.

Achieving Social Inclusion

As discussed, Gram Vikas being an area-based social enterprise multitasks to empower communities who are expected to take control over their own lives. During one of the group discussions, it was revealed about the multitasking of Gram Vikas that:

> They helped us in getting housing loan. Then sanitation system was based on the '*Jaladhara* programme'. Accordingly we have got latrines and bathrooms. This has resulted in protecting the dignity of our women and girl child. Then they have established school for all children. Now functioning of the school has been stopped as government has initiated a new school in the locality based on the Right to Education Act. The centre has become non-formal education centre. Further, they have also helped us in forming SHGs. There are six groups in this village at present. All of them got benefited by Gram Vikas. We have initiated pineapple small scale industry and procured a pineapple juice machine from the loan we have received as part of SHG.

This narration gives a glimpse of the activities and social value being created by Gram Vikas.

Through investing to improve the local infrastructure and living standards, Gram Vikas has become a focal actor in revitalizing the rural economy in which it operates. It sets forward a living standard for the stakeholders. Those who never witnessed their social and economic participation now take active role. Especially the economic independence among the various social groups, including Dalits, tribals and women, has enhanced their social independence. As a result, their voices became instrumental in village level development. Kasturba narrates that due to her active participation in SHGs, her voice is being respected beyond the community. Earlier she was just a mere daily labourer and she could not even convince her husband to take a decision related to her own family matters. However, with the guidance and support from Gram Vikas, she became a leader of SHG and undertakes a small business, out of which she manages profits. Taking inspiration from the success, many women in and around her village have started looking into SHG as a potential medium to achieve financial and social inclusion. This further led to the revitalization of the local economy and amplified the thrust to intensify the involvement of women in businesses. It also helped women to become local leaders. As Padma explains:

> I have been an active member of SHG. After attaining financial independence from my SHG involvement, my group has started looking into other developmental structures in our villages. We have raised our voices against various social problems at village level meetings and represented to the taluk and district officers. We were able to get some of the developmental works done in the village. Later, I myself became a leader in the local government. Now we take active participation not only in financial activities but also equally in political and social life.

The enhanced visibility which started with financial and social participation moved to political participation and decision making. In fact, these three conditions are interlinked, which demonstrate a larger practice such as social inclusion.

The elevated financial independence has attributed to the overall growth of the communities. Prosperity and social participation have increased. With the infrastructure development including structured houses constructed under different schemes, villagers are happy about the way their lives have transformed. Social capital has also seen new heights as people come together more often and share concerns. Especially this move has been vital for the development of the once deprived communities, such as Dalits and tribals. Though the social inclusion of various sections within their social structures is ensured, unfortunately, it has not resulted in systematic social change where the rights of the Dalits and tribals are respected in the larger context. As Das puts it forward:

I come from a Dalit family. Though we have benefited from the innovative projects carried out by Gram Vikas, our participation in social life on a larger look is not achieved. My family is happy living with the services we receive; however, our voice is not being respected in social life.

This explains that while individual/family-based concerns at society level are taken care of, when it comes to empowering the deprived, the efforts will have to be much more robust and have to aim at the core of the cultural settings.

The organization also agrees that the social equity across different sections is believed to be a strong mechanism to attain social justice, which has somehow not been achieved due to the rigid systems in place. As Dutta, who works as a manager in the water and sanitation section narrates:

I have been working here since last 15 years. We are trying to bring social equity among different communities. However, due to the strong social misbelieve and caste system, we are unable to do it as communities from the upper strata still follow their orthodox beliefs. However, it has not isolated us from improving the social living of the deprived.

Many projects undertaken by Gram Vikas specially focus on benefiting Dalits and tribals in areas where other castes are predominantly present. As a respondent pointed out:

Water and sanitation programme has come into effect because of our efforts to include socially deprived sections in the developmental planning. We have realized that it is difficult to negotiate with the predominant social structure unless otherwise it is proven that the participation of everyone present in the scenario is imperative to take up the activity and achieve the goals.

The innovative attempts to include social equity and promote social capital among the communities through increased economic and social participation have somehow been successful. The communities are of the view that they are happy about the levels of social capital that exist among themselves. Laxman briefs that with the increased incomes and social participation, the community bondage has become stronger. Thus, the social value creation is achieved in two contexts: (a) through employment generation for the excluded sections and (b) by achieving social inclusion in larger social systems. While social inclusion is achieved to a significant extent, the social systems have not been influenced in order to achieve larger social change.

Sustainability Concerns

In order to facilitate the activities undertaken by Gram Vikas through community-led local institutions, the democratic decision making process has been deep rooted. Gram Vikas takes crucial steps to educate villages to excel in principles of good governance and democratic governance which have been worshiped in the areas where Gram Vikas inspired village level institutions. Moreover, the approach to achieve the goals pertaining to social equity through community participation aims at empowering communities to take active participation in decisions that improve their living conditions. The more the participation of people in local governance, the more sustainable the initiatives can become.

The capabilities of communities and local institutions established to look after the needs of the communities are boosted with various training methods adopted from time to time in order to improve their management skills. For example, the VEC undertakes the entire charge to run the water supply systems in villages, including its operation and running expenses. The funds are mobilized through community contributions in addition to the innovative methods to use the resources available locally such as village ponds, forests or community plantation that aim at maintaining the water supply system.

When we talk about sustainability, it is essential to bring contribution from the communities. Here, communities are not just enjoying the fruits but they also contribute quite actively in their own growth. All the activities undertaken by Gram Vikas have been supported by the communities benefited from the programmes. For example, in sanitation alone, about 60–70 per cent of the total resources required are collected from communities. The remaining resources come either from the government or funding agencies approached by Gram Vikas from time to time. In water programmes, government offers 80 per cent of the total required funds. In housing programmes, communities contribute to achieve the total requirement. In case of all the activities undertaken, about 40 per cent of the resources come from the communities, which makes the SO quite effective. This approach further gets boosted with the corpus fund mobilized from each household. As discussed earlier, every household contributes on an average INR1,000 (USD17) towards corpus fund. This fund is deposited as a term deposit in the local bank. The interest generated from the corpus is used to support new families inducted under various schemes once Gram Vikas withdraws from the village, in addition to using it for maintenance. Though INR 1,000(USD17)/- is a minimum benchmark set forward, the richest may contribute more while the poorest is allowed to contribute less with greater labour participation. In addition, Gram Vikas encourages people to pay for the services they receive. For example, water meters are installed for water consumption from the borewells is one word. Please place together. This allows them to pay according to their use. However, the charges are nominal and only cover the running costs. This not only brings sustainability of the initiative to the forefront but also allows communities to understand the value of water. Gram Vikas intends to make sure that the initiatives continue to exist and social value continues to be created even when the funds are most likely not available or when Gram Vikas withdraws from the activities concerned. The efforts are being laid down to sustain the initiatives once they fall under the community ownership.

The organization also firmly believes that anything given away free without any effort from beneficiaries may result in its misuse, and further it may benefit communities but will not guarantee their active inclusion. The other significant contribution of Gram Vikas for the cause of social entrepreneurship gets manifested in the way certain programmes are initiated without having any financial source. For example, initially there was no funding available for the water and sanitation programme; however, due to the magnitude of the social problem, Gram Vikas had decided to take up the issue with limited resources that they had apart from the greater community participation. In fact, government did not support the initiative despite the repetitive representation as it could not believe a mere fact that 100 per cent sanitation with a toilet, bathing room and 24-hours running tap water were something feasible in villages where basic facilities do not happen to be seen in such areas. Once Gram Vikas has made possible what was believed to be impossible in more than 40 villages, government got convinced to sanction fund to scale the activities in other villages.

At the organizational front, Gram Vikas has, over a period of time, acquired huge corpus fund raised from different sources. Especially, the biogas programme had earned enormous corpus. As discussed earlier, Gram Vikas has partnered with the government to scale up the biogas programme. It had altogether constructed about 54,000 plants. As a result, Gram Vikas has secured the term fee from the government for constructing the plants. The term fee had been put in the corpus fund raised from time to time. The corpus fund is deposited in the banks which get multiplied in every seven years. In addition, organizational support for building corpus has been quite useful. For example, the Ratan Tata Trust and Dorabji Tata Trust have offered a significant portion of funds to build the corpus. The other major contribution for corpus building came in the form of awards. For instance, through Skoll Award, the organization received about USD1 million as one time grant, followed by USD150,000 every year for five years. Such resources have been highly useful for the organization to concentrate on the activities it undertakes and be assured about the funds required. Everything put together, Gram Vikas has developed about INR65 crores (USD10 million) corpus as of the date.

The major aim of creating the corpus is to take care of different activities when the organization decides to scale the reach. In addition, during the financial difficulty, the corpus is expected to look after the running costs of the initiatives being undertaken. For now, the organization runs on the funding received from government, donors or philanthropists, apart from major community contribution. Whenever there is a scarcity of such funds, interest from the investments in various banks is used for undertaking the activities.

Gram Vikas has been quite ambitious to run all the activities with its own SO. There are three ways an organization can be sustainable when we talk about income generation and SO: (a) maintaining huge corpus and the interest that comes from such corpus, which can be used for running the activities, (c) initiating a mission-related enterprise in order to protect the interests of the social organization and (c) mobilizing government or community to invest and contribute. Joe propels about the sustainable plans Gram Vikas envisages that with the declined interest rates, maintenance of the corpus is no more a viable idea. The scenario of maintaining endowment in India with the current inflation rates has turned to be a totally unviable option, while government generally does not involve until the activity is scaled significantly and has achieved greater social value, whereas the communities are most likely unable to contribute to a greater extent. However, the best way to move with regard to preserving the corpus is to push it through the second option—investing in some business which would result in better returns. However, the existing policies do not allow non-profits to undertake such activities. Especially when the income on investment exceeds INR25 lakhs (USD40,000), the entire organization becomes taxable. That is the reason, as Joe clarifies, "[w]e had to withdraw from running three enterprises that were started some time ago including brick, bamboo and cane unit."

The other notable financial problem experienced by Gram Vikas is folded within the way in which government handles its activities. Most of the activities undertaken by Gram Vikas are funded by the government at both state and central level. However, due to the unaccountable delays in government releasing the fund, Gram Vikas faces several problems. For example, government has yet to release (in 2013, when the field work was carried out) the amounts sanctioned in 2010–11 financial years. As Joe narrates:

We undertake the activity once we get approval from the government agency. However, due to various administrative reasons, the release of fund always gets delayed beyond bearable time. Finally, our reputation will be at stake if we do not deliver to the communities. So, we go ahead and advance from our endowment or corpus and then even take money from the bank to finance the activities. The primary reason we identified for the delay is our policy not to comply any illegal means including corruption to get funding.

Another respondent from finance department mentions that, "When you begin to work with people, the momentum cannot be stopped half way, because the promised funds from government do not materialize. You spend your own or borrowed money. As work progresses, the debt burden increases until it almost crushes you." It supplements a common understanding that the participation of government in the activities cause enormous delay. However, the active participation of government is always welcome as it makes sure that government, which is primarily responsible for the well-being of the people, takes active participation to fulfil its objective through the social entrepreneurship approach.

As discussed in the beginning of the chapter, Gram Vikas is one of the first social organizations to start business in the form of brick, bamboo and cane industries. However, it has failed to run business due to the lack of a clear strategy. Moreover, being in rural areas, Gram Vikas always used to attract officials from income tax and forest department demanding bribe for running these businesses. Hence, the momentum and interest of the employees towards profit making was lost. As a result, the enterprises created to support the social enterprise have been leased out or sold to outsiders. However, Gram Vikas overlooks the other alternatives available which have been widely accepted throughout the sector; these include creating an entirely different for-profit organization where tax implications matter for the separate entity. However, capital has to be raised. While Gram Vikas claimed that they are open to initiate ways of unleashing different options available to promote SO, the analysis of the interaction yields that such options are rarely explored by the organization.

Mitigating to Avoid Risk

Social entrepreneurs are familiar across the globe for their risk-taking behaviour or at least for calculated risks (Light 2006). However, Gram Vikas, which has been focal for undertaking continuous innovation within the given structures, seems to avoid taking risks beyond its control when it comes to creating SO. Gram Vikas is largely stuck with a notion that creation of an enterprise may lead to negative externalities. The largest fear surprisingly comes from human resources related issues. "Best of the employees from the social enterprise may need to be transferred to the business entity," Joe expressed his concern. Especially during the time when there is a lot of struggle that organizations experience in order to get qualified and motivated employees on board. Hence, the best people working with the social enterprise may get transferred to the for-profit business which may result in compromising social value creation. In addition, there are a lot of prejudices prevailing in the organization. When the researcher spoke to a few employees, they were of the view that creation of a separate for-profit enterprise and pulling its surplus to run the social activities may dilute the whole intention to create social value. Further, it may create rift between employees of the different entities where employees from profit-making industry may claim their superiority over their counterparts from social enterprises with a view that the social enterprise is sustaining with the support from the business enterprise. The fear further emerged that the situation may lead to a case where the organization may split into two different parts.

Even the cane industry established earlier has had tremendous production which led to profits. In addition, local artisans were trained to create income generating activities in small-scale industry. The products manufactured by artisans such as handicrafts, homemade food items and agro business had substantial demand in local markets including Berhampur, Pralaka, Mundi and Rayaghada. It has resulted in increased visibility and unwanted guests in the form of tax officers, who approached the organization for bribes. In spite of the no-bribe policy, the organization had initially entertained such guests. With the passage of time, it was found that more than 50 per cent of the total profits were spent towards paying the bribes. "In order to sustain in the business, we had to entertain them," said an employee in the finance department of the organization. However, later the organization has attempted to resist demands for bribe which turned to create several problems including objections being raised by the government neither to sell the forest products nor to import the cane. In addition, a lot of taxes were leveraged on the products. Hence, finally Gram Vikas had withdrawn from all the engagements of profit making including cane, bamboo, brick industries and decided never to venture into such activities in the near future. This learning has been crucial for social enterprises. Social enterprises are expected to be mature and clear about the transparency and accountability, unlike their other third sector counterparts. However, the participation in illegal activities for the noble cause is still a wrongdoing. The lessons learnt from such failures made sure that Gram Vikas never re-enters into market-based approaches.

Neoliberal Sanctity

The social transformation Gram Vikas rendered is to be highly appreciated. However, on the other hand, the fact that remains important is the withdrawal of the state from basic service delivery in the areas where Gram Vikas is active. With the active participation of Gram Vikas in providing basic facilities, it is said that the government has adopted a no-look policy into those villages where Gram Vikas serves. It unveils a practice that active social entrepreneurship would promote the reduced Welfare State. Joe emphasized that, "Government has started hesitating to look into the 1,090 villages where Gram Vikas actively undertakes various developmental activities." State offers all facilities to the remaining villages excluding those that are served by Gram Vikas. Now, the villages where Gram Vikas is present are the only villages which pay for the running water supply. Though the running water system or sanitation is not so robust in the remaining villages, government takes care of the expenses incurred in the process, whereas it overlooks the villages where Gram Vikas offers the service. Joe further opines that, "I would say this practice is only to smoke us out. However, we sustain on our credibility and trust we have built over a period of time among the communities." In fact, it is much beyond than mere smoking out. It has to be critically understood from neoliberal orientation.

It is further disclosed that the government has not offered its support to the activities undertaken in good faith. An employee adds:

> Government does not want anybody to do excellent work. It just expects us to do what is prescribed by them or what has been conventionally carried out. In addition, they expect about 10–35 per cent of the total grant in the form of bribe. However, we neither encourage any involvement of government in our activities nor offer bribes. In spite of it, we are able to sustain ourselves in this scenario, due to the reputation that our model has acquired worldwide, and our strong presence in the developmental discourse has been well received by both local and global communities. Notwithstanding with any of the views, still we believe that the government is responsible to people and the resources of the government are the resources of the people. So, we continue to fight and aspire to get the funds from government.

Joe being reputed in the field of water and sanitation in the country, influences government policies as a member in the national sanitation committee. He attempts to achieve his vision by influencing the government policy.

Gram Vikas experiments show a lot of momentum about how dedication and continuity in undertaking multiple issues contribute to achieve social transformation. Gram Vikas offers simple solution for the most pressing social problems. Continuous innovation, dedication and engagement with communities would make the idea of creating alternative social realities possible. Attaining social change may not be possible in the first experiment alone, nor were the communities impressed there. However, with continuous experiments and efforts to reduce the gap between communities and social enterprise, it is evident in the current context. In addition, the commitment of the social entrepreneur and his team, in spite of the discouraging environment at times, has resulted in achieving better social transformation. Down the line in a few months, Joe will retire and he would like to take this experiment forward. Joe tells:

> I will take this forward. North east, Himalaya region, wherever the induced gravity water system is possible, where most of the women do not need to trench down the hill and up for water. I would like to take it to the other states in eastern and central India. That would be what I am interested to do before I walk into the sun set.

It propels that social entrepreneurs do not rest until their innovations reach out to different corners. Their commitment, ambition and passion aim at better living for the excluded and the marginalized.

Gram Vikas as a social enterprise is well described with the incremental innovation it has initiated since beginning in order to chip into the community ties and to explore ways to unleash social problems. In the process, initially it went on initiating several enterprises on its own in order to achieve its own sustainability. However, with short success, the operations went into distress when the enterprises were shut down due to the legal barriers that came up. With the fear of facing troubles from the legal mechanism, it is to state that the organization has become cynical to explore other options available to initiate further market-based enterprises. Notwithstanding the SO that it misses out, it is found that the organization has been instrumental in innovating in various fronts in order to cultivate inclusive growth. The community contribution and their participation somehow ensure sustainability of the activities undertaken, and advance its SO.

This chapter highlighted how dedication and continuous innovation, in addition to commitment, lead to create inclusive growth. The various processes Gram Vikas adopted from time to time offer rich understanding about different processes ranging from trust building to fostering alternative social realities. The next chapter discusses about another innovative attempt from a Delhi-based social enterprise to contextualize how clothing, as an issue of human dignity, is promoted by using innovations at the core of its operations.

5

Goonj: Clothing as a Right

Chapter 4 conceptualized on continuous innovation and its implication for social transformation, whereas this chapter focuses on in-depth innovation in a single issue—clothing. The case explains how in-depth innovation results into developing the best solutions for some of the depressing social problems associated with clothing. One of the problems with the growth and development in developing countries is the growing gap that exists among different classes. In particular, the gap between urban and rural population within a given context is a significant setback for any society to achieve inclusive growth. In India, while plenty of policies aim to make both urban and rural areas independent of backwardness and deprivation, none of them talk about reducing the gap between these areas. On the contrary, the rampant disparities within the cities due to the divide between rich localities and slums have already led to social trauma and exclusion. However, the debates on reducing the inequality gap among various sections of the population require due attention as this will bring obstacles in the growth process. Goonj (meaning 'echo') attempts to reduce the gap through connecting the various sections as partners in achieving social growth. The philosophy of Goonj is built on a belief that a piece of cloth would bring change among the most marginalized and excluded. Anshu Gupta, the founder of Goonj, argues that clothing is one of the most significant developmental issues that has been adequately sidelined by the mainstream developmental trajectory.

Goonj is an issue-based social enterprise located in the capital city of India—New Delhi. Its reach is motivated by the philosophy drawn by its mission. Goonj, as an idea, has managed to convince youth and environmentalists who, in turn, have opted for an active role in its day-to-day operations. The major objective of Goonj is to operate a 'cloth bank' that provides clothes to millions of poor and needy who face greater hardship and indignity besides health risk due to the lack of proper clothing in far-flung areas of the country. Goonj was started by Anshu Gupta in 1998 with 67 personal clothes and currently it is channelized to produce over 70,000 kg of material every month. The existence and growth of the organization is driven by passion and commitment for a cause, in which initially an individual, rather a family, and later a team believed to demonstrate the social change they have sought after. As a result of the passion and commitment, Goonj has grown quite rapidly with cloth collection stores in eight Indian cities and is currently operational in 21 states. In addition, several volunteers have come up in large and semi-large cities to form groups and spread the philosophy of Goonj to extract support.

Background of the Social Problem

Clothing is a basic human need. It not only offers dignity but also helps individuals to protect themselves from different climates. Lack of proper clothing has become a significant social problem especially during the winters, as a majority of poor and deprived cannot afford winter clothing. Anshu first came across Habib, who used to guard and cremate abandoned dead bodies near Lok Nayak Jai Prakash Narayan (LNJP) Hospital, New Delhi. Habib himself was in the clutches of poverty and deprivation, which resulted into great hardship. His little daughter used to hug dead bodies in order to keep herself warm during the winters. Anshu also witnessed, when he travelled to Uttarkashi to help victims affected by the 1991 Uttarkashi earthquake, that the victims were wearing jackets made of gunnysacks. He learnt that their only request was not food or money but warm clothes.

Usually, rich and middle-class people from urban areas respond to various natural calamities in terms of donating their used clothes. However, such a donation drive is restricted to the period of unexpected natural calamities, such as flood, earthquake and tsunami. Generally, a number of volunteer groups are formed for this purpose. They assemble in nooks and corners, especially in the cities, to collect unused clothes and other daily grocery and to distribute them among the victims. This also offers opportunities for those who would like to donate their unused clothes. Otherwise, until a natural disaster strikes, people do not know where to donate their clothes even if they are interested, leaving no scope to recycle or reuse the material. As a result, they tend to dispose them in the waste-collection boxes, leaving a lot of scope for environmental degradation due to traditional ways employed in the management of waste, especially the burning of the waste. Moreover, it rather creates another social problem that is linked to the environment. A significant segment of the population in villages and urban slums does not own dignified clothes which leaves them at the crossroads. The scenario is that, on the one hand, there are people who do not often have accessibility to proper clothing and, on the other hand, there is a stock of unused clothes with the privileged sections of the society who in turn are left with no option but to dispose them in an environmentally distracting manner. These two scenarios open up an opportunity space where the demand and supply created by these scenarios could be employed to address the problem. This is where Goonj came up as a connector: it collects clothes from aspirant cloth donors and reaches out to the neediest in both rural and urban localities. It emerged as a strong mechanism in an institutional form, unlike other earlier temporary attempts. The supply chain of Goonj comprises a variety of stakeholders, and in most of the cases volunteers inspired by the initiative play an active role.

Idea of Goonj and Growth of the Social Enterprise

Anshu Gupta, as a volunteer during the Uttarkashi earthquake that struck North India in 1991, witnessed traumas of the marginalized affected by the disaster. He was mostly touched by the fact that a lack of adequate clothing was one of the significant problems that the affected people faced. Unlike most of his classmates who accompanied his visit, Anshu took the issue further by exploring how problems faced by affected people could be addressed. Clothing, as an issue, was what struck Anshu the most. It did not take much time for him to understand that clothing is not only an issue of dignity but it also has a larger implication for social development. Being an urbanite, Anshu knew the fact that urban people tend to respond to these disasters by largely offering their unused clothes that quite often do not reach the needy, or even in case they do, the mismatch between the need according to the local customs and the clothes donated make them unsuitable for the areas in which they have been distributed. In addition to the Uttarkashi earthquake, several incidents that he witnessed later in the capital city of Delhi provoked him to start an innovative venture that would address the need of the most vulnerable during their difficult days.

One such incident that he always shares had occurred in Delhi. During the early hours of a winter night he came across an unidentified dead body at Khooni Darwaza near Delhi Gate. The body was covered just with a thin cotton shirt, but it held a packet of food. This is one of many such incidents that made him realize a fact about the importance of clothing. The man had not died due to the lack of food as he already had it, but due to the lack of proper clothing in the freezing night. This fact emphasizes that sufficient clothing is as important as the food and other basic needs. Accordingly, a start-up that he came up with aims at providing clothes to the poor and needy. It not only talks about access to proper clothing, but also aims at making clothing a human right (Balakrishnan 2009).

In the current context, the social entrepreneur has set up a system that aims to transfer used clothing and household goods from urban households to the poorest communities. The used clothes, before reaching the end user, are recycled at Goonj collection centres. Of these, all usable ones are cleaned and the ones that may not be worth using are recycled to manufacture other products such as sanitary napkins, school bags, conference pads, purses, etc. However, all such varieties of cloth-made items would reach their way to poor households through different programmes envisaged for the purpose. One of the many other unintended outcomes of the process include reducing the expenditure on cloth purchasing and further expanding the purchasing power of the poor and the marginalized to spend on other useful household items.

Their first major contribution came from the tsunami waste. When the southern coastlines in the country were struck with the tsunami, one of the strongest disasters to have occurred in human history, there was tremendous support from across the country to provide basic necessities to the victims. In such a scenario, as already discussed, communities from across the country started offering clothes to the victims. A lot of clothes were collected by various civic organizations, but the lack of interest among the victims to accept the collected clothes accounted for the distribution being far difficult than the collection. A mismatch between the need and the donation was a major cause for the rejection. Meenakshi, Anshu's wife, believes that there is a lot of mismatch between what people donate and what the need of the region, where the donated clothes are sent. In most of the cases, the donations coming from the people of Tamil Nadu or Andhra Pradesh in South India during a calamity in North India do not satisfy the needs of the people there as the cultures and dress styles of both the regions are very different. So, Goonj acts as a mediator and creates the match between these supply and demand conditions. "We recycle the clothes as we receive and stitch them according to the need of the communities in which we distribute them," Meenakshi further narrated. For example, in South India, women wear saris whereas the donations from other parts of the country consisted of a large collection of Punjabi suits and salwar kameez. As a result, the collected material was dumped in the beaches across the coastal line. Goonj collected the material that was then counted as 2 million pieces from the beaches and converted every single piece into a valuable cloth product such as attractive attires for children, youth, men, and women. Unlike the other cases discussed in this book, the supply chain of Goonj is quite unique and moves through different phases, and a variety of actors are involved in the process. Figure 5.1 explains its context and the discussion thereafter deliberates its flow.

The supply chain of Goonj, as described in Figure 5.1, starts with the collection of clothes from the urban residents who are capable of making donations. The collection takes place broadly in two ways: (a) during the campaigns led by volunteers in different parts of the country on different occasions and (b) by cloth collection centres created for the purpose in eight cities of the country. Volunteers play a crucial role at different levels of the supply chain. A much detailed discussion about their contribution is discussed in the next sections. The collection of the clothes is basically a continuous process. The collection centres not only collect clothes but also accept household items necessary for daily living. The exhaustive list of goods that Goonj collects includes old clothes which are in usable condition such as trousers, shirts, saris, woollens, salwar suits, kurta-pyjamas, children clothes, bed

Figure 5.1

Supply chain of Goonj

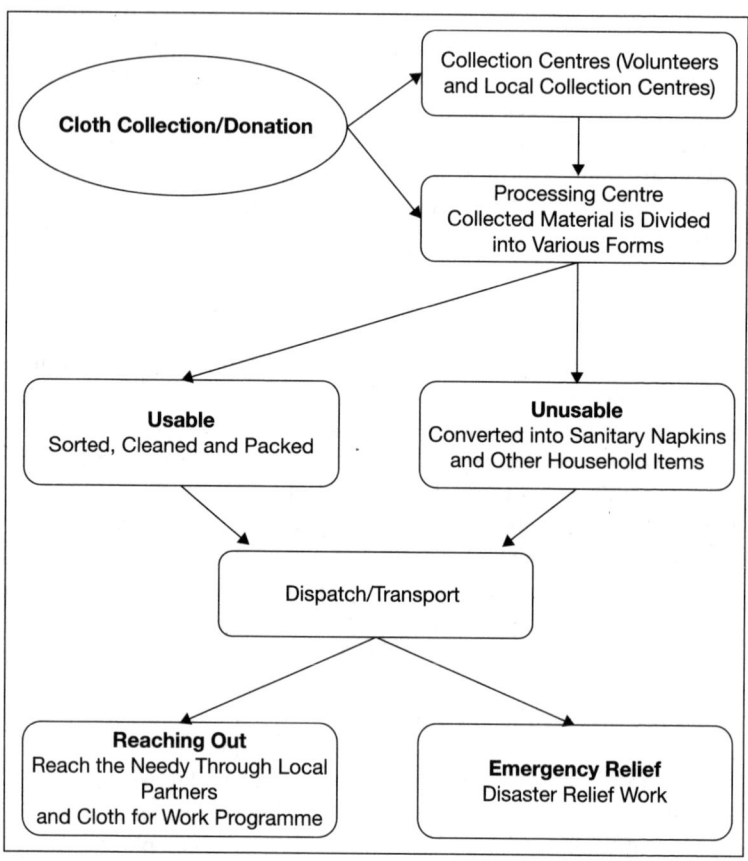

Source: Nanath (2011) and Pruthi (2012).

sheets, blankets, footwear, new pans, plates, bowls, glasses, spoons and ladles, cookers, cups, tongs, lunch boxes, water bottles, etc. In addition to these, stationery in different forms such as old/new school bags, pens, pencils, sharpeners, erasers, rulers, etc., are collected in order to support its back-to-school initiative. Apart from these, newspapers, magazines and one-side-used papers are also collected. They are sold in open market, which makes sure that Goonj is able to recover some costs incurred in its activities. In order to manufacture sanitary napkins and undergarments, large quantities of surplus/waste cotton and hosiery clothes are collected. Cash donations are also encouraged for communication, collection camps, storage, sorting, packing, travel, transportation and local distribution of the manufactured cloth-related expenses. On collecting a sufficient quantity of goods, they are transferred to processing centres located along with the collection centres. During the process, the clothes are segregated into different streams ranging from usable to unusable. The usable clothes are dry washed and later necessary minor repairs are carried out. The unusable clothes are recycled to manufacture other products such as sanitary napkins, clothes for children and other household items. Once the products are ready for dispatch, the processing centre takes care of dispatching them to the necessary locations according to the order received from the head office in Delhi. Reaching out to communities again broadly involves two ways: (a) disaster relief, for example, the victims of Uttarakhand floods in 2013 were timely reached by Goonj and (b) reaching out to the communities through local partners. Under this process, developmental activities are carried out at the grassroots level.

Various Activities Initiated by Goonj

In order to facilitate its mission, Goonj has initiated several activities within its reach to educate, inspire and motivate the urban population to understand that a disaster is not indeed necessary for donating their unused/old clothes. Several activities have been initiated to promote the right intentions. Vastra Samman is one such activity which demonstrates that the accessibility to better clothing is a basic need of the poor. As part of this initiative, volunteers across cities in 21 states take up several street plays and adopt other popular ways to promote awareness among people to understand the significance of donating unused clothes and the essence of Goonj as an organization in creating social value.

Table 5.1 narrates how various items collected are remanufactured to distribute among communities. The usable clothes are, as usual, distributed by undertaking minor repairs, if necessary, whereas the unusable clothes are manufactured into different items as prescribed in the table.

Table 5.1

The list of products manufactured from donated clothes

Donated Clothes	Products
Suits, bed sheets, blouses, petticoats (Cotton)	Sanitary napkins
Jeans and trousers	School bags
Saris	School, yoga mats
Chunris (dupattas)	String for ladies suits
Children clothes	Front portion to be added as design in bags
Old T-shirts and other hosiery items	Undergarments for women
Old non-cotton bed sheets, towels, sofa covers	Bags
Old shirts/non-cotton material	Sheets and covers for baby beds
Jeans and pants	Half-pants or school bags
Western clothes	Design and colour in products
Last bit of small pieces	Mattresses for babies

Source: Balakrishnan (2009).

Cloth for Work

Goonj, like any other social enterprise, believes in a philosophy that guides that rather than charity-based offering, it is recommended that the capabilities of the communities are enhanced wherein both the needs of individuals and their enhanced capabilities go together. The innovation practised at the receivers' end includes promoting an initiative 'Cloth for Work' (CfW). As part of this initiative, various developmental activities are carried out in rural areas to address the daily problems of the villages; for example, construction of bamboo bridges, development of small irrigation canals and dug-up wells, building village schools or repairing roads, cleaning up water bodies and developing water harvesting systems, etc.

Historically, the marginalized have not gained much with the traditional way of service delivery, where they are given basic needs free of cost, rather than elevating their capabilities, which could be used to make sure that they are well participated in markets. With this traditional service delivery approach, communities have been identified as passive beneficiaries from the activities undertaken for their benefit, rather than being perceived as a source to address a social problem. That is what makes a social enterprise unique. In the case of Goonj, the innovative service delivery system adopted clashes out with the traditional way. The poor are inspired to work in the villages towards undertaking developmental activities in their locality for which they receive clothes as remuneration. Initially, village-level development activities, employment generation and the provision of dignity have been noticed as value addition to the whole discourse. With this approach, the social value created is not only restricted to cloth distribution or promoting dignity, but also expands over other developmental activities that promote the participation of the poor and the excluded in social life.

Under this initiative, several developmental activities have been undertaken in far-flung areas. For example, the local residents of the village Salidhana in Madhya Pradesh had to struggle every day for water due to the existence of only a single hand pump in the village. It was then under the 'Clothes for Work (CfW)' that a new well was dug by villagers to cater for their long-awaited need. Initially, it was started with a few people participating in the discussion process, whereas towards the end the entire village joined when the actual work took place. In return, clothes and dry ration was offered to the villagers who showed interest. Another classic example of CfW is the construction of a bamboo bridge in rural Odisha. Villagers and children in Tadapada village used to face extreme difficulty while crossing River Gobri in the absence of a bridge for going to markets and schools, respectively. Requests made to various government agencies to construct a bridge were all in vain as the political representatives were never touched by the fate of the villagers. As a result, attracted by the CfW programme, a total of 35 families came together to construct a bamboo bridge of 300 metres on the river. Finally, the work was completed in less than a month. Every participant received rice and clothes for their contribution. The villagers are now happy about the initiative, as the children can easily go to schools and elders can make various work-related visits to the nearby towns.

Another example of CfW is that of the Assam and Bihar floods in 2004, when a road in Morigaon, Assam was damaged which seriously affected the region. Goonj, which believes in self-reliance, asked the villagers to repair the road and in return the villagers were rewarded with clothes. Starting from then, Goonj adopted this process in its philosophy. However, it was not just restricted to post-disaster rehabilitation, but the practice further widened to other areas as part of its developmental activities. Projects are identified in collaboration with local organizations such as NGOs or local government, which could demonstrate the local need and accountability on the activity initiated. Rather than restricting its focus to a single activity, the social enterprise has been driven by its passion to extract social change by incremental innovation that it preaches in order to benefit societies in which it serves.

School to School

Another prominent activity that has been undertaken by Goonj is the promotion of rural schooling. Here, urban school kids are encouraged to donate their used school kits so that the same are recycled to produce valuable assets that are distributed in rural schools where children lack basic needs. In fact, this is not restricted to rural schools alone, urban schools based in disadvantaged locations also are part of it. Goonj has developed a two-step approach to promote the waste into usage by adopting different styles of recycling for urban and rural counterparts. Simple school bags, tents and mats are developed for rural areas, whereas a range of fancy bags, wallets and yoga mats are developed to accommodate urban demands.

Addressing the Women's Need: Sanitary Napkin Project

As Ashoka stated, social entrepreneurs do not rest until they revolutionize the industry in which they enter. Taking the success from its initial activity of cloth distribution and linking clothing with developmental activities, Goonj has started an attempt to address one of the most vulnerable problems that women face. Anshu and his team has struggled to know answers to a basic question as to how women in rural India manage during the menstrual cycle without having access to basic clothing to even cover themselves and, thus, have realized the shocking ways used by women in different parts of the country.

Every woman needs proper care during the menstrual cycle, at least for five days in a month. Most shockingly, it was observed by Goonj that millions of women in India use sand, ash, jute bags, husk and newspaper, etc., where otherwise a clean sanitary pad is needed. This biological cycle is considered as a social taboo in India to such an extent that women are even not allowed to see birds, permitted to visit a newborn baby or see men before bathing. Further, they are restricted to offer prayers to God and visit temples. It is this shocking state of mind and lack of purchasing power that forces them to stay away from a piece of clean cloth. Moreover, in a country like India, women are not expected to speak in public about these natural needs. As a result, they frequently face health problems that affect the families' incomes. Women tend to face multiple problems as they sometimes forgo their health problems owing to their family needs.

Due to the predominant backwardness which prevails among women and many cultural constraints which do not permit them to speak in public, efforts to address their necessary needs are most likely unfruitful. As a result, many issues that require special attention or special provision do not come to the forefront. One such issue that Goonj has brought to the forefront is making sanitary napkins available to women coming from deprived backgrounds. The incremental innovations that Goonj has undertaken over a period of last one-and-a-half decade have widened its operations from distributing mere old cloth pieces to the recent sanitary napkins and many more.

Anshu and his wife Meenakshi have decided to take up the issue to the next level and offer necessary interventions. However, it did not take them much time to realize that not even a single philanthropist was interested to fund the project to manufacture sanitary napkins, in spite of numerous representations from the team. The main reason portrayed for the lack of interest was that the proposal for manufacturing sanitary napkins was out of their funding objective. This scenario further helped to grow curiosity and enthusiasm in Anshu and his team and to demonstrate on the issue as an activist. It offered them to move beyond just offering clothing to the needy and opened them to another potential area which continues to be ignored by the mainstream social debate and policy. However, understanding the need, Goonj has introduced the manufacture of low-cost sanitary napkins from unused cloth. These sanitary napkins are much economical in nature and illiterate women from rural and deprived backgrounds have been educated to use them. After years of involvement, Goonj has succeeded to the extent that women have realized the need and started adopting the practice. The movement in turn broke the ice that negates cultural orthodoxy and the basic needs.

While establishing a manufacturing unit has been a mammoth project in itself, convincing communities that are distant from discussing the issues related to menstruation was a far more difficult task. Anshu propels that women neither use good cloths during menstruation, nor are they interested to discuss about it within the families, including their husbands. This is the kind of cultural taboo that they had to break. It took them some time to understand the communities, and due to the reputation of Goonj within the communities, they managed to chip into the community culture and explored methods for transforming the social settings. At the same time, it has never been an easy act to talk about this among the communities. Even women did not show any interest to avail the sanitary napkins, in spite of knowing the fact that they need them. However, Goonj used various strategies to reach out to women. One of the best mediums is to employ women volunteers where the sanitary napkin project is being run. The most challenging task with regard to this project is related to creating awareness about its usage and the advantages it offers to health. Village-level meetings with women from different communities are arranged frequently to facilitate free flow of discussion. Volunteers from different academic institutions in various parts of the country took active part in awareness building.

In addition, Goonj partners with various NGOs and village-level developmental organizations to get communities on board without investing much time in convincing them. Due to the intervention of Goonj, people have started discussing the issue which was earlier considered as a social taboo. A respondent from Dharwad district in Karnataka who works as a volunteer for sanitary napkin programme felt, "After we started the sanitary napkin programme, it is found that women are able to work without any constraint during their menstrual cycle. Earlier they had to face a lot of troubles. Moreover, their health conditions are now being improved." This programme helped Goonj and communities to penetrate each other easily. As discussed in the last chapter, it becomes easy for organizations that initiate work on community health to create trust and penetrate communities.

Though initially sanitary napkins were distributed for free to the needy in the communities, later as the organization transformed its approach about development and charity, a nominal price was set for each sanitary napkin. Lakshmi, a volunteer from Karnataka responded that the nominal prices collected towards selling the sanitary pads are an indication that the communities feel proud about their purchasing power. She further states:

> Communities may expect us to give goods for free when they cannot afford. But when the prices are within their reach, they would be happy to pay. Sanitary pads experiment we undertook is a clear example to prove their interest to purchase. As a whole, it uplifts their confidence and their market participation. In addition to improvised health, we also see their increased confidence where work participation of women and subsequent earnings are multiplied.

Thus, the intervention benefits women in multiple folds ranging from health to work and economy.

Vasanta is a villager who comes from SC social background in the caste-dominated Odisha state. She claims that since last four years Goonj has been familiar in her village due to its involvement in various activities. It was in 2012 that Goonj volunteers first visited her village. The village has a significant proportion of deprived sections including people from SCs and STs, which account for about 70 per cent of the total population. Accordingly, except a few, most of them are deprived and daily wage labourers. One day's absence from work would mean that the family needs to forgo at least a meal. Earlier, during the menstruation cycle, it was too difficult for women to attend work as they were not aware of the implications of not using sanitary napkins. However, after the availability of sanitary napkins for such an affordable price, now they can easily participate in their day-to-day activities. Hence, the involvement of Goonj in other activities related to clothing, especially sanitary napkins that have larger implications for their health and work participation, has been well received by communities. It has created a culture where needs of women are addressed while protecting their dignity.

Strategy and Operations

Resource Mobilization: Volunteers Sharing Sheer Amount of Workload

The organization which is one-and-a-half decade old is successful in inspiring a range of youth across the country who take active part in all its activities from campaign, collection of clothes to the final reach of the product to the end user. The volunteers support is crucial in connecting different dots in the supply chain, although there are a few social enterprises in market which do not believe in sharing the work with volunteers with a belief that they may fail to accomplish the duties assigned due to the voluntary nature of the work (Thomas and Kummitha 2013). The experience of Goonj has been entirely different. In fact, most of the activities undertaken by Goonj would not have been possible without the generous support it receives from its volunteers. Anshu elaborates:

> We receive splendid help from our volunteers. Our volunteers comprise of both Indian and foreign nationals, the ratio of which is about 90 to 10 per cent, respectively. In some of our collection centres, we do not have any full-time staff and all our activities are taken care of by volunteers in a professional manner. They come with a lot of passion and commitment to generate some value for the society. Most of the youth inspired by our philosophy are those who visited our organization or processing centres in various cities or those who learned about our initiative elsewhere. We get a lot of social networking support for all our activities. I must say we could achieve the success only due to the active youth participation.

The volunteers organize themselves into various levels. For example, they have state-level committees for each state where Goonj operates. These committees are headed and maintained by young volunteers. They take up door-to-door cloth collection on various occasions and are responsible for the collection camps. As a whole, their support is vital in each and every activity of Goonj. By attracting and retaining young volunteers, Goonj has overcome human resource constraints. Further, it has reduced the costs involved through minimizing the need of recruiting employees. With merely 200 full-time and part-time employees, one can imagine how significant would the volunteers' contribution be in undertaking activities which are spread across most parts of the country. For example, there are about 30 cloth-collection centres located in Delhi alone which are organized and monitored by volunteers regularly.

Goonj has succeeded in maintaining accountability and transparency which has resulted in the youth taking up significant roles and responsibilities. Further, its philosophy that is surrounded towards waste and recycling has been the key instrument in attracting youth. Kaushik, a student at IIT Mumbai who actively volunteers the Goonj Mumbai collection centre, stated that he was part of the Jagriti Yatra[1] when he first visited Goonj in 2009. Since then, he was inspired by the innovative ways employed at Goonj in addressing complex yet different social problems. In addition, Kaushik elaborated that the supply chain at Goonj is very actively looked after by a handful of both formal employees and informal volunteers.

Volunteers celebrate every New Year by collecting clothes and the day is declared as Goonj's Cloth Day. Anuradha Gupta, a school teacher in West Delhi proclaims in support of the Goonj's Cloth Day that she could not start a new year on a better note than joining Goonj's efforts to distribute clothes to the needy. Another volunteer who has just graduated in her masters' said that she would not go out of her house on the first day of January like all her friends because her residence address has been printed as one of the collection centres on the Goonj pamphlet. Because of this, she has to receive a good number of people who would turn to donate clothes on the day. Anshu narrates that among all age groups, youth and young adults have been asserting for the growth of the organization and to extend its reach. The accuracy in usage of technology, time management and the passion they show towards the objectives of the organization have together added value to the functioning of the organization. Further, their active participation has enhanced visibility due to their strong presence in social networking sites such as Facebook and Twitter.

---

[1] Jagriti Yatra is a nation-wide train journey which is participated by about 400 selected youth every year on an 8,000-km-long train journey in India to interact and learn from the innovative grassroots experiments carried out by well-known social entrepreneurs. By doing so, the youth are inspired to take up entrepreneurship and nation building as their career choice.

In-depth Innovations

Clothing as an approach to address basic human problems is an innovative attempt adopted by Goonj. This particular aspect related to in-depth and incremental innovations are clearly witnessed among all the social enterprises covered in this research. However, yet all of them undertake a variety of ways for invention and promotion of innovation and assure the communities whom they serve. However, clothing which may not be an immediate developmental response, at times as argued by Goonj, may become a significant aspect that hampers other activities someone would like to take up.

Unlike many social enterprises, the strategy adopted by Goonj has earned enormous support from different social groups in the country and abroad. As a result, it is not surprising to know that most of the dots in the supply chain are filled by volunteers who have shown continuous passion and commitment towards the social value being created. For example, Jagriti Yatra that visits Goonj in Delhi in addition to 13 other social enterprises in different parts of the country every year with its 400 young participants believes that Goonj is a remarkable experiment and everyone wants to volunteer in its various activities. Moreover, its positioning in the capital city also attracts a significant media attention. As a result, Goonj gets predominant publicity in social circles and in academic institutions which often invite Anshu to speak in their forums. Predominantly, the innovations involved in the organization attract volunteers and other enthusiasts to support the cause.

In addition, the strategy that Goonj has adopted from time to time in revamping its association with communities, partner institutions, governments at different levels and international networks have been useful for the organization to mobilize resources and volunteers. Until Goonj entered the space, clothing was never considered as a significant social problem. The social value created by Goonj and the investments made for achieving it are not comparable with the SROI created by other organizations, as Goonj is established with the required resources coming from waste that does not have any financial value. So basically, the resources tapped to run the venture and to solve the social problem are worthless.

Scaling and Partnerships

Goonj never wants to spread itself beyond 1,000 employees or have offices beyond 12 cities in the country. Its intention is to replicate its idea with networking and partnerships. Anshu believes that he is interested in making neither a sanitary napkin production company nor an old cloth distribution company. His intention is to just open up the subject for discussion and deliberation and, thus, influence the policy for better ways of reaching the poor. Goonj always envisaged growing as an idea rather as an organization. That is the reason why it partners with various organizations including governments at different levels, corporates and grassroots organizations. In order to maintain accountability, transparency and to stay strong, the partnerships entrust a clear due diligence. Partnerships with local-level governments, local organizations and communities are the key to engage in continuous innovation in order to promote social transformation. Corporate ventures enhance their brand value through partnering with Goonj and accordingly look after all transportation and logistical needs of the organization. However, Anshu believes, "The corporates may cut down their budgets or totally pull out from offering logistical support, so we will have to be ready with a profit making venture to support the cause." Thus, it is all about continuing to explore alternative and better ways of doing the same thing to create a social value and achieve SO.

Goonj persuades its mission across several parts of the country through its 250 networking organizations. Furthermore, it uses the Indian army to distribute necessary clothes in places such as Jammu and Kashmir and northeastern states where the transportation of goods is not possible due to both human and natural calamities (Balakrishnan 2009). In addition, it also trains NGOs and communities to learn how to manufacture sanitary napkins in order to spread the movement.

Governance and Structures in the Organization

When it comes to the organizational structure, like any other case we have discussed in this research, Goonj also follows a democratic set-up where hierarchies are eliminated. Though every employee is assigned a specific task to undertake, everyone is efficient in handling multiple tasks in the organization. It facilitates them to switch their roles whenever it is required. Decisions in the organization are taken in accordance with the consensus gathered from the employees present in the meeting. It is further embedded within the transparency principle and valuing human capabilities based on the performance and commitment showed in the organization. It has resulted in high retention rates in the organization. The social capital developed among the employees is another key that has developed bondage. Often when employees are in need, either other employees or Anshu helps them with whatever is required. The reputation and popularity that Goonj has attained over a period of time must be credited to the positive word of mouth that spreads across the civil society through Anshu's presence in networking events and his amicable discussions with youth in various events.

In addition to taking up development interventions, Goonj builds awareness among people that donating the unwanted is not a mere privilege but a responsibility towards society. Especially, the donation of clothes should not be just restricted to disaster relief as the lack of proper clothing is a major social problem throughout among the poor and the excluded, especially during the winters when this problem creates much disaster. The venture which was created out of passion from an individual, today collects about 70 tons of clothes every month and distributes recycled products in 21 states.

Goonj dominates the social landscape especially for the poor and the marginalized by adopting and practising innovations at various levels including (a) understanding the social problem, (b) employment generation, (c) approaching and awareness building among the communities, (d) product/service innovation, (e) innovation in impact orientation and (f) innovation in processes. It has been strong in creating a social value through various attempts embedded within the focus towards clothing as a mean to promote development. Goonj which is the first of its kind has inspired a large proportion of people to extend their hands in the process of cultivating the poor and the marginalized. In order to strengthen its operations, it needs to create better ways through which robust ways of community involvement is encouraged in the activities of Goonj which may further widen its impact. In addition, market penetration through enhancing their direct market participation or mission-centric approach would further this impact.

Social Value Creation

Employment Generation

In addition to undertaking the activities as discussed, Goonj also generates employment for about 200 people coming from various deprived backgrounds. In fact, similar to all cases that are part of this book, Goonj also adopts the WISE approach where the deprived and the poor from communities are encouraged to join its team. Employees are selected from communities that demonstrate extreme hardship in leading their lives. Out of the 200 employment opportunities generated, about 70 per cent of the employees are women. A larger number of the employees of Goonj come from extreme poverty; in the head office itself there are about 150 people employed. Out of the total 150, about 80 come from deprived backgrounds and about 60 of them are illiterates.

Gowri, an employee at Goonj's head office at Delhi, lives in Sangam Vihar, one of the slums where 52 per cent of people live without having access to basic amenities. She narrates that Goonj has initially approached them to help in reconstructing a road that leads into the slum. In return for the work they carried out, they were promised to offer good clothes. The entire community was very much inspired by the initiative. She further said:

> Though mere clothing may just look simple for outsiders, we know the value of those clothes that bring dignity to our door steps. Generally, we have to spend a significant portion of our incomes towards clothing for the family. In case of joint families it becomes too difficult to manage different expenses involved. Hence, we liked this activity. Moreover, they were not offering us anything for free. I would have not preferred to receive anything for free as donation. In fact, the clothes were remade, even if someone wanted to donate, my family would not want to take it. But, we showed interest only when we learned that we would get it in return to our hard work. Finally, on the day when it was decided to build the road, hundreds of slum dwellers had gathered and showed keen interest in constructing the road. We all enjoyed the occasion together like a festival. And finally by end of the day, we could build the road and in return received clothes, which were better than what we had expected. The clothes looked like new. We all were delighted to receive such good-valued clothes. Then, I personally visited Goonj's office and

the collection centre in order to understand what they do clearly before approaching them for a job. Instantly, I was offered a job in the processing centre where I have been working since last six years.

While different respondents had different stories to narrate, the most common among those who come from deprived background is that they are given a job not because they are well trained or skilful but because they are in need.

The association with Goonj helped several employees to get dignity in the communities and acquire social mobility where their choices are respected. Rani is an employee who works at one of the processing centres. She narrated that she approached Goonj through one of her neighbours who was already working there. She enjoyed the work at Goonj because of the nature of her work. She considered herself as a social worker who contributes for the community's well-being. Earlier she was not considered as someone worth to listen to by the community, but now they respect her presence and allow her to speak in the community meetings. She could clearly observe the transformation in the community's perspective.

For many people employed at Goonj, it brings supplementary income that improves their families' conditions. Employees are happy about the salaries they receive and are proud to work with Goonj due to their conscience which often encourages them to work for a social cause. Sarika is an employee working at Goonj's collection centre at Mumbai. She comes from one of the slums in Mankurd. She said that after being employed by Goonj, her family's condition has improved. With her earnings, her children could afford to go to school. While her husband is an auto driver, whatever he earns is hardly sufficient for running the family. Hence, her employment supplements the family needs, the most crucial one of which is education of her children. She further narrates that she finds herself happy working with Goonj as it serves for the cause of social development of the deprived sections. Being someone who comes from the same background, she contemplates the importance of clothing as one of the need which quite often gets lesser priority among many other household priorities due to the lack of proper income. While asked about her experience with Goonj as an employer, she felt that Goonj pays her well and it is far ahead of what she used to get when she worked earlier as a domestic labourer.

Promotion of Social Equity and Inclusion

Though the contributions of Goonj are significant like other social enterprises studied in this research, it has not been able to achieve constructive or visible social transformation as it is witnessed in other cases. However, Goonj demonstrates its success by emphasizing on increased infrastructure in rural areas and enhanced dignity among the masses. Goonj, like any other social enterprises in this research, promotes social inclusion through two different streams: (a) by providing employment generation for the most needy among the communities and (b) by facilitating services required for the communities.

It has been evident that the communities show respect to the activities undertaken by Goonj due to the strong effect it has in promoting dignity and social inclusion. Mohan, a villager from Srikakulam district of Andhra Pradesh, proclaims how the Goonj initiative helped him to send his daughter to school. He says that it was in 2009 that due to extreme floods he had to migrate to a nearby government shelter. It was then that Goonj had helped many families affected by floods in terms of offering a variety of household usable items such as clothes, rice, dal, etc., which were useful for minimum sustenance. Later, once they relocated to their original village, Goonj further helped them with required clothes. This is how he could control his spending on household items and use the same money for his daughter's college fees.

The role of Goonj in post-disaster relief is well regarded. It was found while interacting with the respondents that Goonj also looks after offering daily consumable goods required, which has not been highlighted by any literature or the employees of the organization during the discussion. Bijaya proclaims that the recent floods in 2011 in Odisha, which affected 2.1 million people in 3,000 villages, forced her to migrate to a safe place in a nearby town in Kendrapada district. She proclaims that it was relief work by Goonj that helped them during and after the floods and so they were not much bothered about their daily needs. It was volunteers from Goonj who were as helpful as the relief team from the government. She further said, "Goonj had also organized a school in their relief camp where her children were educated during their stay in the camp." Some of the respondents have also mentioned that apart from the financial value that they gained by involving with Goonj, they now also believe that they are more empathetic about other social issues.

Sustainable Orientation

Like any other social enterprise studied in the research, Goonj as an organization depends more on philanthropy for the organization's running costs, maintenance and salaries of the staff. Though innovations have been employed time and again to reach out to the excluded, Goonj has been operational as a social enterprise from social innovation school-of-thought perspective. Though there were initially efforts invested in order to generate incomes to cover some of its costs through their marketing methods, due to the lack of sufficient attention in planning, the proportion of income raised from such efforts remain nominal. However, the in-depth innovations and interest to excel in garnering the earnings is a crucial attribution which is expected from an organization that is under the transition process towards a sustainable social enterprise. It is to further emphasize that most of the investment for Goonj comes from waste which demonstrates high level of social return. In addition, it has been able to reduce the operation costs significantly by establishing processing centres adjacent to the collection centres (Balakrishnan 2009).

Goonj basically requires two kinds of investment.

1. *Investment in terms of waste.* The innovative operation model of Goonj allows it to operate with nominal financial requirements. The waste collected from urban areas is recycled and remanufactured with a nominal expenditure in order to achieve its mission. In addition, it also allows them to undertake various developmental activities in rural areas with help from locally available resources.

2. *Investments required for running costs.* This requirement is tackled by using three methods.

    i. Philanthropy-based investment: Due to Goonj's global reputation, it receives a credible attention from global actors. Due to its high-level SROI, as most of the resources come from voluntarily collected waste clothes, any investments will reflect in high impact. Hence, there is a strong feeling among the philanthropists that investments in Goonj are worth.

    ii. Market-based approach: Through this approach Goonj undertakes a few activities to integrate itself in market orientation, though the approach as it stands is a minor contributor in the process that has to operate in its fullest form.

iii. Awards and prizes: All successful social enterprises part of this research are reportedly successful in winning major awards and prizes, which bring significant cash incentives. Goonj utilizes all the cash awards it receives towards building the social enterprise.

However, there is a twist in the tale that would prologue our discussion about the sustainability of the organization. If we understand the philosophy of the organization, it is clear that the organization's basis itself is structured in such a way that it runs on the donation of clothes from urban areas. It is found that old clothes do not hold any value among the holders. It costs 97 paisa (USD 0.02) for Goonj to re-manufacture a piece of cloth, right from collection to turning it as the end-user product. The clothes which are of no use for a section of people are being used as an investment in order to create value. Hence, the fundamental source of the investments made into Goonj come from waste. Tackling waste in cities and serving the rural population is altogether an impressive initiative. In fact, by collecting waste in cities, Goonj significantly contributes to prevent environmental protection. Among several contributions of Goonj, promotion of environmental sustainability takes a predominant role, though it is not one of the objectives of Goonj. Environmental sustainability is being attained by avoiding wastage of material and land where the material is disposed (Mashelkar 2010). Thus, ideally the sustainability element gets overwritten by larger social value creation with relatively less investment and the environmental sustainability.

However, the key source of resources required initially to start Goonj did not come from philanthropists or donors, but from a small venture that Anshu and Meenakshi had initiated to support their larger goal. As part of the venture, small art and crafts items were manufactured and sold. These received impressive attention in the local markets and the profits of these were used to transform the idea of Goonj into practice. This small-scale venture helped the duo to attain a variety of skills and approach a larger group of people.

As it stands today, about 50 per cent of the total financial requirements come from individual donors. Anshu claims, "The individual donations are the key for our activities. We are able to attract a great number of individual donations which we feel proud of. We get such response without any fundraising attempts from our side." It explicates the interest of various sections of the society to promote social development activities based on rational of social innovation. However, the last few years have seen a drastic change in the way how people think about the organization. Individual donations have sharply fallen due to an impression that the organization has gained significant level of publicity and recognition which might have increased its funding options. Hence, the individual donors have started showing less interest (Balakrishnan 2009).

There are cases when the help expected does not reach on time. One of the respondents proclaimed:

> Our task becomes so hectic that we need to make every stakeholder understand our value proportion. It is all due to the mindset that is associated with the traditional and social norms. First we need to convince donors who consider offering used clothes as donation and needs appraisal; however, the actual situation is different. We must thank the receivers for accepting the used clothes. We also take the responsibility of convincing the receivers sometimes. It becomes a question of dignity and distress.

Thus, the vibrant problem space opens up a scope for an innovative mechanism for a dialogue and brings various actors to experiment innovative practices.

The ways of understanding social realities and employing various innovative methods have helped the venture to pioneer in adopting rigorous ways to approach communities for both collection and receiving the clothes. The main concern Goonj poses is limited within the ways in which people opt to donate. When approached to donate the used clothes, the donors sometimes offer clothes with poor quality, without even bothering to wash the material before donating. This situation has helped Goonj to be particular in order to make sure that the clothes come in good and usable conditions. That is where it has started reducing the collection camps and encouraging people to visit the nearest collection centres run by volunteers for donating the clothes. This change has helped people to modify their priorities and to understand the dignity and need of the receivers.

When it comes to skills with regard to managing finances, Goonj has failed to nurture the skills, especially pertaining to fundraising. For example, recently Goonj has introduced a programme that resulted in soliciting funds from general public. The response for the programme has been quite impressive till now and a significant portion of individuals have registered to contribute. However, Goonj has failed to follow it up with those who register and send reminders to contributors to solicit contributions every year. It is further found that the organization has neither a fundraising department nor someone who can work for the purpose. However, it is quite normal in social entrepreneurship space that the social enterprises do not have any dedicated fundraising departments. Thus, there is a need for Goonj to build skill sets among its employees in order to not miss opportunities.

In a nutshell, this chapter highlighted how in-depth innovations lead to a creative ways of exploring problem space. Further, it helps the teams involved to locate resources for realizing the dreams set forth. Chapter 6 brings forth the last case of the research in order to understand how community participation and involvement in the entire process of building alternative realities is worth understanding.

6

Barefoot College: Empowering Rural Communities

In Chapter 5, we understood how an important, yet much ignored social problem, is addressed using in-depth innovation. The current chapter focuses on how communities are trained to become engines of their own inclusion. Barefoot College is a rural social enterprise located in Rajasthan. It empowers the poor and the marginalized to build their capabilities to ensure the existence of their inclusion in mainstream society. Barefoot approach strives to promote skills and capabilities of the excluded to earn respectable social living through fighting against poverty. It opts for training and educating the rural poor as a means of their inclusion, which brings employment and facilitates income generation, lack of which is one of the major reasons for the existence of social exclusion. In addition, the employment generated is used to facilitate basic services for the poor and the marginalized, whose existence is largely ignored by both state and market.

Barefoot College is located in Tilonia village in the Ajmer district of Rajasthan. Tilonia is rather known for Barefoot College, which primarily works for the poor and has been striving for their inclusion for the last four decades. The term 'barefoot' had first evolved when Chinese leader Mao Tse Tung launched a programme to train farmers to become health workers and replace the doctors. Having opted to take inspiration from such an experiment, Barefoot College has evolved with undertaking various activities in a more sustainable manner.

Barefoot College was formally registered as Social Work and Research Centre (SWRC) in February 1971 in Tilonia. The college was established by educationalists from different parts of India in order to bring aspects of social work to rural India, which, by and large, was in the tight grip of urban social workers. Initially, the main purpose of the college was to listen and learn from the poor and deprived. Especially during the 1970s, the college was interested in both urban professionals and farmers, between whom there was a possibility for exchange of ideas, experience and expertise. Hence, initially it was conceived as a joint venture of both literates and illiterates. Its emblem depicts one person holding a book and the other a plant. It was envisaged that these two sections work together and understand each other to create a better place to live.

Background of the Social Problem

The concept of Barefoot College was initially started when Bunker Roy[1] and his team visited Tilonia to study the village and villagers. They studied the basic social structure of the village, way of living and share of contentment among the villagers. Earlier, Roy had attained an expensive education from one of the elitist schools in India. Despite having such an elite profile, he still decided to go and work with the villagers. When Roy first entered Tilonia, the questions he faced from people were: "Are you running away from the police? Did you fail in your examinations? Didn't you manage to get a government job? Is there something wrong with you? Why are you here? Why have you come from city to this village?" (Roy and Hartigan 2008, 70). These questions explain the rural scenario in India where villagers do not expect an educated person to come to their village to study their plight and serve them. There is a strong assumption that educated people do not usually go or would not want to go back to the villages. In fact, even the government officials including school teachers who are appointed to serve in the villages are not willing to perform their duties. Most of the questions Roy faced came from women and adolescents as the men and youth have migrated to nearby towns for livelihood.

The youths from village who have completed certain courses from some of the nearby institutions in towns are usually not respected by the employers because of the general perception and most often

---

[1] Mr (Sunjit) Bunker Roy is the Founding Director of the college. He is more familiarly known as Bunker Roy.

a fact that these institutions fail to offer 'quality education and good infrastructure.'[2] Hence, this situation imposes on these youth a forced exclusion from the employment sector. Apart from that, Roy was frustrated by the fact that most of the youth who migrated to the towns end up living in slums due to unemployment or underemployment. Especially when village youth migrate to bigger towns and cities and fail to get good jobs, they would never want to go back to their villages because of the fear that the villagers and family members would not respect them. So, the whole situation pushes them to end their lives in slums, where the minimum human existence is at stake.

Furthermore, Roy had witnessed that villagers were facing a series of social problems ranging from lack of proper clean water to lack of skills to earn two square meals a day. Moreover, these villagers are always seen as inferior in the social hierarchy compared to urban educated people. That is the reason experts from urban areas would never want to serve the villagers. Further, the larger question Roy poses is that whether these illiterate villagers are any less to the urban educated folks when it comes to dedication, self-respect or capabilities. Roy, who has seen the two extreme situations, decided to initiate social activities that pertain to solve all the social issues that come across in the way.

Idea of Barefoot College and Growth of the Social Enterprise

There is a general observation that poor and illiterate voices are most likely ignored by urban 'paper' qualified experts.[3] Often villagers are not encouraged to speak in public where urban educated are present. Simply, they do not own the right to speak. Hence, Barefoot

---

[2] We can also witness a similar scenario in contemporary South India where hundreds of engineering colleges produce a million engineering graduates every year who often end up without jobs. The situation is due to the lack of sufficient infrastructure and expertise in the educational institutions.

[3] Urban paper qualified experts are those who come with expertise based on their education from urban areas with a poor knowledge about rural population and their living.

questions this attitude and mindset. Initially, Roy and his group had spent a significant amount of time in understanding local issues by deliberate discussions with villagers and learned several issues from illiterate locals who possess traditional knowledge. After speaking to them, Roy and his team had gained systematic knowledge and realized that the community knowledge should be utilized to ensure their own inclusion in the mainstream. They have learned that the traditional knowledge of the communities is far superior to the knowledge of the urban experts. Because the community knowledge is grounded in social realities which is quickly useful to understand local realities and to explore solutions. Thus, they realized that it is essential to learn from communities about what they know. Such learning can only be robust when it is accompanied with an open mind. So, they believed that it is essential to unlearn what they already knew in order to understand the communities. After a series of discussions and debates with the villagers, they established SWRC. People were encouraged to share their experiences, ideas and knowledge through which several villagers were motivated to take part in the activities. Following SWRC's philosophy of 'learning by doing', people approach, learn and become professionals such as computer engineers, hand pump engineers, solar engineers, architects, masons, etc. The poorest of the poor, illiterates without any paper qualifications have been trained and given knowledge to employ themselves. That is the reason the entire set-up is called Barefoot College. Without formal degrees, diplomas or education, they gain knowledge through mutual learning. That is how the concept of Barefoot has evolved and is being successfully implemented since decades. The excluded have been given space to enhance their capabilities and further secure their life with dignity. Furthermore, they have become focal actors in the development of the community. However, initially in the process of learning and reflection, there occurred a strange situation which led to transform the priorities of the organization over a period of time.

Initial Setup and Transition

Initially, in order to understand the concerns of the illiterate and uneducated for whom the entire process had been initiated, it was decided that:

The urban-educated professionals had to go through a de-schooling process because whatever they have studied in their university education system was conflicting with what was happening in the field. There was a feeling of getting into a process of understanding the inherent value of human beings and working with them. (O'Brien 1997, 74)

Between 1975 and 1979, the enterprise faced various crises including the founder educationalists leaving the campus due to the problems related to ideologies as well as decision making.

In the initial stages, qualified professionals from urban areas were given utmost priority and were paid high salaries which had resulted in the creation of a gap between educated professionals hailing from cities and illiterates from the villages, whereas the major objective of the institution as discussed is that the urban-based experts and villagers come together, share expertise, knowledge and ideas to solve practical problems. Very often, the rural masses did not open up in gatherings and meetings where the experts were present. Thus, the social enterprise decided to leverage the positions of everyone in the enterprise as equal, irrespective of their qualifications and, thus, decreased the job descriptions of the urban-based experts in order to balance the hierarchies. Adding to this decision, lack of infrastructural facilities in remote Rajasthan where the college is located pushed professionals to leave the college. Therefore, finally, the college was only left with farmers. In fact, it has resulted in settling on an understanding that it is not wise to depend on outsiders to address grassroots problems as they may leave the initiative at any given point of time. In addition, initially following the influence and expertise of the paper qualified engineers, the enterprise solely involved itself in digging up of wells in search of water for five years, but found no water. Then the rural masses suggested that trapping of water would be more effective during rainy seasons. That way, they have located ground water bodies easily. In fact, the rainwater harvesting programme has become one of the most successful activities run by Barefoot College till date. This scenario helped Barefoot to decide on the action plan to be taken up. Making beneficiaries participate in the decision-making process of the project would produce better results, because they have been associated with the problem and are aware of the problems, consequences and possible solutions, better than any other expert. "We have looked at the problems that the poor face from their point of view and not from the point of view of a so-called expert looking from outside," Bunker Roy clarified. He elaborated further, "We have come to the conclusion that by using their own knowledge, skills and practical wisdom, it is possible for them to solve their problems themselves" (Coles 2002, 42). Today, as a result, the college has 95 per cent of its staff coming from rural Rajasthan.

With this background, Barefoot has taken a transcendental approach in which the poor were given priority both in decision making and implementation. In general, Indian villages are classified based on several identities; villages in Rajasthan do not hold any exceptions. As discussed in earlier chapters, caste plays a crucial role in dictating the social norms. Hence, Barefoot was in dilemma whether its aspirations with such hierarchies in place would leave any scope for maximizing the capabilities of the villagers as a whole where the facilities are enjoyed by all inhabitants. For example, while providing solution for the problems related to water, they realized that the caste hierarchy would never allow any member from SC/ST community to draw water from open wells. Thus, after identifying this lacuna, it was decided that the Barefoot College must work only on the broader agenda of poverty alleviation, offering no space for discussions related to other deprivations in the decision making. Adopting poverty as baseline protects the interests of SC/ST as majority of them represent the BPL category, thus, leaving no scope for social hierarchies to dictate the terms. Hence, the policies were made to serve all social groups such as marginal workers, landless peasants, marginal farmers, rural artisans, women, children, SCs and STs (O'Brien 1997). That is how caste hierarchy, which is one of the cause and consequence of social exclusion in India, has been tackled by Barefoot approach.

So, the entire structure of the social enterprise has been transformed to help those who are excluded and need assistance to lead their life. The Barefoot approach, hence, started adopting a bottom-up structure. The main aim is to assist or guide the poor to depend on their own capabilities rather than on urban paper qualified outsiders or on philanthropy for their development. So, an 'outsider' is termed as the one who holds a paper qualification from urban areas. An 'insider' is the one who does not hold any paper qualifications and is not much aware of modern tools but has traditional skills or talent which he/she gets from his/her families, communities and societies. Furthermore, Barefoot wants to be an institution which is owned by its beneficiaries; the stakeholders are asked to be more active and take part in the construction and development of the college. It aimed at facilitating reverse migration from cities to villages by enhancing skill development and employment opportunities in the villages which give a positive value to the whole notion of 'village'.

Post Transition

With the crucial transition, strategically the target population has been identified as the poor, the impoverished, the economically and socially marginalized and the physically challenged who earn less than a $1 per day. All activities undertaken in the organization are made poor friendly. Though the salaries paid to employees are nominal which are above the market wages, the employees are provided with other facilities required to live with dignity. When a member of an employee's family has some health issues, a doctor is available on the Barefoot campus; schools are made available for the children of the employees; for higher studies Barefoot College funds them in terms of educational allowances. For those who stay on the campus, a house, electricity and water are provided on nominal rent basis. Ratan Devi, an illiterate employ, reiterates:

> We are experiencing how to be more dignified and happy without having more money. That's why I always feel that one has to be happy with whatever he/she has, and finance never remains a topic of discussion. I have lots of faith in the Barefoot system, because I am one among those who have framed it.

The ideology of Barefoot College as mentioned by Roy and Hartigan (2008) has four key components, that is, alternative education, valuing traditional knowledge and skills, learning for self-reliance and dissemination. In order to pursue them, the college adopts: (a) training the deprived sections, especially the illiterate youth and women, on solar electrification of the night schools and the remote villages; they are also trained to repair and maintain them; (b) provision of safe drinking water with continuous water quality tests, locating the hand pumps in needy areas and maintenance and repair by the barefoot hand pump mechanics; (c) training and employment generation of artisans; (d) educating children through night schools and pre-primary schools in villages, and training semi-literate youth to become teachers in these schools; (e) achieving women empowerment by allowing their presence in all the initiatives mentioned here, and to ensure their participation in the movements against social evils; (f) transforming technologies in order to enable communities to control them; (g) promote traditional communications including puppet shows to spread awareness in villages on issues related to social and environmental concern; and (h) provision of basic health facilities through community health workers.

To reach the aspirations as mentioned above, Barefoot College has so far trained Barefoot doctors, teachers, health workers, solar engineers, hand pump mechanics, accountants, designers, communicators and architects. All these positions are held by the local youth, women and people from deprived sections who are illiterates or semi-literates. Upon successful completion of the training, the trainees are expected to serve their own communities.

Barefoot College is managed, controlled and owned by the poor. The thrust areas that one must hold before entering into Barefoot College include "honesty, integrity, compassion, practical skills, creativity, adaptability, willingness to listen and learn, and ability to work with all sorts of people without discriminating" (Roy 2011, 3). The college cultivates the deprived and excluded to exist as a 'Barefoot winner' who strives to improve not only his/her personal life, but also of the community. The college does not provide any paper degrees after the training, because it believes that paper qualification may influence the trainee to migrate to nearby town or city in search of livelihood which has two larger repercussion: (a) they may end up in promoting urban slums upon failure to get dignified jobs and/or (b) the needs of the communities will not be met as those who have been trained generally migrate to urban areas. Thus, the college never provides paper degrees in order to make sure that the trainees are working with their communities to improve living style. In this regard, Chota Singh says:

> Certificates are not needed. Whoever goes to the college, they come for training or employment which is always available, provided that he/she falls within our target group. For those who are uneducated and deprived, certificates are anyways not useful. What they need is mere support to get two square meals a day.

This approach is said to promote reverse migration, which, is very much required in order to create sustainable rural and urban social order.

Migration is one of the prioritized areas that has occupied a predominant role in the Barefoot approach. Reverse migration is made even possible with the Barefoot's initiatives. Reverse migration in this regard reflects people coming back to their villages; for those, especially the youth, women and men, are given training in order to attain employment. If the employment is available in rural area itself, migration can be easily tackled, which is one of the basic principles for the existence of the Barefoot. Kazzidevi, an employee in the Jawaja Field Centre, explained:

> If we migrate to the cities, no one gives us jobs, we are not educated, and there is no guarantee that our choices would be respected. We are not even sure whether our lives are secured. They will certainly reject us because of lack of education.

Altogether, the Barefoot strives to render sustainable solutions to the seemingly unsolvable problems of the rural areas, such as migration, lack of education, technological ignorance and health and water problems. It is a movement that aims at maximizing rural capabilities.

Various Activities Initiated by Barefoot College

The objectives of Barefoot College highlight its orientation as an area-based social enterprise. The objectives include but are not limited to (a) providing sustainable solutions to improve the quality of life of the poor and rural communities, (b) reducing migration by generating employment within the villages, (c) providing vocational training to semi-literate and illiterate men and women, through the process of learning-by-doing, (e) reducing drudgery of rural women and girls by providing them access to education, vocational training, health care, etc., (f) empowering rural women socially, economically and politically, (g) encouraging community based, owned and managed initiatives, (h) demystifying technologies and decentralizing their uses to improve the quality of life of the villagers, and (i) using and promoting traditional knowledge and skills that have been passed on from one generation to another. All objectives put together talk about the holistic development of villages and communities in which Barefoot operates. Apart from adopting several innovative strategies and processes, Barefoot College aims to sustain the empowerment achieved through its advocacy. Thus, identifying all lacunae, Barefoot strives to promote education. Education here is not about mere literacy. It gradually makes an individual capable of making his/her life more secure; the whole notion is based on Mark Twain famous axiom, 'Don't let schooling interfere with your education'. Thus education is seen as a broader concept, where life-long and everyday learning is considered as a part of it. Accordingly, learning by doing is the broader philosophy adopted by the Barefoot. Barefoot College undertakes a variety of tasks in order to make rural life dignified. A glimpse of them are: (a) provision for running night schools for those who could not attend day school; (b) drinking water supply from rain water harvesting; (c) maintaining a clean environment by spreading awareness about environment-related issues to the villages; (d) empowering rural women by securing dignified jobs; and (e) fighting against social taboos by performing communicative traditional puppet shows and propagation of the traditional communication system through the community radio.

Barefoot works for those who have failed to recognize their latent capabilities and work for their own upliftment. Unfortunately they have not been guided properly as of now in many parts of the world. Facilities such as drinking water, lighting, education, health, employment and housing can be earned by them without depending upon any external agencies. In order to attain it, they need proper guidance and mentoring. Hence, Barefoot provides the poor people an opportunity to realize their dreams by utilizing their maximum capabilities in order to sustain their efforts. There are various activities undertaken to make sure that rural communities get access to greater social participation. The discussion below narrates them in detail.

Solar Technologies

Barefoot Solar Engineering has been owned by Barefoot College since 1984. It started off with a small experiment of solar electrifying a community health centre. Under the social design, usage of solar photovoltaic cells is promoted on a massive scale. Barefoot disproves the notion that rural illiterate poor cannot become engineers. It further envisages that lack of literacy must not be a problem to become an engineer. "If we believe in the capabilities of the individuals, everything is possible. What we need to do is to just believe in them," one of the employees at Barefoot College narrated. As of now, Barefoot Solar Engineers (BSE) have built solar electricity systems that generate power equal to that of a large centralized solar power plant in India and the statistics of the organization shows that it has benefited over 90,000 poorest households in India alone. Himalayan areas, which are well-known for their coolest temperature around −40° F, are not covered by electrical grids. These areas have been chosen by Barefoot to solar electrify. Nominal contributions from each family for repair and maintenance are collected in order to sustain the venture. The BSE experiment has generated significant proportion of employment including for women from rural areas. Providing electricity to the unreached areas has decreased health problems and elevated the living standards. They targeted elder women from communities in order to train as BSE. Though earlier men used to be trained, most of them ended up in cities in search of employment. This destroyed the commitment of serving the communities. Hence, Barefoot has been trying to get more participation from women, especially those who are elderly, thus guarantying to serve the communities. "Once a man gets trained or educated, he migrates to a town or city. This defeats our purpose." Laxman Singh, who has worked with Roy for more than two decades, says.

BSEs have so far solar electrified several villages across the continents. Krishnalal, a beneficiary explains the process. In the first phase, Barefoot representatives inquire with communities whether they want to solar electrify their households. Once communities accept, they are expected to represent the most excluded to be trained and recruited as a BSE. To maintain the solar electricity equipment, each beneficiary household has to pay a small amount of money and then a monthly installment in the later days to enable the BSE to properly maintain them. Village Energy Environment Committee (VEEC) has to be created to work as a mediator between Barefoot College and the community concerned. The money collected is deposited in the local bank account which is managed by the VEEC. Several steps have been employed to ensure transparency and accountability. The money has to be used for repairs, changes of battery and salary for the BSE. For maintenance, each household has to pay around INR50–60 per month (around $1 or less). The solar electricity provided to each household includes two lights and a mobile charger.

Since 2003, the college is training people from other countries in Global South. In 2004, for the first time people from Ethiopia, Sierra Leone and Afghanistan have visited Barefoot training facilities and undergone training to become BSEs. Barefoot college offers not just training, but also promotes programmes to boost the confidence levels of illiterate women as leaders who can also work in other developmental activities. Many women educated in Tilonia have created history through solar electrifying their own villages in their respective regions. Bagwathnandan, the coordinator of solar section, explains:

> We are working in 35 countries in Latin America, Asia and Africa. Since 2008, the Government of India has started funding the international training. Ministry of External Affairs has been taking care of it. Women have been exposed to external cultures. In some African countries, there are cases where one man is married about 4–5 wives at a time. In fact, when women from African countries come here, they realize that it is wrong. In a couple of countries, we have started Barefoot College's associations. In 2007, two women from Sierra Leone were trained here and they have gone back and convinced their government to solar electrify their respective villages. Today, they are fixing around 40 kW solar electrification equipment in villages. The Government of Sierra Leone funds them and we are sending them the instruments. We face several obstacles in the process, as we have only uneducated women and our system is *learning by doing*. Solar energy is one of the vital entries that we could get into the communities.

Barefoot College is able to access resources to scale the initiatives across the African countries, due to partly its successful impact creation in India.

Solar usage has also resulted in reducing the emission of CO_2 and other greenhouse gases. Solar energy has been substituted for cutting the trees and shrubs for cooking, heating and lighting. Diesel and kerosene consumption has also been minimized. The massive installation of solar systems has also partly contributed to bring down global warming by reducing the consumption of several thousand litres of diesel and kerosene. As a result, it is estimated that 1.2 million tons of carbon emission has been stopped from entering into the atmosphere. Cases of respiratory diseases due to toxic smokes, emitted while burning kerosene, coal and wood for cooking and lighting indoors, has also come down significantly. In Africa alone, an average of 1.6 million women and children die or suffer due to this problem. The solar solution has been a proven model to eradicate the said problems in the poorest African countries (statistics obtained from Barefoot College on 8th November 2011).

But before installing a solar system, the community must be willing to undertake tasks related to maintenance and repair because Barefoot believes in achieving sustainability of the initiative. In this context, Lalita clarified, "For solar energy, except the case with the battery, everything works fine. Battery has worked for as long as 11 years in some areas. So, we will have to be more careful. Two lights work for five hours in the night". Electricity has been provided with limited charges, which even the poor can afford. Poor and excluded communities have gained a chance to enjoy the electricity supply through solar energy. Meghanath, a beneficiary, states that his village was not provided with the grid-based electricity supply. He hails from a very poor family where they used to invest significant portion of their financial resources to buy kerosene. But with the help of Barefoot solar energy initiative, they have been using the solar energy for last 12 years without any problem. "The fee we have been paying for the usage is also nominal, which is much lesser than what we used to pay for kerosene lamps", says Meghanath.

In some places, the solar system has worked well and in others it has not. It depends upon the strength of the community and their commitment. Dorji, a solar engineer, says:

> I would not say that the solar venture is 100 per cent successful; there are some cases, which we need to critically examine. We have such villages in Sikkim, which are solar electrified, but later the community is not interested, because they have also got hydro power in the recent past. They are not willing to return even the instruments.

As a whole, the Barefoot solar technological initiative has contributed significantly to solve several problems such as usage of kerosene, lack of power supply in the remotest places and environmental degradation. During the discussions with the villagers, they claimed that this innovative approach has contributed successfully to enhance their access to electricity.

Education

Education is one of the major thrust areas of the college. The College runs pre-primary and night schools to educate the children. The youth selected as teachers must undergo a residential training camp for 30 days. The target group to become teachers is again those who are out of employment in the villages, and the neediest. Curriculum in the night schools is decided by the teachers, based on practical learning methods, which mostly fit the local environment and needs. The curriculum, for example, includes information related to common civic needs, such as how does a post office function, how to use a bank and a police station, etc. The Barefoot teachers are selected by rural communities, wherever the night schools are operated. The target population is in most of the cases unemployed rural youth. The main intention to initiate the education system under the Barefoot approach is to adapt the education system according to the needs of learners. The schools are reoriented, in terms of mutual learning, where teacher learns from the children as well.

Barefoot night schools have been spread across six states, which include Assam, Bihar, Madhya Pradesh, Odisha, Uttaranchal and Rajasthan. These schools have been maintained and educated by 714 Barefoot teachers including 200 women teachers. Nanda Ram, one of the night school's alumni specifies:

> Children from poor and marginalized backgrounds have been provided an opportunity to study in the night schools. For them, accessing the day time education is impossible, because of their involvement in the family activities. I used to take care of my livestock in the day time and attended night school.

This is a general scenario where children from deprived backgrounds cannot afford to go to daytime schools due to the poverty trap. Thus, the night schools approach addresses a very significant social need. If we critically analyze, this approach is neither sustainable nor feasible. In other words, there are better ways of addressing this issue. For example, one way could be that the livelihoods of the parents can be enhanced in order to convince parents to send their children to schools. This is a more sustainable option; however, it is found that given the limitations involved in creating livelihoods for a large number of people, Barefoot had to compromise on the quality of the outcome. However, this initiative also encourages parents to send their children to school on a later date, when they realize that their children are well talented.

Every year, more than 3,000 children in a single batch in various schools attend the night schools in which 2,000 are girl children. The larger scenario depicts that girl children have been ignored from providing basic amenities including education. Such a situation is alarming in tradition-bound states like Rajasthan. It is for this reason that Barefoot prioritized girl child education and empowerment as its primary objectives in order to ensure social inclusion on a sustainable basis. Hansi Swaroop, coordinator of Jawaja Field Centre, clarifies:

> Women are so backward in terms of education! That's the reason, girl child education has been given the topmost priority in our night schools. As a result, most of the children in the night schools are girl children. This is because families are generally not prepared to send their girl child to schools, instead they are retained in the work places. If not, during day time they either have to take care of their siblings or buffalos or goats. Now, communities realize the importance of girl child education due to the presence of night schools.

The prime motive of Barefoot is that every girl should be given basic education. Later, it is up to the family to decide whether to send their children for higher education or not. The whole scenario has brought a sea change in the traditional outlook of the mothers. With the help of night schools, girls as well as women started studying and participating in the day-to-day social activities. This has changed the outlook of men, family, village and society. These girl children who learn in the night schools about political, social and economic empowerment share their learnings/experiences with mothers, who indeed realize that when the girl children are gaining knowledge from night schools and showing maturity in various household activities and social life, what's wrong in learning such techniques by elderly, especially women?

Village Education Committee (VEC) in the areas where the night schools are located coordinate the activities of the night schools with the Barefoot College, Tilonia. So far, as a whole, 235,000 children (among them 170,000 are girls) attended schools in six states and 714 night schools in 673 villages. Apart from empowering the children, the night schools approach has provided employment to 3,140 Barefoot teachers, so far. Badrilal, a Barefoot night school student, confessed:

> The knowledge that I have gained from the night school was an effective tool for me; whatever I have learnt has been used to earn a respectful job in Barefoot College. Today, my elevated social status has to be attributed to the Vth class that I have studied in the night school.

Those who work in the Barefoot as teachers are also very happy about their own empowerment, as well as about their task towards offering a better life for the underprivileged children. Gishalal, a teacher who teaches students in the night school, stated:

> I am a teacher in one of the night schools. I have witnessed that many students have studied beyond, whereas some have stopped after night school. A few of my students have gone to Mumbai for jobs and others are working in Kishangarh. In fact some people even got government jobs and many are working in Barefoot College itself.

Apart from educating the underprivileged children, Barefoot night schools have also become more prominent for their 'children parliament'.

The functioning of night schools does not take place in isolation. Communities in the form of VEC, look after the activities. Lakshmi, a 40-year-old respondent, who happens to be a member of the VEC states that, earlier, she never went out from her house for any public meetings. But with the help of Barefoot night schools, she has become a member of VEC through which she came to know about several problems that school-going children face. She believes that if the concept of Barefoot night schools was absent from their villages, most of their children would not have earned the minimum education standards, especially the girl children, who might have been most vulnerable to the situation. She further felt that the VEC, which comprises representatives from all communities in the villages, is given utmost freedom to decide the functioning of night schools in the villages. Communities owning control give them greater responsibility not only to run the school but also to make sure that the children in the village attend regularly.

Children's Parliament (Bal Sadan) is another institution of Barefoot that has been recognized globally. The Children's Parliament is meant to create awareness among children of the night schools about the political aspects and democracy. Once in every two years, elections are held to elect the 'parliament' which has a 'cabinet' of its own. It has functions to supervise, monitor and administer night schools. Children in the age group of 8–14 are given the right to vote and elect their peers as the representatives. The practical experiences of governance have been imparted in the children with the help of Children's Parliament. In order to ensure that they are learning political aspects, 'parliamentary' elections are given priority where democratic aspects like voter ID cards, electoral committees, nominations, withdrawals, campaigning, no-campaign day, polling, counting, declaration of winners, forming the 'parliament' and then the 'cabinet' are duly followed. It characterizes every aspect of Indian democracy. The ballot boxes are carried to the Barefoot campus after the elections in order to count the votes and declare the winners. These parliamentarians and the cabinet make sure that the teachers are playing an active role in classroom activities, and basic amenities in the school are provided. About a couple of years back, a girl was elected as 'prime minister' who had to take care of her goats in the day time. In the nights, she acted as a prime minister. When talking about Children's Parliament, people might not realize its importance, but it is working better than many democratic institutions in the country to tackle the emerging problems and decide on actions. The Barefoot College feels that sometime down the line they might produce Barefoot politicians with help from the Children's Parliament approach.

Ratan Devi talked about the history and working style of parliament. She explained that when she was teaching third standard children in one of the night schools, there was a small lesson on *Chalo Panchayat Dekhiye* (Let's visit Panchayat).[4] In that lesson, there were a number of pictures placed in the textbook in order to create awareness among children about political practice. She thought of teaching the same practically. Hence, an election in the school was planned in

---

[4] Panchayat is a local democratic institutions elected as per the provisions furnished in the Constitution of India.

order to give a proper understanding about the parliamentary system. Her school did everything needed practically and she asked all children to take part in the election. The intention was just to give a practical turn to the lesson. In the process, she observed that the children were very keen and participated in each and every activity. She then raised the issue in one of the weekly meetings, where another teacher also agreed to take up this activity as these elections had taught children about the real election system.

Slowly later, Children's Parliament was created. Teachers came from all the night schools located in different districts and decided to teach clean politics to the children, in the form of elections. "When we speak about children's rights, we will have to practise them as well", a teacher in a local school proclaimed. Barefoot College has taken up Children's Parliament to the next level. Posts like 'prime minister' and several other 'ministers' have been created. Elections for the parliament are held once in two years. Roy clarified that all the section in-charges in Tilonia who look after sections such as education, solar energy, water, etc., also act as secretaries to the 'ministers' concerned. If there is no water in the school, Ram Karan, who coordinates the water section in Tilonia, has to answer them as a secretary.

There was a 'minister' in one of the night schools, who insisted upon constructing a pipe line in his village. Barefoot College told him, arranging a pipe line is a big task, it can be done only through the Panchayat. There was a lot of debate. He said, he will collect *chanda* (voluntary contribution from community) from public, "they will listen to me and at any cost, Barefoot College must construct the pipe line". For six months, the struggle continued. Finally, he collected around INR10,000 (USD170) from the community. Then it was realized that the whole village has faith in the small kid. Why did the college fail to understand? Barefoot College then decided to get the pipe line. The leadership qualities imparted among children help them to understand and influence larger social systems.

Once, one of the 'education minister' insisted that there should not be any wine shops near the school. Everyone thought it was correct. Then they had a doubt, how to support her cause and remove the shop? She said girls are scared to go to the school because of the wine shop located on the way. It used to create a lot of tension. Then, with the help from women groups in the village, they approached the Sub Divisional Officer, and asked him to get the shop removed. It was found that the shop was being run without any license. Then their task became easier and the shop was closed. In another incident, a sarpanch (village-level political representative) of a village had given a building to run a night school, but in the next election he lost his post and another one was elected as the sarpanch. The new sarpanch was not happy about the school, and wanted to close it down. The children carried out a dharna. Finally, the children were able to meet the District Collector for a solution. He gave orders to reopen the school. The struggle to attain rights have been in forefront since childhood with this approach. It has opened space for families and communities to understand value proposition the kids talked about. Furthermore, they became part of the healthy political discussions.

The elections are being held in a free and fair atmosphere. Once, a contestant offered a chocolate to one of his classmates during the campaign for election. The organizers came to know about it and enquired, then he said, "yes, it is after all a chocolate," then he was questioned why the chocolate was given during the election campaign, whereas earlier he never did so. There was a continuous debate and the organizers thought of debarring the school from elections. But then, the concern was that the children from that particular school will be excluded from the noble intention. So they cancelled the entire election process and initiated another election in the same year. Because of this, children got to learn how valuable a free and fair election is for the success of democracy. It gave them a strong message about democratic structures and processes.

Ones, there was a debate on an issue, in which a child was not allowed to take water from a pot by another child as he was from a lower caste. When the issue came to the notice of Children's Parliament, there was a lengthy discussion among them on the issue, as it was very important and finally there was a clear verdict that everyone is equal and must enjoy same privileges. As a whole, the concept of Children's Parliament may sound quite unusual, but its operation and results represent its noble form. "Barefoot College has received an award for Children's Parliament in Sweden. Roy, along with Children's Parliament 'prime minister' and two other 'ministers', went to Sweden to receive the award," Ratandevi recounted the incident.

As a whole, Barefoot night schools and its allied initiatives including Children's Parliament, offer a success story, which has a

great potential that may be replicated elsewhere to maximize awareness and let children understand the democratic process from their
childhood. Night schools have helped the children from poor families to gain nominal educational qualifications on the one hand, and
on the other, in addition to the education, they are also well trained
in the political aspects to become responsible citizens in future. This
particular venture has helped to raise the awareness levels among
children and families.

Rain Water Harvesting

Being a desert land, Rajasthan is always in deep crisis related to
availability of water resources. Water is often the biggest problem
for both drinking and irrigation. Thus, preserving and developing
water sources is the main objective of any organization that works
on water-related issues. Accordingly, providing drinking water has
been identified as one of the high priority areas for the Barefoot.
Barefoot has promoted piped water, hand pumps and groundwater.
Barefoot's experience in the initial days was that many engineers that
they invited to tackle water problems insisted that problems of water
shortage could be solved only by digging big, expensive, deep wells or
getting piped water supply from the areas where water scarcity was
not persistent. In fact, Barefoot did try this in the initial days but in
vain, as a lot of money and valuable time was wasted. Fed up with the
suggestions that civil engineers from urban areas offered, the villagers were asked to locate a solution. Then the villagers suggested that
the rainwater harvesting was a better solution for the water problem. Rainwater harvesting has to be operated through Rooftop Rain
Water Harvesting (RRWH). The villagers were asked to trap the rainwater. Rooftops of the schools and buildings became channels to trap
water in order to store it in underground tanks and use it when the
water sources exhaust. These RRWH tanks have been used wherever
the night schools and crèche schools are located. Even community
needs have been met with the RRWH system. It has worked very
effectively with high returns on investments. The whole system has
been useful for the communities when they are affected by droughts.
"The credit must go to the villagers who have given the very natural
and most viable idea", Bunker stated.

It is noticed that the percentage of children attending schools has risen after the RRWHs were introduced in the schools. Around 50 per cent increase in attendance has been found throughout the year. School buildings have been used to trap the water which is used to fulfil needs of children in the school. Lack of water had been one of the reasons that prevented girl children from attending schools. Neena, a beneficiary, says that the concept of rainwater harvesting in the school buildings has motivated her to send her daughter to school. Earlier, her daughter used to just take care of the household activities in which carrying drinking water from 2.5 kilometres had occupied most of the time. But with this initiative of Barefoot, her daughter has been sent to the school and in return she was allowed to take water from rain water harvesting tank (RWHT) in the school. She further claims that, as a result, her daughter need not walk for miles to get the drinking water and, more importantly, she can go to school. Neena was proud to claim that her daughter is the first girl in her family who has completed 10th class.

It is very interesting to note that all Barefoot night schools have underground tanks in order to trap rainwater to meet the needs of children who attend the schools. The children who attend the school are given water to take home as 'gift', which allows the parents to send their children to schools. The RRWH approach was turned down by many urban-based engineers, including Sikkim State Chief Water Engineer (SSCWE) once. But challenging the prejudice of the SSCWE, the Barefoot architects have constructed one with a capacity of over 160,000 litres on a rooftop of a village school, and the chief minister (CM) and SCWE of Sikkim were invited to inaugurate it. Impressed by the efforts taken to complete the structure, the CM approved 40 more rooftop rainwater harvesting tanks. As of now, a total of 1,000 RRWH's have been constructed by Barefoot water engineers in 16 Indian states,[5] with a capacity of trapping nearly 50 million litres of water. This has helped about 20,000 villagers to get seasonal employment (statistics obtained from Barefoot College on 19th November 2010).

So far, around 3,140 hand pumps have been installed through the Barefoot College and 5,000 water quality tests have been carried out in 3,300 drinking water sources in 318 villages by 34 village

---

[5] Sixteen states include Jammu and Kashmir, Himachal Pradesh, Uttarakhand, Bihar, Sikkim, Assam, Rajasthan, Gujarat, Madhya Pradesh, Odisha, Andhra Pradesh, Kerala, Nagaland, Manipur, Meghalaya and Jharkhand.

technician in six Indian states.[6] The hand pumps have been installed in about 764 villages, which are spread across seven states,[7] through which, around 1 million people are benefited. Water quality tests by Barefoot technicians reached around 1.28 million people. Piped water supply has reached 52,000 people in Rajasthan. Devi, another beneficiary, mentioned that:

> The Barefoot rain water harvesting system must be prized a lot. Earlier I used to walk for miles in order to get drinking water because of which my health deteriorated and, most of the time I used to suffer from several health problems. But with the help of this particular approach, I am absolutely doing fine now. Earlier I was of the view that my health problems existed because of some other reasons, but when I stopped walking for miles for drinking water, my health problem has been resolved.

Rainwater harvesting of Barefoot has reached to benefit 230,000 people to date. Apart from them, 1,286 schools collecting around 93 million litres of rainwater provide drinking water to about 400,000 children going to schools. Interestingly, with the use of rainwater harvesting models, around 3,100 hectares of wasteland was developed in 77 villages in four states.[8] A total of 1,686 toilets have been constructed in 1,286 schools for 200,000 school-going girls. Practices of rain water harvesting have yielded greater results than merely solving water problems. Women and children have systematically benefited from this initiative as the time that they used to spend to carry drinking water from long distances earlier are now being utilized to find and enhance their livelihood sources.

Communication and Crafts

Various communication devices are being used by the Barefoot College to ensure that villagers are aware of social taboos. Communication is a key element to ensure that people are well aware of transparency and accountability. In order to avoid any gaps, Barefoot College

---

[6] Rajasthan, Madhya Pradesh, Odisha, Andhra Pradesh, Bihar and Sikkim.
[7] Rajasthan, Madhya Pradesh, Odisha, Andhra Pradesh, Bihar, Sikkim and Jharkhand.
[8] Rajasthan, Madhya Pradesh, Bihar and Jharkhand.

launched a communication section in 1981 using puppets to increase awareness related to social stigmas. Social messages are disseminated to audience through puppet shows, especially where the target groups are rural illiterate people. Issues taken up so far include child marriage, bride burning, legal rights of women, right to education, right to information, exploitation of the poor, equal wages act for both men and women, and child education. Each year, they have a target of 100 to 150 plays reaching about 100,000 people in around 100 villages. "The main intention of the communication section is about creation of a better place to live. We undertake activities on various social issues in order to create a better world especially in rural areas," Ramniwa, the in-charge of the communication section, explained.

In 1985, immediately after a puppet show on *roti* (bread), which emphasized on consuming liquor and its consequences in one of the villages, a person among the audience responded:

> Did you listen to the play carefully? That happened to me. You all know how liquor totally destroyed me and my family. You have opened my eyes. Where were you all this time? I have a request to make. From now on, whenever you perform this play elsewhere, please tell people that this is the real story of a man in the village called Chota Narena. (Roy and Hartigan 2008, 88–89)

This is the kind of response that the puppet shows evoke with their reality in order to motivate the illiterate and semi-literates.

There were even instances where the impact was very dramatic and results had appeared immediately. Ram Narayan mentioned:

> Earlier, I used to vote to those whom my parents voted. But after I attended the plays by communication section on the importance of vote, I have realized the blunder I had committed by misusing my vote. And from then onwards, I started to vote for those who just work for us.

That is how the villagers are made aware of various social issues like caste, dowry, importance of the vote, children's education, etc. People started gaining knowledge about wages, political participation, women empowerment and student–teacher–parent relations after attending the plays performed by the communication team.

Villagers even pointed out that the communication section has improved their awareness levels. Earlier, they used to practise several traditional cultures that were harmful to social harmony. In fact, they claimed that they did not practise them intentionally. They had learnt from their elders and used to practise without having knowledge about the cause and effect of that particular social evil. But the efforts of the communication team have been impressive in dealing with them. Several practices including caste and gender discrimination have been reportedly reduced. When the researcher was curious to know whether they have been totally abolished in practice, the villagers admitted that the practices had just been minimized and could not be totally abolished.

Recently, about five years back, the communication section came up with a community radio initiative. Community radio helps to communicate with the villagers more systematically, with relatively less costs. Though community radio is a technological venture in which the staff of the communication team has no knowledge, the section has not left its operations to any outside professionals. They have learnt how to operate it, and they have proved their success through running various programmes. Ramniwas shares his experiences while working with this new section. Community radio was initiated in 2009, but he was little sceptical of working in this section, because it entirely depends upon technology involvement. He is still not a technical man. However, he wanted to interview different segments of people on various issues, largely development-related, and telecast them on radio. He is responsible for content development and rest of the activities are taken care of by others in the section. He further elaborated:

> The main intention of the community radio is about propagating rural culture among villagers. It allows us to take pride in village culture and ask people not to destroy it. If any untapped talent in the villages is found, then it will be popularized through interviews and performances.

As a whole, the use of community radio as an instrument for the communication section allows them to minimize their cost and experiment innovation more economically and, at the same time, reach a greater number of audience.

Handicrafts

Handicrafts section, under Hatheli Sansthan, a registered for-profit entity, deals with handicrafts production, its sales in foreign market, and organizes stalls in various exhibitions to sell the products. Around 18 people work in the handicrafts section. Apart from them, there are about 300 part-time artisans who develop the product line. The weavers, traditional craft persons and leather workers have been promoted under the Barefoot emblem. Though the crafts are traditionally made at homes, Barefoot has trained 1,850 women who specialize in the area. They have been provided markets in India and abroad with the help of Friends of Tilonia. Friends of Tilonia[9] is helping out the college to market the products that the college produces across the globe. In order to facilitate the same, a website—www.tilonia.com—has been created. It is registered in US under 501(c)(3) non-profit organizations. This is an enterprise that Barefoot has instituted to make profits in order to emerge as a hybrid venture. The profits are expected to pull to run the Barefoot College.

Strategy and Operations

While the strategy of Barefoot College has been integrated into each and every section discussed in this chapter, this section explores to understand the role of communities in the entire strategy and operation processes. We have already learnt that Barefoot works together with active participation from the concerned communities. The main motto of the college is that the control over villages must be in the hands of villagers. If any problem persists in villages, the villagers have to come together and take a feasible decision. During the course, they might adopt some of the innovative solutions that the Barefoot has been familiar with or come up with an entirely new solution. Barefoot, as an organization, facilitates their tasks and advises them about how to proceed. Ramcharan, who is presently working in Harmada Field Centre, expressed his views:

---

[9] Friends of Tilonia is a US-based initiative which partners with Barefoot College in order to maintain Barefoot's online store and channel the products in markets outside India. By doing so, it builds business capacity and entrepreneurial skills among the artisans under Barefoot College.

Whatever programmes we undertake must get approval from the community, without which we will not initiate the work. With a few resources at our disposal, we have to get the best out of them. That's the reason why we involve communities in their empowerment.

Hence, community participation is identified as one of the best practices to make sure that they engage in the process of their own inclusion. Thus, community participation is ensured in each and every stage from proposal writing to the completion of the task. Villagers are asked to take active part in all the activities. Shyam Karan, a beneficiary from Harmada village, gushed:

> I have been staying in Tilonia since the last 55 years. We are familiar with the college since around 30 years. We are very happy with the services provided by Barefoot College. They gave us solar energy, when there was no electricity. We are provided water through rain water harvesting method. They have been giving education to our children and our women have significantly benefited from their activities. As a whole, I can tell you that we are very happy about the services that we receive from the Barefoot College. What I like most from the College is that they provide us the best at the cost of the cheapest methods employed.

This narrates a scenario which is considered by developmental experts or initiatives as a hard task to follow. However, systematic and minute planning helps to develop the innovation and development of the deprived.

Before writing any proposal for funding from external sources, they have a community meeting intensively, where, after deliberate discussions, they start to write a proposal. Community gives ideas and participates actively in the entire process. The roles of Barefoot College, of the Government and the community are all discussed in the meeting before preparing a proposal. Once the grant is awarded, immediately it is transferred to the Village Development Committee[10] (VDC) in accordance with the project guidelines. The committee is asked to open a bank account so that the money can be transferred to its account. Communities are not only responsible to control the work, but they also have control over the resources. For example, Barefoot runs 150

---

[10] VDC is a local governing institution established by the community members who are in turn part of it. Barefoot College instructs the villagers to create a VDC as a precondition to start any developmental activity.

night schools in 150 villages in a sub-district. Officials from Barefoot will not be able to visit and check everyday whether the teacher is present or not. Hence, the power of control has been given to the communities. On behalf of the community, Village Education Committee (VEC) has been formed. They supervise the school during its working hours. If a teacher is absent, VEC deducts wage during the absence from his/her monthly salary. In case of constructing RRWH tanks, communities purchase the goods required, pay the bills and complete the construction. So, control is decentralized across the communities. The committee looks into the day-by-day activities, and tackles problem that may arise in the process. "We have learnt several things from the communities; and, of course, we have taught them several aspects. Your capacity might be different from mine, but when both of us work together, we can create something useful," Ramkaran, coordinator of the women empowerment section, added. The philosophy of the employees justifies the major transition which the social enterprise had undergone.

Initially a meeting is conducted in all the villages before initiating any work in which every villager is invited to participate. The VDC is elected in the meeting. VDC comprises equal representation from both men and women with 10 members each. Among them, a man and a woman are authorized to manage financial transactions. Ramcharan, one of the respondent beneficiaries of the college, disclosed that:

> The account is opened in the nearest post office or bank so that they will not have to take any risk while operating their accounts. Money power plays a predominant role. For example, village teacher has to stay in the village and has to listen to the communities. For this to happen, the community must have control over the teacher. Hence, Barefoot has decided that the committee will pay the teacher based on the performance.

If a school needs to have solar electricity, the money will be deposited in the concerned VDC's account by Barefoot College. Labour comes from the community. Engineers also come from the community. What Barefoot College does is just to support financially and train the person who represents the community. Shama says that earlier there was no electricity in her village. Her community in the village selected her and sent to Barefoot College to learn the processes and patterns involved in solar energy. She learnt various aspects related to solar technology. During her training, there was another training programme on solar cooking, and she was asked to learn the solar cooking systems as well. In Rajasthan, generally women do not work on welding-related works, but she has worked on welding in order to manufacture solar cookers. With that effort, she also later started to train other uneducated women.

Promoting the participation of VDC in specific issues related to development is a key indication of active community participation. Krupakaran, a beneficiary mentioned:

> I am a member of the VDC in Kardala village. I have been associated with this committee for the last 12 years. A school building, several rain water harvesting tanks and solar electrification of several households have been taken up so far. Everything has been done with a committed involvement of the community. I do not have any relation with the Barefoot except that I am a member of the VDC. I have been inspired by the way how our roles are assigned.

In fact, communities are given freedom to allocate their own roles within the philosophical boundaries as prescribed by Barefoot College.

Engaging communities in the processes is not an easy task. They have to be convinced. They might be having several questions about the activities that Barefoot College proposes. Everything has been clarified in a positive frame of mind. According to Sushila Devi, when she used to go to the villages, all men and women were very much concerned about what she should teach them: whether she is going to influence them positively or negatively? Not everyone in the village thinks in a single direction. There are several women in the villages who have never been out of their houses so far. So, creating awareness among such women about their rights and entitlements is a difficult task, which she had to fulfil several times. They have to be made aware of all the relevant government policies and programmes. Lack of awareness among the villagers is the biggest obstacle that she observes. There were several doubts about her in the village. However, within no time, the entire situation changed. Women have been encouraged to participate in the day-to-day decision making, as well as political activities. They are now striving for empowerment at all levels. All this became a reality due to the trust the college has built among the communities.

The normative aspects of the work style are considered as key, which resulted into its continuous association with the communities. In fact, the community interaction and participation also make sure that the organization does not slip away from the mandate it has set forward. Ratan Devi says:

> We never compromise on our non-negotiable values like equality— equality in caste, gender equality, religious equality and, of course, everyone is equal in work. Honesty is also a necessary quality of all the beneficiaries: honesty towards work, honesty while dealing with money and honesty with the communities.

She further says that they have been sustaining the organization by tapping local resources available in the villagers. They collect ideas from communities and villagers so that the ideas could be implemented. It is all about establishing partnership with communities for their own inclusion. Participation of communities is given utmost priority and it could be seen as the basic foundation of Barefoot College. Without community involvement, it is quite impossible to eradicate the problems on a sustainable scale. Collective decisions are encouraged. "We don't negotiate with our non-negotiable values," Ratan Devi stressed. The strategy and operations of the Barefoot College largely include the ways in which it interacts with communities and ensures their participation. In fact, Barefoot reinforces that community integration is a crucial aspect for social entrepreneurship to sustain the activities undertaken and so the social value created.

Social Value Creation

While developing the skills of the poor and deprived and promoting them to serve the communities in need, Barefoot provides them with relevant employment. Bata, an employee in the audio visual section explains that:

> If you are poor and want to take home minimum wage, you can come here. There are no gates to prevent you from being with us. Of course, you can leave whenever you lose interest. It is also very simple. If you want to make lots of money, you are strictly advised not to choose joining us, because it is not going to work out. If you

really consider to work out of your own interest to do some good work for the society, then you can be accommodated happily in our Barefoot family. We would not need paper qualifications, unlike any other place. We will trust you and respect your capabilities.

It is further claimed that many people that the college employed since beginning are those who initially migrated to urban areas in search of livelihood. The principle of reverse migration is well adhered to by such approach.

Ramkaran, who has been engaged with the college for more than 35 years, says:

> Barefoot College is a community-based volunteer social enterprise. People participate in various activities voluntarily. For their voluntary services, a little amount of honorarium is paid. Everyone [Barefoot College] knows the principles and non-negotiable values we respect. Whoever is comfortable with them, can come and join. Many people come even from other states. They learn from our activities and go back to their respective places to start their own organizations. Barefoot approach has been replicated by as many as 20 different organizations in 13 different states of India.[11] Slowly this approach is expanding globally.

The interview for the recruitment of the poor and the excluded largely focuses on the deprivation of the candidate and need for an employment. Naru shared his experience:

> Before they handed over an appointment letter, I had to attend an interview in which they asked me questions such as what did you study? How much beega [beega is equal to 1/3rd of an Acre] land you own? How many dependents do you have? What does your father do? Based on my answers, they realized that I was in need of a job. They wouldn't have selected me, had I been someone from a wealthier family.

A need-based approach is followed in which only those who may not have a dignified life without a job will be appointed. Capabilities, qualifications and backgrounds are generally ignored while selecting employees. Like any other WISE, Barefoot College determines its basic existence on enhancing skills of the poor and deprived. The

---

[11] Rajasthan, Sikkim, Jammu and Kashmir, Himachal Pradesh, Uttarakhand, Bihar, Gujarat, Madhya Pradesh, Assam, Orissa, Kerala and Andhra Pradesh.

process not only enhances their skills but also makes sure that some of them get employment and serve the community needs.

Community Participation and Social Integration

As discussed earlier, those whom Barefoot College trains and encourages to serve the communities largely come from deprived and excluded backgrounds. The trainees witnessed that their lives have been transformed. Their families have been sustained with secured employment. Their awareness levels have gained momentum with regard to many social issues, their children have been educated and their awareness of political, cultural and social issues have been elevated. In this regard, one of the respondents, Bata, explained:

> One thing I must tell you that I was two years old when my family came to Barefoot College. Apart from many activities, it works for women empowerment, girl child education, it asks people to step away from the faults and proceed in the direction of exploring truth. Women have to wear veil in rural settings, girl child should not be sent to the schools—these were few rules that occupied a predominant role in lives of women during my childhood, but our parents questioned them and took a radical step, which resulted in our empowerment. They allowed us to be free from chains and to enjoy freedoms. I should mention here that if we grow in a good environment like Barefoot, our thoughts would be noble. We are four sisters, our marriages were not held when we were 14 years like all my other friends. We are given full freedom to excel, and we have broken the rule of villages, cultures and societies. My friends in the village who have grown along with me were married long back and they have children, they are largely restricted to guard their homes and families. I mean, their capabilities have been restricted to safeguard their husbands and in-laws. They are totally disempowered. Their life was guided by parents before marriage and now by their husbands and in-laws. Our life is different because we have grown up in such a good environment.

In her view, the kind of environment that she has come across in the Barefoot structure has certainly helped her to gain access to social institutions which ultimately brought inclusion in several forms.

Children of those working in Barefoot College have been attaining good education. Parents concede that it is possible only because of the continuous support they receive from Barefoot College. Suneeta, a child whose parents work in Barefoot College, had her education entirely supported by the college. Not only she but all the Barefoot employees can send their children to nearby towns for higher studies; the expenses are paid off by Barefoot. When she was in school, Barefoot College helped her in terms of fulfilling her needs. Another respondent has mentioned that she has two daughters; both of them have completed their Masters' and then teacher training courses with the extensive support she received from the college. "Without the support from college, it would have been quite an impossible task to give them a dignified education," she concluded.

There are some respondents who have approached Barefoot because they had earlier lost their livelihood due to adverse circumstances they had come across. One of the respondents said that he had become physically challenged while working in an industry. His wife was already working in the handicrafts section of the college. He used to depend on his wife to run the family, in the absence of his job. He has become physically challenged and it was highly impossible to work outside the Barefoot structure for him as he could not find anyone to offer him a job. He felt very happy after he was included in the organization, because he got a chance to meet several kinds of people and to do entirely a new mode of work which he had not even imagined before. People can work according to flexible working system, irrespective of structured working hours. It has opened a new space and new mode of working from which he has drawn much inspiration.

There are even cases where the employment secured in Barefoot helped some of them to have their own families. For example, one of the respondents mentioned that Barefoot is an institution which has given him a family. Earlier, he did not have any family of his own. Because he got a job in Barefoot College, he was able to get married. Today he has a son. Earlier he was not at all sure for having a married life. He is physically challenged, and he challenged the status quo by demonstrating "who bothers about the Physically Challenged in outer society, whereas their welfare is taken care of at the Barefoot College." He insists that if he divides his life into two parts, the first part is before he joined Barefoot College where his life was not secure. Now in the second part after joining the college, he has attained most of the requirements which have fulfilled his life.

Those who are not aware of the magnitude of the Barefoot approach became aware of Barefoot's philosophy once they are accommodated into the structure. One of the respondents who works as a BSE said that he is very happy about his present work. He had not even studied 10th class, but got an opportunity to work in an innovative venture. He emphasized that many people who studied with him during the school days had completed their higher studies and some of them had even completed their degrees and secured various jobs. But he claims that they are not as happy as he is now. They work in the marble industry and they do not even know what solar technology is all about. He has friends working in police whom he often tells, "See, you guys never get a chance to go anywhere. I have been visiting several places and learning several things." So, the respondent feels privileged about the exposure and subsequent learning he undergoes.

The Barefoot philosophy helped the respondents realize what their roles should be in family, college and society. Ramswaroop, who presently works as an accountant in Barefoot College mentioned that when he listened to Roy in the first meeting about what Barefoot College does, he became conscious of its ideology, its importance and how it offers its services to the poor and the marginalized. His words of inspiration have brought a realization to him, who was otherwise exploring to switch his job. Then, he decided to stick with the college. Starting from such a scenario, where he thought of quitting because of less salary, to the current scenario where he became one of the key employees, he could witness a true transformation in his life, as he narrated. The salaries are directly credited in his bank account. He further states:

> Several of my friends and relatives always enquire why I am still working here, when I do not receive proper remuneration? They always ask me to go along with them, so that a better job will be provided with better facilities and salary. One friend, who earlier worked in Barefoot College as an accountant, left for the marble industry because of higher salary offered there. He asked me several times to join him so that I will get three times more than what I am paid here, but all are in vain, because I am not interested at all. I said whatever I get here [Barefoot College], I am satisfied.

The innovative environment and learning-by-doing structure helps the employees to experiment innovatively. Furthermore, the equal preference to its employees and its innovative organizational structures encourage them to continue to work with the organization.

Sometimes, this transformation has also helped them to develop entrepreneurship among employees. One of the respondents spoke about an innovative instrument that he had developed. He fabricated an instrument for LED lamps which lights better and consumes less battery. He developed the idea and there are companies that manufacture the instrument. He met with one such company in Delhi and explained the prototype. The instrument has been manufactured, based on his idea. Apart from that, the Delhi-based company also prepares several other new instruments according to the needs of Barefoot College. The illiterate solar engineers have developed several such new innovative instruments. "Technology changes rapidly, that's the reason everyone has to adjust accordingly," he further justified. Barefoot College's innovations allow them to go for any modifications in the instrument in accordance with their needs. In such cases, even repairs are also very easily taken care of. Earlier, he did not even know how a computer works. Now, he uses it regularly. He has studied only till 8th class. He works on PowerPoint, types in Word and performs many other tasks on the computer. This is all that he has learnt in Barefoot College. He has an email ID, and he gets approximately more than 10 emails daily and he also replies to them on his own.

For several women who work in Barefoot, this is all a new and life changing experience. Another respondent mentioned that earlier she used to just take care of kitchen and household activities. After she visited Barefoot College, she has learnt many things. She had never seen a computer before. Now, she is a professional in the operation of computers. She has gone to the school for just six years, and barely knew alphabets, but now she handles all activities of her section with a computer. It all started, when she saw uneducated women working on computers in solar section and realized that she could also do it. She was given training for six months by those uneducated professionals. Later on, she started practising on her own. After receiving long hours of practice and guidance, she became a professional. Another respondent mentions that earlier she did not even come out of her house, hence, she was not aware of her rights and was always frightened to talk to others. She had even gone back to home several times during the training, because she was worried. Now, she handles various tasks both at office and at her home. The key informant narrated about Nirmala, an employee:

> People sometimes wonder how she would be able to cope up with her work without having any educational background. Before coming to Barefoot, she never even thought of going out from home and speak to men. However, now she is confident while speaking and earned skills to convince people easily. In her entire family, she is the first woman to go out for work.

Transformation in the life patterns of respondents have been instrumental in multiple ways. Their social settings, behavioural aspects, children's education, health conditions have all been transformed. Respect and dignity in society and empowerment in case of women and Dalits have been attained. Employment and financial stability that they have attained help them to be more dynamic and face exclusions bravely. Villagers who earlier treated them with disdain have now started respecting them. More than anything else, social equity has been made possible among the excluded sections. For example, Ram Nivas, a respondent from scheduled caste background clarified:

> In our society, we are neither allowed to sit with others on chairs, nor take tea in the roadside shops in the villages, nor are we permitted to be part of social discussions in villages. But Barefoot College never allowed any such discrimination. That's the only reason which has bonded me here for more than 25 years. If I go back to my village, again I will have to face the untouchability which I have avoided while staying at Barefoot. Hence, I am not interested to go back to my village.

Working against caste hierarchies in Indian rural settings is not an easy task; it needs strategic attention. Barefoot has done the same since beginning, in terms of not looking into the upper strata or rich populations, it has been very keen to promote solutions for problems that the most deprived have been affected with. With their effort, the Barefoot approach has provided space for deprived sections such as Dalits and women to fight against social evils. Moreover, this attempt has allowed them to keep themselves away from the magnitude of exclusion.

Sustainability Orientation

Barefoot College receives funding from external funding agencies as well as several government agencies within India. But the crux in case of Barefoot College is about generation of finances on its own or self-sustenance. Though the college was established as a non-profit voluntary organization, it is in the process of becoming a hybrid organization. The Barefoot College is evolving as a full-fledged social enterprise by adopting an array of entrepreneurial activities. The social venture denotes its capability from: (a) its own finances that have been secured through contributions from communities, beneficiaries that are empowered and the products that are manufactured in the Barefoot College, (b) contributions from the funding sources and (c) awards and recognitions it receives. One of the crucial aspects with regard to the contributions accepted by Barefoot College is that it neither bends its ideology nor compromises on its mission for extra resources. It allows Barefoot College to work on its activities without negotiating on its objectives.

As Bornstein (2004) specified, Barefoot College demonstrates their capabilities to realize its strong commitment towards projecting itself as a social enterprise. Furthermore, it has broken free from established structures. Barefoot College is a unique example to realize how to chip into the social fabric of village settings and stand on its own capabilities through employing various innovations. Furthermore, Bornstein specified that social entrepreneurs are willing to share credit. Accordingly, Roy always concedes that nothing in Barefoot College is being done by him. Everything has been built and maintained by community members. As Bornstein further envisaged, salaries/payments may not be impressive, but the credit that the employees get is immense under the Barefoot approach.

Though Barefoot receives funding from various external sources, it is understood that the principle of non-negotiability is what directs its existence. In addition, funders are not encouraged to influence the process of achieving social development. Roy (2005) maintains, "We never let an expert come into our organisation. We don't allow anyone from the World Bank, we don't allow any UN types to come into the organisation" (p. 184). He further mentions that apart from the money, they do not have any quality offerings to the value creation process; they do not have the humility; they do not have the patience; they are so arrogant, it is unbelievable.

Hence, the stereotypes are not entertained. Another typical example in this regard is the Aga Khan Award which Barefoot College had received for its innovative architecture built by illiterate architects. The award included a cash prize of $50,000. The award and cash received as part of it, was returned back due to the wrong citation (against the interest of the college) given by the award granting body, which claimed to underestimate the work of the Barefoot architects.

In the process of mobilizing resources for activities that are proposed by communities, initially, Barefoot College approaches them to contribute for the proposed project. Accordingly, around 15–20 per cent of the total estimated budget is collected from the community. For example, in case of RWHT, villagers are required to dig the pit to lay concrete, in addition to monitory and material contribution. Apart from that, everyone is encouraged to own the activity in order to create a feeling of ownership. This perspective has helped Barefoot to maintain the structure for a long period. For example, Ramkaran says, "We run crèche. If there is no nutrition to feed the children, we will collect grain from community and feed them. People are encouraged to donate according to their capacity, including but not limited to fruits, vegetables or rice." This proves the difference social enterprises bring on board when compared with NGOs. Social enterprises continue to operate in the absence of resources required. In order to control the situation, they may involve all the stakeholders in the process. "It is not about resources, but about inclusion that is required to improve the living conditions," a respondent opined.

After estimating community contribution, BC sends proposals to various funding agencies. In case the proposals are rejected by agencies, contributions are collected from communities and the task is accomplished. So, the completion of the identified task is important, not the finance. Planning, implementation and maintenance are undertaken by the community. "Many governmental welfare activities have failed because the significance of people's participation was ignored by them," says Ramkaram. Another example of active community participation is mentioned by Bagwanthnandan, the coordinator of solar section.

> One of our field centres selected a village for solar electrification.
> It is an interior village and about 200 families were selected by the
> field centre. They are provided solar electricity in Barefoot style. They

are asked to pay INR3,000/- (about USD50) each as their contribution, which they are allowed to pay in installment basis. Whether the family should pay in installment or at a time is decided by the community. We do not have any say in it. We just listen to them.

Accordingly, communities are expected to own the activities in order to achieve sustainability.

While Barefoot College receives funding from various sources, the continuous increase in contributions raised from own sources including sale of services/products is an indication for its transformation towards a hybrid venture. For example, during 2008–09 financial year, it had accounted for about 40 per cent of the total finances coming from own sources, whereas 54 per cent from abroad and 6 per cent from various domestic donations and contributions. In fact, the figures had seen its peak during 2003–04 financial year where the financial sources raised by Barefoot College on its own—from selling goods, community contribution and the awards that it received—accounted for about 62 per cent of the total finances. The steady growth of own financial sources from approximately 1 per cent in 1993–94 financial year is an indication to claim that Barefoot is strongly emerging to achieve its SO.

Barefoot College, through its innovative and path-breaking experiments, penetrated the local settings and contributed significantly to the sustainable development of rural areas where it operates. The involvement in multi-leveraged activities is to claim its existence as an area-based social enterprise. Unlike many social enterprises in India, Barefoot College pioneered in employment retention and community integration with various innovative processes that have evolved over a period of time with continuous discussion and deliberation among the communities. In fact, Barefoot is one of the first institutions in India to question the conventional methods of social development, and brought incremental improvements in the ways how problems have been solved.

In the last four chapters, we have discussed how various social enterprises address social problems, create social value and strive to achieve SO. The next chapter aims to build a framework which explains the process of social entrepreneurship and contextualizes various phases and stages adopted for the successful functioning of social enterprises.

7

Social Entrepreneurial Conceptual Framework

While the last few chapters offered rich understanding about the processes involved and strategies and innovations adopted to address social problems in different social contexts, the current chapter undertakes a normative approach and offers a discussion on what worked best and how the social innovations or social entrepreneurship can be better facilitated by promising or budding social entrepreneurs or social innovators. The chapter synthesizes factors that influence social enterprises to be successful from the cases studied in this research. A framework will be introduced in order to analyze the scenario and offer a context. Furthermore, it narrates how success can be replicated in different contexts based on the learnings from this research. Since all the four cases studied as part of this book come from high profile social enterprises which have already started creating social value through their innovations, it is appropriate to draw imperatives that offer better understanding of the social contexts in which success can be replicated. Such understanding may also be useful for enthusiasts in the field to realize what works in an ideal scenario. In a way, this chapter can be considered as a learning guide for practitioners, enthusiasts, academicians and researchers.

While the case analysis narrates that the area-based social enterprises are grounded in communities, the issue-based social enterprises adopt in-depth innovations to strengthen their focus. It is to say that there are different sets of learning in case of area-based and issue-based social enterprises; however, the analysis from this chapter draws from successful factors applicable across the cases. That means the framework created is contextualized based on the cross-case analysis. This book proposes that the process of social entrepreneurship can be explained using a framework from sourcing to scaling and replication of social impact. This framework which is discussed later offers a case for understanding the process of social entrepreneurship in consistency with the social innovation framework which is developed by Murray, Caulier-Grice and Mulgan (2010) as discussed in the second chapter.

As depicted in Figure 7.1, the proposed social entrepreneurial framework has six phases that include (a) sourcing, (b) setting the hook, (c) strategy, (d) social value creation, (e) sustainable orientation and (f) scaling and replication.

Sourcing

The sourcing phase unveils the process of social entrepreneurship where a social entrepreneur or a team of social entrepreneurs

Figure 7.1

The social entrepreneurial framework

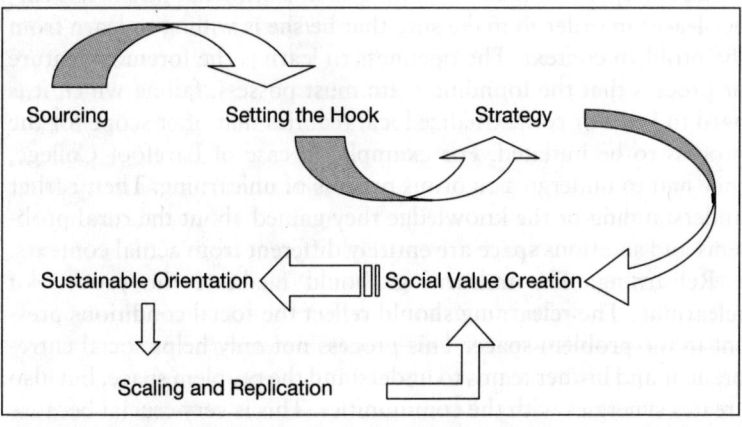

Source: Author's own.

integrates him/her/themselves into the social context where inspiration for finding the source is located. Source, in the context of social entrepreneurship, can also be understood as a social problem or social need identification in social terms or opportunity recognition or exploitation in the market terms (Archer, Baker and Mauer 2009; Fuglasang et al. 2010). Notwithstanding the terminology used, the social value creation principle dictates its normative stand which makes the terminology irrelevant. However, the source phase creates synergies for social entrepreneurs to take up the social entrepreneurial process. While identifying the source which is known as social problem or opportunity identification, the social entrepreneur opts subjective modalities. In fact, such subjective understanding emerges from the realities witnessed in social space. The process of locating the source involves seven stages: (a) unlearning, (b) relearning, (c) community penetration, (d) immersion in the problem space, (e) setting up a vision, (f) social innovation and (g) personal sacrifices. We will now discuss each step in detail.

Unlearning: Since all the social entrepreneurs in this study come from external contexts where they have later induced themselves in the problem space, there was a need for all of them to unlearn what they have already known. The knowledge gained from external environment may not allow the social entrepreneur to understand the problem space as it is located in the local context. Thus, the social entrepreneur must be willing to unlearn what he/she has earlier learnt in order to make sure that he/she is willing to learn from the problem context. The openness to learn is the foremost feature or process that the founding team must possess, failing which it is hard to learn or contextualize local realities that offer scope for the process to be initiated. For example, in case of Barefoot College, they had to undergo a rigorous process of unlearning. Their earlier understanding or the knowledge they gained about the rural problems and solutions space are entirely different from actual contexts.

Relearning: The unlearning should facilitate the process of relearning. The relearning should reflect the social conditions present in the problem space. This process not only helps social entrepreneur and his/her teams to understand the problem space, but also creates synergies with the communities. This is very crucial because we are already aware that the prevalent top-down approaches or the approaches successful at certain context may not represent local realities; thus, relearning the knowledge about the local contexts and the cultures would pave the path for the right way where understanding the process becomes quite easier for those who are involved. Relearning has been an essential element to identify the right problem context. For example, Gram Vikas had to relearn from the local contexts and employ continuous innovation before it could understand the local need and cultures.

Community penetration: The relearning process would become quite easy and the process of social entrepreneurship in general becomes quite impressive when social entrepreneur and his/her teams penetrate the communities. We have realized in this study that community participation not only allows a social entrepreneur to carry out frequent interactions, but also makes sure that the activities become sustainable over a period of time. At this phase, social entrepreneurs may interact with a set of community members from different groups based on the need. The community penetration has several benefits for both social enterprise and the communities involved as it creates and enhances synergies between the two groups. In fact, from community penetration to actual setting up of a social enterprise, social entrepreneur and their teams need to have sufficient time to make sure that the communities come on board to take up the activities and share the responsibilities. The community mobilization stage in the next phase will make sure that the social enterprises sufficiently position themselves in the contexts in which they are present. In case of Barefoot College, Enable India and Goonj, the community penetration element has offered unconditional support to the process of social entrepreneurial value creation. In fact, communities were cynical about entertaining the social enterprises in the beginning; however, with their active involvement in understanding the social problem and possible exploration of solutions in addition to dedication, communities have later started to show interest in sharing their problems and concerns.

Immersion in the problem space: The unlearning, relearning and community penetration would facilitate the social entrepreneur to immerse in the problem space. Interactions with communities on a daily basis and providing space for them to participate in the planning, decision making and implementation of the various activities, social enterprises create such environment for their own immersion.

The teams involved in both Barefoot College and Gram Vikas have had their presence in each local contexts and understood the structures meticulously. In fact, after identifying the need for such immersion, Barefoot College had took a significant stand by paving the way for more robust and rigorous immersion, whereas Gram Vikas had to constantly engage itself with the communities before they could really understand what they needed to do to achieve their mission. In case of an issue-based social enterprise, the immersion has been an act of continuous process as they interact with new groups in different geographical locations.

Setting up a vision: Exploring and understanding the problem space offers scope for envisaging a vision. The social entrepreneur in general takes responsibility for envisaging such vision. The vision comes from interactions with the subjects in the social settings. The vision once set, would continue to play a crucial role in dictating the value proposition it aims to embark. The vision which comes from the relearning and continuous interactions with the various parties involved would dictate the various activities social enterprise may need to undertake in order to achieve objectives set forward. In further stages, vision may be enriched based on further probing. The envisaged vision which dictates the overall context of the enterprise at this stage gets operationalized by the mission that sets the whole process into motion. In this stage, the envisaged vision may deal with addressing immediate problems. However, it may lack a larger picture, which will be probed in further phases. For example, in the initial phases, Enable India just aimed at providing training and finding employment for those whom it trained, which is envisaged in its narrowest form. It, in fact, reached its fullest form when they introduced WPS in support of the actual work carried out.

Social innovation: Adoption of social innovation becomes an integral part of each phase of the social enterprise. In the context of source, it revolves around understanding the context, envisaging the initial vision and setting up the mission of the organization. As someone rightly said, good planning is an indication for half success. Accordingly, proper understanding of the social problem and identifying the factors that cause such problems and the ways in which these problems could be addressed using various innovative mechanisms make sure that the processes is innovative, and so are the results. For example, social innovation has been quite intense in all contexts across the social enterprises studied in the research. Especially in the sourcing phase, innovations are involved in the way the problem or opportunity space is defined.

Personal sacrifices: It is quite obvious that everything happens in this universe at a cost. The cost in the context of social entrepreneurship for social entrepreneurs is that at least during the beginning of their social enterprises, they will have to forego the pleasure of being comfortable in their own living environment. In fact, this engagement or involvement takes away their energies and minimizes their income sources. Furthermore, it comes at a point where families start discouraging and disowning them. For example, in case of Bunker Roy, his mother had in fact stopped talking to him, while for Anshu Gupta, his in-laws were shocked to know that he quit his comfortable job. Though close ones come on board and start supporting once success knocks their doors, the initial conditions or personal life may be devastating.

Nevertheless, sourcing phase in the context of social entrepreneurship is a continuous process. The initial ideas in the phase help social enterprises to set the process in motion, whereas the ideas that emerge in the later stage enhance the depth of initial ideas or extend the focus to entire new areas. We have learnt in this research that social enterprises continue to look for sources in order to strengthen their social value creation on a later phase. Accordingly, the social value creation gets multiplied as the social enterprises engage in multiple social value creation processes. The next phase of the framework deals with setting the hook, which is a key process to step up the processes to the next levels.

Setting the Hook

The successful sourcing of the problem and opportunity space and the relevant background work as specified in the earlier phase leads to the second phase of the process which is called 'setting the hook' phase. In this phase, social entrepreneurs or their teams advance in their planning to institutionalize the processes. This phase has five stages that include (a) community mobilization, (b) trust building, (c) enhancing vision, (d) team building and (e) resource acquisition.

Community mobilization: One of the first stages while setting the context is to mobilize communities. It goes on to include various activities such as to sensitize, educate and mobilize them to be part of the process. One should not be confused about this stage with the community penetration stage in the earlier phase. While the community penetration helps the social entrepreneurs and his/her team to understand the social contexts, community mobilization in this phase helps them to get communities on board and take active part in day-to-day activities including planning and execution. In fact, the rigour should make sure that communities believe that the social enterprises exist to look after their welfare. For example, as discussed in the community penetration stage, initially communities show interest in sharing the problem. But to take this interest to the next level, social enterprises have to actually show them their vision and the initial processes of organizational building.

Trust building: The community penetration and mobilization stages help social enterprises acquire the much needed 'trust' within the local contexts. One of the major problems for social enterprises, for that matter any other grassroots level organization, is to win the trust of the communities. It is one of the preconditions for social enterprises to exist and to sustain in the long run. Thus, community mobilization enhances such trust which is initiated through community penetration. We have realized in this study that trust building and community participation enhance the much needed breakthrough in terms of acquiring resources and sustaining the initiative or activity for a long time. For example, all cases in this research show that communities trust the concerned organizations and respect their activities, which would eventually ensure their success. Since trust building has implications for sustainability, discussion related to several other practices involved in such adoption are covered in detail in different phases.

Enhancing vision: The stage of envisaging vision, as discussed in the earlier phase, gets hooked here to the organization in an enhanced or enriched form. In fact, at this phase where communities become an integral part of the entire process, there are all reasons to believe that they support and enhance vision to enrich and integrate in the process. In fact, with the community mobilization, the vision in this phase is set to integrate different stakeholders involved at this stage. For example, during envisaging vision, the social entrepreneur may aim or focus on narrow objectives such as in the case of Enable India, just to train and provide them suitable employment, whereas when the process becomes quite intense, the entire process shifts to aiming at a larger vision, which includes achieving well-being of individuals and families involved and achieving social inclusion, which is the overall aim driven by enhancing social, political, cultural and financial participation.

Team building: While the initial teams might have already been built for social enterprises, as we have witnessed in the cases studied, the process becomes intensive at this stage. Initial few people who joined the team in case of issue-based social enterprise are the family members, whereas for the area-based social enterprise, these are friends and associates who have extended unconditional support. In this case, it shows a clear understanding that while issue-based social enterprises are individual-driven from the beginning, the area-based social enterprises are team-driven. However, the success path of all the social enterprises are driven by individuals with the help of their teams and stakeholders involved. The teams which enter the organization on a later stage are required to take up the difficulties and success and contribute for its growth.

Resource acquisition: This is one of the crucial stages of the entire venture creation. While all the stages as part of this discussion are crucial for building the venture inch by inch, resource acquisition plays a significant role. Initially, social entrepreneurs acquire resources from the friends and family members and individual philanthropists. In the later stage, resource acquisitions are boosted by the philanthropic agencies, enterprises initiated, awards and recognitions achieved and active contribution from the government. Especially the community penetration remains key for the ventures to make sure that they contribute in building their own lives. At this stage of the venture growth, social entrepreneurs especially use bricolage as a means to acquire resources. The need and essence about the resource and its association with SO would be discussed in a separate phase in this framework.

This phase helps the social entrepreneur and his/her team to shape the processes and create space for the organization to form its basic structures. This phase is succeeded by another crucial phase called 'Strategy'.

Strategy

Strategy building and venturing into operations in order to achieve what is being planned is a crucial phase. As part of this phase, the social entrepreneur and his/her team in consultation with communities and other players involved move forward in actualizing operational issues, and make sure that the venture gains all the required support and resources it deserves. As part of this phase, there are eight stages which include (a) enhancing capacities of communities, (b) WISE to enhance trust building, (c) WISE to enrich SO, (d) adoption of social innovation, (e) involvement of volunteers, (f) building partnerships, (g) partnering with government and (h) enterprising social value creation. Each stage in the phase is crucial for venture growth. Let us discuss about each stage in this phase in detail.

Enhancing capacities of communities: One of the successful strategies social enterprises adopt is to enhance capabilities of the communities. The existing systems and structures negate this principle and do not focus much on enhancing the capabilities as it is necessary for them to make sure that the communities depend upon them. This is the way the existing third sector manages to acquire grants or donations. On the other hand, social entrepreneurship, being a superior breed of the third sector, aims to enhance the capacities of the communities in order to make sure that they become part of their own inclusion which eventually leads to their inclusion in the mainstream. For example, all the cases attempt to avoid freebies, so that the communities own the activities undertaken by the social enterprise, which builds their confidence levels. In case of Goonj, which generally does not focus on charging the beneficiaries, started to focus on 'CfW' programme in order to create the ownership feeling which leads to enhancing capabilities of the communities.

WISE to enhance trust building: As part of strategy building to enhance trust among communities and create the feeling of ownership, social enterprises employ the deprived and excluded among the serving communities in various job roles. In order to do so, all the social enterprises in this study emerged as work-integrated social enterprises. This experiment not only places them in a strategically comfortable position, but also makes sure that the community members' deal with the communities using local language and culture. This has worked well in case of all the social enterprises.

For example, in case of Enable India, prioritized recruitment of PwDs create synergies among the beneficiaries and the employees which facilitates the integration or empowerment principle quite significantly. In other cases including Barefoot College, Enable India and Goonj, this principle has strategically placed them in the helm of the communities.

WISE to enrich SO: In fact, the other element of employing the WISE approach by social enterprises has roots in creating their own SO. The community mobilization stage in the earlier phase gets boosted by the WISE approach in order to make sure that the sustainability elements become an integral part of the social enterprises. When social enterprises employ community members, they institutionalize the organizational mission and vision within the community culture. In fact, they take part in the planning and integrate cultural paradigms within the strategy and the operations related to the venture, which enhances the prospects of achieving SO.

Adoption of social innovation: While the adoption and practice of social innovation could itself constitute a separate phase of the entire process, given its contribution to several phases in this analysis, its practice is integrated and clustered as necessary in several phases. As part of adoption of social innovation in strategy building, social enterprises embark on social innovation in the very planning and building the pillars of the organization including but not limited to (a) adoption of WISE through training masses, (b) setting up structures such as WPS, which makes sure that the process does not get stuck due to the systematic failures which may come up in the process and (c) work for cloth as a potential approach that came up in the process of strategy building which has suppressed the freebie concept.

Involvement of volunteers: As part of strategy building, the key element is the utilization of resources economically. In the process, attracting volunteers for the various activities that are carried out is an important aspect. In fact, attraction of volunteers in the initial phase may turn out to be a difficult practice due to their invisible nature. However, those involved in the initial sourcing and setting the hook stages work as volunteers without having any remuneration. Thus, the contribution of volunteers in social enterprises is quite significant. Given the innovation and successful social impact creation, the successful social enterprises attract external volunteers quite actively, especially after they gain recognition or initial success. Social enterprises, after gaining certain visibility, attract volunteers quite easily. As part of the building base for voluntarism, social enterprises need to aim at attracting the youth, who mostly constitute the volunteer force in the social service sector. For example, while all social enterprises benefit from volunteers, Goonj in particular has gained the most. It could spread its activities to more than 20 states within no time and the success should be attributed to the increased participation of volunteers.

Building partnerships: Building external partnerships takes roots from the strategy phase. In fact, the process becomes robust when the social enterprise succeeds in creating initial social value. The initial recognition facilitates them to gain awards, which positions them in the global scenario. Such recognition also enhances their partnership curve in both national and international arena. In fact, partnerships with community-based committees which are created for the very purpose of enhancing their participation is also an important aspect. This also goes well with a perception that it is necessary for social enterprises to maintain healthy relationships with various entities in the ecosystem. For example, we have learnt in this research that the corporate companies are eager to partner with Enable India due to the value addition or brand image it creates. In addition, Goonj partners with various corporates to act as its transport partners, while the established area-based social enterprises have successfully partnered with organizations of global repute which not only brings financial resources on board but also other connections and reputation. Partnerships with the community-based committees such as VDCs and VECs creates supportive environment at the local level.

Partnering with government: While claims are in rise that partnering with the government is a necessary evil, social enterprises maintain healthy relations with the government. In fact, government has emerged as one of the biggest financial supporter of the social enterprises. Partnerships with various government agencies and ministries at different level and participating in their schemes and programmes benefit, social enterprises in a number of ways. While it has its own drawbacks such as corruption, legal restrictions and delay in disbursement of funds, it is highly opined by social entrepreneurs that it is otherwise the responsibility of the government to address the social problems, which actually they undertake. Hence, they consider that it is their right to get support and resources from the government sources. In fact, such partnering also enhances their positioning in local and community contexts. For example, initially Gram Vikas had partnered with the local health departments in order to build trust among communities, while Goonj partners with the Indian Army to reach the unreached, and Barefoot College partners with the Ministry of external Affairs to facilitate its operations in Africa.

Enterprising social value creation: While reducing the dependency on external funding, social enterprises aim to create mission-centric social enterprises. While for some, the mission-centric approach aligns from the very beginning of the venture growth, for others, it becomes part in the process. However, the underlying practice is that all the social enterprises aim to enhance their vision through enterprising their activities. Though the successes are context specific, the inherent desire to become self-dependent inspires the social enterprises to be entrepreneurial. For example, the initial success has lived shorter in case of Goonj and Gram Vikas, whereas Barefoot College could succeed in nurturing its entrepreneurial vision in the process of social value creation. While all the social enterprises aim to reduce their dependency on external funding in terms of building their own mission-centric social enterprises, most of them do not venture due to several institutional limitations. Social enterprises have to excel beyond their aspiration to enhance the prospects.

The strategy phase offers a clear context for building the social enterprise operations through the spirit gained from the earlier phase—setting the hook. The several stages discussed in this phase create the necessary momentum required for social enterprise functioning and set the stage for social value creation where communities ripe the results from the various processes adopted. The next phase of the framework is related to social value creation. This phase talks about the output or outcome of the entire process which is what the overall aim of the social entrepreneurship movement is.

Social Value Creation

The whole aim of the social entrepreneurship process is to address social problems and create social value. Social value creation is a robust process which may result from the very beginning when social enterprises educate the communities or stakeholders involved or from the time when the stakeholders start benefiting from the process. The phase talks about the various stages in which the stakeholders gain momentum and start benefiting from the process through either service or product provision or directly benefiting through the elevated social status. The phase has four stages that include (a) social participation, (b) political participation, (c) work integration, and (d) economic participation. Let us discuss each of these stages in detail below.

Social participation: Across the cases studied in this research, it is proven that social enterprises, by addressing the social problems, enhance prospects for social participation of the poor and deprived. In fact, in the earlier contexts, when social enterprises were non-existent, these socially excluded groups had no significant social participation. For example, the PwDs within the purview of Enable India, and the poor and deprived in case of Goonj, Barefoot College and Gram Vikas have had no basic facilities, which restricted their social participation. It includes Dalits and PwDs who are not having space in social activities and access to basic facilities. However, with the realities rewritten by embracing new institutional forms and approaches, these deprived and excluded sections could enhance their social participation.

Political participation: Social enterprises while operating at grass-roots contribute to the political participation of the communities. Often the strategies to enhance political participation start from as nominal as just educating or awareness building among communities about their political rights. In addition, the elevated social living and community integration help them to advance from their earlier political participation levels. We have witnessed in case of both area-based social enterprises that the elevated social and financial status help communities to advance in their political life. Even there are cases where illiterate women take up political roles including the role of the head of the village or town. The children parliament offers scope for children to understand the political ethos since their childhood.

Work integration: The work integration aspect in the social entrepreneurship space aims to achieve two objectives: (a) to enhance trust building among communities and (b) to benefit the most deprived and excluded with a job. In order to facilitate the process, the social enterprises train the potential candidate in the skills which are required to undertake job roles. The work integration element helps the job holder to work as a connector between communities being served and the concerned social enterprise. For example, all the cases discussed in this book employ work integration. As a result both, the communities and the social enterprises, benefit from employing this strategy.

Economic participation: While work integration is an output, its value gets visualized through economic participation. As stated above, the second aim of employing work integration is to enhance the economic participation of the deprived and excluded who are given priority in the job roles of the organizations. Thus, most of the processes in the social value creation are interrelated and contribute to each other. For example, the economic participation enhances social and political participation. In addition, the product or service delivery to the poor and deprived makes sure that they can participate in markets with relatively less financial resources that they are capable to access. All the cases in this book have contributed to enhance economic participation of the varied stakeholders ranging from excluded and deprived employees to other community members through providing flexible product or service delivery.

While social value creation itself is a crucial outcome in the entire process, the social entrepreneurial adventures or activities do not end there. The other two phases including SO and scaling and replication of social impact for larger social change are key and significant aspects in the process of social entrepreneurship and social value creation. In fact, these two phases take the impact to the next level with a focus on rapid and systematic social change. Thus, the social value creation gets promoted to the next level, that is, social change with help from the next two phases. The next phase discusses about SO.

Sustainable Orientation

The social value creation phase brings hope for social enterprises to adopt innovative methods to enhance the value created. This is where social enterprises differ from traditional organizations. Traditional organizations in third sector get relaxed when they appear to achieve certain level of social value, or they go for finding more donors in order to scale the successful activity. However, social enterprises take inspiration from social value creation, and advance in the process to sustain the activities that foster social value and to enhance the social value being created. In fact, the various stages discussed in this phase might take place from the sourcing or setting the hook stage. Thus, this phase is quite dynamic and can take place any time in the venture creation and growth based on the strategy adopted. This phase comprises five stages, including (a) creation of enterprises, (b) awards, (c) grants, (d) government and (e) market penetration.

Creation of enterprises: It is found that all the social enterprises would want to strengthen their financial self-dependency. This stage is capable of facilitating three practices, including (a) to enhance community participation, (b) to initiate sustainable activities and (c) to achieve organizational sustainability. Accordingly, there has been considerable interest shown to create and promote mission-centric enterprises. We have, in fact, realized in the cases as part of the study that all social enterprises at some point of time started their own enterprises with a philosophy to achieve organizational sustainability. Though some efforts went in vain, others have been successful. The aspirations are promising and they set the stage for achieving SO.

Awards: All the social enterprises that are part of the research have received several awards in both national and international circles. Early stage recognitions, including Ashoka and Global Development Network, offer considerable material and non-material support including global recognition, connecting to different networks and high profile individuals. On a later stage, three of the four social enterprises which are part of this research are recognized and awarded by Schwab awards which offer considerable grants apart from global recognition. While the early stage awards are crucial to build the enterprise, the later stage awards offer the much needed support to initiate or run various activities. In case the activities are already sustainable, the financial support is useful for social enterprises to introduce a new service or a new product. In fact, in the case of Enable India, recognition from Ashoka has helped it to move to a bigger space where it could expand its initial organizational set-up, whereas in the case of Barefoot College, the World Children Prize which was awarded by World Children's Prize Foundation in Sweden has been used to strengthen the Barefoot Parliament.

Grants: While grants are crucial for the success of social enterprises, it is found that they have reduced the level of innovation in social enterprises. In other words, due to the availability of excessive funding, social enterprises which were once highly innovative in terms of creating mission centric enterprises have now moved away from such priorities to concentrate only on social mission. Thus, the excessive availability of grants may lead to compromising social enterprises on their entrepreneurial orientation. On the other hand, grants are crucial for early stage social enterprise building. Not compromising with the grant-based approach, social enterprises require to move on and explore market-based innovative methods to reduce their dependency on grants. This not only helps them to be sustainable, but also makes sure that the available grants can support other social enterprises which are in need of such support.

Government: When it comes to SO, government also plays a crucial role. It is considered in the social enterprise circles that the grants from government must be seen as part of the revenues and thus constitutes for the entrepreneurial orientation. Though it is a debatable issue whether or not the grants be considered as part of the earnings of the social enterprises, it is proved that the innovative problem solving approaches employed by the social enterprises are well appreciated by the government at different levels. On the other hand, there has been considerable contestation whether or not it is ideal to partner with the government for social enterprises as their existence is a result of the failure of governments and businesses. However, as opined by Joe Madiath, it is after all the government's responsibility to undertake activities that are otherwise actually taken up by social entrepreneurs. Nevertheless, it is ideal to have government on board and make sure that it actively takes part in the alternative realities being created. The other advantage of having government in planning and execution of the social innovations is that it may be able to provide necessary facilities to achieve systematic social change. For example, in case of Gram Vikas, the biogas programme has been generously supported by government which was then scaled up in different areas. So, attracting government is one of the best advantages in order to achieve systematic social change.

Market penetration: Market penetration is a broader activity compared to entrepreneurial orientation. While entrepreneurial orientation talks about creating a market-based enterprise, market penetration talks about usage of market techniques in the absence of an established enterprise. This includes usage of market techniques to impress different players. For example, Enable India uses entrepreneurial language including professionalism and skill-based approach while approaching employers to provide jobs for the PwDs who are trained by the organization. In addition, accountability and transparency are a few key approaches adopted in order to improve the operations of all social enterprises.

While there is a lot of expectations from social enterprises to achieve SO, in reality social enterprises struggle or negate the objectives set forward to become sustainable. However, the social impact created and the innovations employed to achieve such impact contribute to the significant social value creation. Thus, you may find that many social enterprises are in operation without employing any market-based approaches; however, they may create and promote innovative products and services. It is to conclude that this particular phase is crucial in order to help social enterprises to replicate or scale their initial success and enhance the impact, while also significant to sustain the activities undertaken. However, since social enterprises give primary importance to achieving social value, the financial value creation sometimes may be delayed beyond the expectations. This discussion moves to the next phase on scaling and replication of social impact which takes social value creation to the next level to transform larger systems.

Scaling and Replication of Social Impact

Scaling and replication is a key phase in order to enhance social impact and achieve systematic social change. This is important partly because of the fact that successful social innovations should make their way to as many communities as possible in order to create systemic social change. Given the fact that the success rate of the social enterprises is quite disturbing, it is important for the successful ones to scale and create larger social impact. This phase discusses the approaches social enterprises employed to scale or replicate social value. Altogether, this phase has three stages: (a) replication/scaling, (b) persuading or partnering with local institutions and (c) influencing the government policy.

Replication/scaling: Social enterprises which have established their roots in the deeper social contexts aim at quality of the impact, rather than the quantity. That means it is not about the numbers, including how many families are benefited, it is all about the depth of such benefit and its influence on their daily living. In order to focus on the depth of the impact created, social enterprises claim to focus more on the replication of the organizations. After the initial success, social enterprises, instead of scaling the venture, prefer to replicate the success. In other words, instead of growing as an organization which is an intended outcome of scaling, the social enterprises would want to collaborate with various grassroots organizations which are operational in other geographical areas, and empower such organizations to take up the successful activities. In such a way, local organizations take up the task of empowering the communities and undertake the activities. It is an easy way for achieving systematic social change as the trust building alone would take a lot of time, if successful social enterprises would want to scale in other areas. Given the need for achieving social impact in quick times, social enterprises adopt replication as a best method. For example, Anshu believes that it is always better to grow as an idea than an organization.

Persuading or partnering with local institutions: Persuading or partnering with local organizations and institutions becomes key to achieve systematic social change. Especially, the global recognition and credibility the successful social enterprises embark on help them to connect easily with local organizations and build partnerships and networks to persuade them to replicate the successful approaches. In fact, the local organizations also show interest to replicate because of the value advantage they receive by associating with the successful globally recognized social enterprises. For example, Barefoot College partners with local organizations in Africa to train and empower rural women to solar electrify the villages concerned.

Influencing the government policy: Continuous interaction with the government is a striking proposition for social enterprises to enhance the prospects to create system-level change. In addition, influencing government and policy are key in order to educate the government officials about the need for adoption of innovations. The successful social leaders often represent in high level decision-making bodies of the State which are useful for them to influence policy and include the philosophy of social entrepreneurship into the larger policy objectives. For example, with his success, Joe Madiath has become a member of the national sanitation committee, from where he has influenced State policy quite successfully to promote innovation in the sanitation sector.

The six phases discussed in this chapter offer a framework to understand what goes into successful social enterprises. The framework explains that the process of social entrepreneurship starts with sourcing where social problems are identified and moving on to next levels through setting the hook where basic pillars are built to initiate the process. The next phase builds a strategy that takes the social entrepreneurship into the crux of the problem, where the innovations and various other strategies are employed to strengthen functioning of the social enterprises. The fourth phase of the process results into the actual social value creation process where social enterprises start creating value. The successful social value creation enforces the social enterprises to look into different avenues, where they could start focusing on SO which results into the last phase, where they start replicating the ventures to achieve systematic social change.

While the phases described in this framework are binding in social entrepreneurship space, stages described in this framework may differ from one social enterprise to another. It all depends on the local contexts and processes adopted. Thus, the stages discussed in the framework may only be applicable for the current research or for similar social enterprises. However, when it comes to phases, all social enterprises have to undergo these phases at a given stage of venture growth. They need not be present in the similar sequence as represented in this book, that is, the actual sequence may differ. For example, social enterprises may first aim to attain SO before venturing into social value creation, or some social enterprises may attain both the SO and social value creation simultaneously. The growing 'for-profit' orientation in many social enterprises shows interest to adopt the later process where both social and financial value is created simultaneously. However, all the phases discussed in this framework are binding on the social entrepreneurship practice. Thus, the aspiring social entrepreneurs may learn from these successful practices before initiating their ventures. The following chapter concludes the book and draws a cross-case analysis.

Conclusion

While the previous chapter presented a framework for the process of social entrepreneurship and discussed what works in the practice of successful social entrepreneurship, the current chapter aims to analyze the case representation and offers the actual social and organizational contexts at the grassroots level. Overall, the research offers an outlook into existing practices of social entrepreneurship, which enhances the social participation of certain communities whose interests have been overlooked by social and market institutions. It envisages the need for innovative existence of third sector in order to address social problems while manifesting the interests of the excluded and deprived. In the process, the emergence of social entrepreneurship and the various processes adopted by selected social entrepreneurs in India have been highlighted to capture the social transformation created. The four cases, namely Enable India, Gram Vikas, Goonj and Barefoot College, represent four different geographical locations in the country. The cases selected have offered rich insights with various innovative attempts that they have undertaken in the process to facilitate social integration. Such processes have been restlessly working to promote alternative realities in order to bring the interests of the poor and the marginalized forefront. With this backdrop, the research highlighted innovative attempts involved in the processes employed and analyzed the impact created with in-depth interviews. Furthermore, the study highlights organizational sustainability as a significant move to stick to the objectives of social value creation without being restricted by any external factors. In fact, this very basic factor differentiates social enterprises with the other third sector organizations (Wallace 2003). The chapter, in a nutshell, summarizes various innovative practices adopted by social enterprises studied as part of the research. The cross-sectional analysis of cases studied in the research and imperatives drawn are discussed in detail.

Inspiration for Addressing Social Problems

As earlier described by several scholars including Alvord, Brown and Letts (2004), Seelos and Mair (2004), Tan, Williams and Tan (2005), Austin et al. (2006), Cho (2006), Harding (2006), Mair and Marti (2006), Mulgan (2006), Nicholls (2006a, 2006b), Nicholls and Cho (2006), Westall and Chalkley (2007), Nwankwo, Philips and Tracey (2007), and Zeyen et al. (2012), it is revealed that social entrepreneurs create social ventures to address social problems that have been largely ignored by various players in society. It is further understood that the social problems have a strong relation with social entrepreneurs in terms of motivating them to get involved. Though none of the social enterprises have personally experienced the social problem, yet all of them were touched by the plight experienced by communities. In the case of a social entrepreneur, it was a family member who had got into the trap of social exclusion, because of which the social enterprise came into existence. All social enterprises studied have emerged out of nowhere in the context of just a social entrepreneur taking the initiative and then later followed by teams of teams to change the momentum and scale the social value created.

Anshu, Bunker, Joe and Shanti have all graduated from reputed academic institutions. However, their passion to strive and address social problems has led them to think about the ways in which they were travelling up to spotting the problem where finally they decided to work. It is then that the momentum has changed which has later transformed the lives of millions, who are stuck up in the cross sections in social and economic deprivation.

Adoption of Social Innovation

This research agrees to a popular notion that prevails in social entrepreneurship research and practice that the social entrepreneurs adopt innovations in the process of community integration and delivery of services and products. Contributions of scholars such as Leadbeater (1997), Dees (1998), Drucker (1999), Dees (2001), Dees and Anderson (2006), Wong and Tang (2006/07), Seelos and Mair (2007), Zahra et al. (2008), and Hill et al. (2010) in this regard are well-appreciated as the ways they defined or explained the process and practices of social innovation within the given contexts of social entrepreneurship prevailed in the practices of cases studied in this research too. For example, starting from problem identification to integration of the excluded in the mainstream, the research prompts that social entrepreneurs innovate to promote sustainable living. The social problems in four cases including clothing, problems related to PwDs and multiple problems faced by rural population have all been tackled using social innovation in different stages. Especially, the clothing and sanitary napkin issues as highlighted by Goonj, which operates in an in-depth innovation space, is a significant attempt. The way how skill development and employment provision are offered in all cases is an indication of the adoptive innovative procedure followed. For example, the PwDs in Enable India or Dalits and tribals in the case of Gram Vikas or rural deprived in the case of Barefoot College and Goonj have been facilitated to find a place in mainstream markets and society through their enhanced market and social participation, respectively. This has been made possible through the innovative efforts carried out from time to time. The processes that innovation adopts to integrate communities also vary from one organization to another; however, they all have shown strong commitment in terms of highlighting the process evolved in structures adopted. For example, the WfC initiated by Goonj is an adequate model to analyze the aspirations and better ways of reaching out to the poor with incremental benefits and social transformation.

Failing to capture the attention of urban-based experts, empowering the skills and capabilities of the poor and deprived in order to address their own social problems is another significant contribution which has opened space for many such interventions to take place across several social contexts. Gram Vikas, which highlights the need for 100 per cent inclusion of households in its sanitation and water programme, is a crucial step to understand the intentions of social entrepreneurs to grasp larger social transformation. It shows that it is not about completion of projects or to impress donors but to create systematic social change. It is derived from understanding various activities undertaken and processes involved which are innovative in nature to demonstrate larger social interest that social enterprises are committed to create alternative social realities. However, it is to highlight, in order to facilitate social innovations in the societies in which they operate, social entrepreneurs and their teams had to face severe constraints from the contexts and social systems existed.

Social enterprises have shown commitment to enhance skills, capabilities and dignity of the stakeholders through curbing the practices of charity and 'giving away'. It is felt that the charity approach does not yield in any betterment for the deprived, rather it enslaves them in the clutches of deprivation and exploitation due to the lack of choices. Communities have also shown their unwillingness towards charity and further emphasized on skill-based development rather than charity-based development. They have also realized that it is largely a question of dignity and self-esteem. As Mair and Seelos (2004) projected, it is not in the communities' interest to depend on the charity-based development model; rather, they are forced to accept it due to their limitation of choices and deprivation of skills. Social enterprises have also shown their commitment in terms of employing various ways of educating communities about the need for skill enhancement and capability building to achieve sustainable social change. Three organizations in the study, Goonj, Gram Vikas and Barefoot College, have moved forward in terms of their dedicated efforts to promote and project skill and capability development through community participation in various developmental activities. This approach has also helped to increase ownership among the communities, which has resulted in the sustainability of the projects. Enable India, however, has failed to nurture its potential to improvise the cross-subsidized model, which can reduce dependency of stakeholders on the charity-based approach. However, while dealing with various employers to have their trainees placed in various job roles, Enable India has succeeded in implementing the skill-based approach.

Achieving Sustainability and Ignoring Potential Opportunities

This study offers insights to support the finding captured in an Intellecap (2010) study which found that the SEs studied have shown continuous commitment towards their entrepreneurial nature which brings a large structural cohesion to attain SO. The

Intellecap study finds that about three-fifths of all SEs have adopted innovative business models. On the similar lines, Gram Vikas and Goonj have evolved with their own market-based approaches since the beginning; however, in the process of value creation, both of them have missed the essential ways of maintaining the structures created. In case of Gram Vikas, though the reason being projected as legal obligation, with a wise decision, it could have sorted out the issue or created mission-centric institutions for promoting market integration. In case of Goonj, it has failed to sustain the initial market-based activities that it planned. Furthermore, it has failed to adopt market-based principles; it has shifted its entire focus to non-profit orientation of the organization, totally ignoring the for-profit side. However, the social value created by Goonj is enormous, because the resources it requires come from used goods which are considered as 'waste'. Waste as crucial investment, Goonj could demonstrate social transformation with relatively better ways. The SROI is far better in case of Goonj. Barefoot College, however, has adopted various methods in the process and has successfully implemented them in order to demonstrate its hybrid nature. In case of Enable India, it is yet to optimize its resources to establish EISPL and facilitate SO within the organizational frame. However, the other ways of potential opportunities which may generate certain portion of incomes are often missed by the organizations.

Highlighting what Boschee (2008) confessed about the two approaches that social enterprises largely adopt, the four organizations studied have met their financial needs through allied sources including philanthropy, subsidies and earned revenues. In addition, social enterprises have also depended on community contributions and awards they have received from various national and international agencies. However, the continuous commitment and their aspirations to embark on a variety of innovations in order to enhance prospects of attaining more resources raised within the organizations is a remarkable attempt. It is found that while the aspirations are strong, the processes to materialize the aspirations require further attention.

Brown and Moore (2001) argue that the absence of earned income may help in maintaining focus to attain the goal and objectives of the social organization. However, in spite of having earned strategies or projecting commitment to explore such strategies in the near future, social enterprises have shown strong focus to attain their goal and objectives. In the case of Barefoot College, Goonj and Gram Vikas, they have already ventured into earned income strategies either through community or market integration. Both the area-based social enterprises,—Barefoot College and Gram Vikas—are capable of running on their corpus in case the external support is seized. In addition, any activity they have initiated was never restricted by lack of funding as their community integration is quite effective. It is proven that in case of failed efforts to receive external funding, communities are ready to contribute significantly for the activities meant to improve their lives. Apart from contributions from communities, institutional support plays crucial role in building corpus or sustaining the initiatives undertaken. In fact, it works as a relief for the organizations to be innovative while undertaking various activities to achieve better results and not to compromise with the philanthropies or donors. The awards and recognitions received by social entrepreneurs and their activities not only bring cash incentives on their own but also inspire others to donate contributions. The other two young social enterprises have not demonstrated any corpus which, one of it claims, is not essential, whereas the other organization could not get any such funds to build corpus. Their activities are strictly related to the availability of funding from philanthropists or community contribution. On the other hand, though the organizations are eager to initiate various business models to support the main objective of social transformation, they are stuck in the policy dialogue, especially Gram Vikas, which has had a record of managing three enterprises initially but is now tangled in the policy restrictions. This is to conclude that while there are aspirations, intentions and passion, it may still take a little while to demonstrate most of their market participation and achieve SO.

Decentralized Decision Making and Employee Retention

An Intellecap study (2012) proclaims that finding and retaining employees in social enterprises remains one of the crucial problems that social enterprises face. Another study conducted by Thomas and Kummitha (2013) has supported the earlier research carried out by Intellecap in which it is proven that the organizations are unable to get employees who will continue to stay with the organization for a long time. The current study has mixed responses from social enterprises where it is found that retaining employees remain the biggest problems for both Gram Vikas and Enable India. Though Barefoot College has structural arrangements to avoid scarcity of human resources, Gram Vikas and Enable India have been stuck up in the process. More than 90 per cent of the employees trained at Gram Vikas left the organization within no time. With the experience they have acquired at Gram Vikas, they aspire to move to reputed global organizations. In case of Enable India, it is unable to find qualified and committed candidates for various roles that exist in the organization. However, in case of Goonj, though the issue continues to hamper its growth, its presence in the national capital and the social media visibility have attributed remarkable volunteer support which complements the need for full-time employees. However, Barefoot College is able to manage the momentum with significant retention. For Barefoot College, finding employees and retention is not a problem due to their strong base in the communities. Some employees have stayed back in spite of lucrative offers from outside due to their commitment to the organization. However, Barefoot College has demonstrated its retention with various strategies as discussed, among which 'valuing the communities and employees' stands out.

The main reason for the failed efforts to find and retain employees has been attributed to their failure to respect skills of the employees with better pay structures or facilities. However, it is found that Gram Vikas, being a strong supporter of employee's welfare in terms of offering better facilities, is still unable to retain or find motivated employees. The other problem that Gram Vikas faces for having skilled employees is located in the geographical location of its existence. "We are placed in remote and resource constrained area. And all our work is in remote areas where there is no proper electricity, no cell phone signal, no connectivity, and no roads, etc.," Joe mentioned. The failed efforts to retain employees have resulted in restricting the organization to scale to other areas. It is further noticed that those who stick to the social enterprises are those who value the work being undertaken. Proper space in decision making and continuous encouragement to be active in the activities turned out to be two of the major reasons for employee retention. However, all social enterprises mitigate issues that arise during employee retention with innovative strategies ranging from training the illiterate and persons with lack of expertise to employing volunteers. For example, Barefoot College trains and employs elderly women to become solar engineers. In addition, it does not offer any certificate after completion of the training in order to make sure that those who are trained do not migrate to cities in search of better employment, whereas most of the activities undertaken by Goonj are carried out by volunteers.

One of the drawbacks of social enterprises studied is their failure to offer competitive remuneration or salaries. This single reason has resulted in many people trained by them leaving the organization. Especially, it is visible in both area-based SEs. The wage scenario is much depressing in Barefoot College where only minimum wages are paid to the employees; however, their retention rate is high compared to Gram Vikas. It is partly due to the presence of illiterate villagers who have occupied more than 95 per cent of the jobs in the organization. Moreover, the equal representation of each employee in the decision making and maintaining same salary structures for all sections of the employees is a key in retaining a large section of employees. Though Gram Vikas pays better than Barefoot College, it depends on urban-based educationalists; hence, they are basically inclined to growth and have high aspirations about salaries and other facilities they receive at work places. Hence, it is found that many of them leave the organization within two to three years of their recruitment.

In case of issue-based organizations, both Enable India and Goonj also face similar problems where their salaries do not match the experience and skills of the employees. As a result, many respondents across all the organizations during the research interviews have expressed the concern about the salaries paid to them. Among all the organizations it is found that many of the employees are ready to leave their respective employer, provided that they get better salaries outside.

Risk Taking

The existing research on social entrepreneurship highlights that the social entrepreneurs are eager to take numerous risks in both social and economic space in order to achieve sustainable solutions for a number of social problems (Bornstein 2004; Dees 1998; Defourny and Nyssens 2008). Though the current research confirms such behaviour in a significant way, there are even cases where social entrepreneurs are sceptical about undertaking economic activities in order to attain SO. For example, Barefoot College has shown tremendous risk-taking behaviour in terms of avoiding experts entering in its activities. It has, rather, developed skills and capabilities of the poor and excluded in order to hand over to them the key functions of the organization in addition to engaging them in addressing social problems. However, the study also came across how both Enable India and Gram Vikas have overlooked prospects of adding income streams to their activities with a fear that it may create risk to the existence of the organization. Though prediction of risk and taking adoptive measures to avoid such risk is a good move, both the organizations have projected to simply escape from opting to take risks. This risk aversion behaviour is quite persistent because of the availability of the generous grants and donations. They have access to the grants because their innovations are appreciated among the philanthropists. However, undertaking various activities to address social problems is not restricted by availability of grant funding. For example, while Goonj is not quite active in undertaking market penetration, lack of support from donors or philanthropists has not reduced their aspiration to start a sanitary napkin production unit.

Though all social enterprises studied have plans to emerge sustainable through market or community integration, outside funding continues to play a key role. Especially both the issue-based social enterprises have been operational with full funding from outside sources. Goonj has had some market integrative operations; however, such attempts just help in recovering some operational costs. Likewise, Enable India fully depends upon outside funding from various philanthropists and donors. Though ESIPL is in its initial stage, it may take a long time to become sustainable on its own. Both the area-based organizations have their own ways of sustaining their activities through the corpus they preserved, in addition to a few market-based initiatives undertaken by both the organizations. Furthermore, community involvement in these organizations create value addition in terms of offering their contributions and sustaining the activities. However, it is found that all the organizations still depend on outside donors or philanthropists for running their operations. It is also found that impact investors in selected social enterprises play no role. It may be largely due to the existence of social enterprises for a long time, whereas the impact investment industry is a recent entry in the field. In addition, the returns on investments in these organizations are not effective and immediate, which could be another reason why impact investors maintain distance from these organizations.

However, in spite of the continuous dependence on the external funding, the organizations have never allowed philanthropists or donors to influence the activities of the organization. Largely, it is found that the donors trust the activities undertaken by social enterprises due to their popularity, strong social presence and social transformation created. Bunker Roy has stated that Barefoot College never allows any funder or donor to dictate or involve in the activities undertaken by the college. Even the case of an unwanted involvement of Aga Khan Foundation earlier, which awarded the Aga Khan Award to the College, had resulted in returning the award and the cash USD 50,000 received as part of it. Dipesh from Enable India claimed that the donors trust them and they value the social transformation being created. That is the reason the donors never had any issues with the organization. Likewise, both Goonj and Gram Vikas have also been entirely independent when it comes to internal freedom where they are sceptical about outsider involvement.

In this research, it is found that social entrepreneurs at least in the initial stages of the organizational establishment have had difficult problems. Especially, lack of cooperation from the communities and resource constraint are the major difficulties. In the process of running the organizations, a different set of problems appear that include lack of resources and professional support form qualified employees and internal transitions, which have been sometimes very depressing. In the long run, issues related to sustaining the social transformation created and scaling or replicating the activities tend to develop additional tensions. However, it is found that in any of the stages, social entrepreneurs have not been demotivated. In fact, social entrepreneurs who are passionate about changing local settings and transforming lives of people have grasped strength from the problems and the resource-constrained environment. For example, Gram Vikas initiated the water and sanitation programme to prove its belief. Neither government nor any funder was of the view that an attempt to achieve 100 per cent sanitation in tribal areas was possible. However, the challenging environment has pushed Gram Vikas to show the alternative reality it believed in. Likewise, Barefoot College also undertakes its activities based on the need. As stated by one of the respondents, when there is no grain to run the crèche, communities support with various food items.

Though Barefoot College is one of the very few well-described social enterprises in India, it had to face many problems, some of which would have literally forced it to shut down. For example, initially when the educated experts left the organization, only illiterate rural masses remained and the bold decision to run it with those who remained in the organization had resulted in its success. It all happened due to the strong motivation and commitment shown in the process. In the case of Gram Vikas, despite its failures in the initial few years, the social entrepreneur and its team had never lost their motivation and showed constant strength while working towards their aim which has benefited most of the excluded in rural Odisha. Goonj and Enable India too have had their share of problems initially, especially their families not supporting them and failed partnerships with local organizations and employers, respectively, led them to distress. However, the continuous belief in their commitment and excelling through the planning as envisaged has moved their vision forward and benefited the targeted communities.

Community Involvement

Community involvement and active community participation are the result of various strategies which social enterprises adopted from time to time. All organizations studied have given freedom to their employees to experiment, innovate and contribute in the process of building inclusive societies. Accordingly, entrepreneurship within the organizations have resulted in attributing for incremental innovations, while in certain cases it has opened up dais for creation of new ventures and activities altogether. For example, in Barefoot College, employees are constantly encouraged to be innovative while implementing their roles and to bring out any innovative product or service which may prove the entrepreneurial orientation. Gram Vikas has also encouraged its employees to take up the biogas initiative in different places of Odisha and establish their own social ventures. Furthermore, it also ensured them that in case if they fail to succeed in their new venture, they would be allowed to return to their earlier jobs in the organization. The incentive offered has helped its

500 employees to replicate its initiative on their own in which only four of them returned due to their failure. On the other hand, the issue-based social enterprises too promote entrepreneurship among their employees. The employees are allowed to participate in the decision-making process of the organizations and explore innovative experiments for achieving better results. Though so far nothing has materialized, yet the issue-based social entrepreneurs are open to encourage their employees to take up entrepreneurship as their career choice and are ready to offer any assistance required in the process. As a result, many of the employees and trainees in Enable India are interested in replicating its philosophy in different locations of the country or in initiating something different on their own while addressing the social problems that they might have come across in the process. In Goonj, employees are freed from administrative constraints to experiment and be innovative to explore new ways to enhance efficiency of the organizations.

The research notes the contribution of volunteers in social transformation promoted by social enterprises. Especially in the absence of professionals in social entrepreneurship sector, their role becomes crucial. For example, the various roles adopted by volunteers in Goonj are remarkable. As Anshu pointed out, "Volunteers emerged as key for the running of the organization. Their active participation in multiple roles talks about the success of various activities we undertake." From creating awareness to reaching out to the communities in the remotest areas, their involvement has been active and a lot of energy is derived from them. Enable India also receives different sections of volunteers from colleges and industry who have been useful for it in performing certain tasks relevant for PwDs. In case of both established area-based SEs, their volunteers come from both India and abroad. Sometimes they bring technical expertise and some other times they come and get involved in the organization to cater different needs that emerge from time to time.

The role of communities in case of the two area-based social enterprises, Barefoot College and Gram Vikas, and an issue-based social enterprise, Goonj, is well described. In fact, communities' active participation propels the success of social enterprises. The communities on whose name social enterprises engage in undertaking various activities initially have had few reservations about the existence of social enterprises; however, with various strategies that social enterprises adopted, communities started taking active part in the processes and further became part of their own inclusion. The contribution of communities to attain sustainable discourse is quite significant. In fact, it is found that without community support, the activities undertaken would have never acquired the level of SO that they achieved in the current context. Furthermore, the way communities became an integral part of the activities being undertaken with their contributions and ownership is quite remarkable.

Both the area-based social enterprises have a well-defined procedure to manage and ensure community penetration. In fact, communities need to take the lead in order to implement various developmental activities. Communities contribute for each project undertaken initially. Contribution could be in the form of either cash or kind, as per the capacity of the community members. Communities are the key to plan and implement, and are accountable for the activities that would promote their social well-being. The various committees established to monitor and look after a variety of developmental activities emerge as the key to the process. In addition, activities to enhance transparency and accountability create trust among communities. In the case of Goonj, community participation ensures various developmental activities in addition to enhancing the social capital. The social capital emerging from the activities initiated by social enterprises highlights community ties and unleashes social participation of different sections of people in the community. In addition, the training offered to communities to build their skills and capabilities also enhances their confidence. The various strategies including WISE helped social enterprises to build trust and achieve a certain level of SO.

For example, it is well evident that all social enterprises studied as part of the research have offered jobs to the most excluded and deprived among the communities whom they serve. It has largely resulted in two benefits: (a) most excluded among the communities benefit from the venture and (b) it further enhanced bondage between the organization and the communities. For example, the community representatives working in the organization for the communities have enhanced bondage between the organizations and communities. In the process, social capital developed has been used to build teams and communities (Spear 2006). In fact, the existence of organizations has had a lot of trust-building process initially. For example, in order to just create trust, Gram Vikas had to experiment with different activities before shifting its focus to health-related issues through which it has easily acquired the trust that was indeed needed. It is found that the social enterprises, irrespective of their area- or issue-based nature, are well aware that winning the trust of the people would consume relatively longer time. That is the reason Enable India does not want to scale its practices or process in other areas as it may involve a lot of efforts to just create trust; hence, they are interested to replicate the idea using local partnerships. Both the rural social enterprises in the study came up with different ways unleashing social problems through their community integration, whereas the issue-based social enterprises pushed through their views into the community.

It is analyzed that efforts of social entrepreneurs in all four places not only offer various services to the poor and excluded but also build confidence among them in order to ensure their social participation. Social, political and economic inclusion enhances the community ties and bring the excluded groups into the mainstream. Especially those who have experienced multiple exclusion or re-exclusion claim significant turnout in terms of enhanced skills and capabilities as a result of their employment. For example, those whom Enable India trains and places in various software companies not only regain their lost glory but also stand on their own, who in turn claim to show how confident they are to their families and communities. The sanitary napkins supplied by Goonj not only enhanced healthy conditions for poor women but also increased their working and social participation without any health problem. The Barefoot College has offered various basic facilities such as water and solar electricity for communities, and continuous employment for most of the excluded from the community. In case of Gram Vikas, it has offered an array of basic provision including 24-hours running water and sanitary facilities, and the dignity of women and girl child is ensured. These activities put together, there is a strong mechanism which proves that the basic facilities and employment offered to the excluded and poor speak about the enhanced dignity and confidence levels.

Social Partnerships and Networks

It is revealed in earlier research that social entrepreneurs rely on partnerships for acquisition of resources and to scale their successful programmes (Pearce and Doh 2005; Thompson and Doherty 2006). In fact, the current study also comes with such an opinion that all the organizations studied have shown strong reason for their continuous partnership building and networking with various organizations and agencies. The community partnerships emerge as key in the entire scenario. International supporting organizations have been a strong support to the growth of the sector in India. All the four organizations studied have been supported by one or more of the three renounced social enterprise supporting systems—Ashoka, Skoll Foundation or Schwab Foundation. Furthermore, the social networking websites have offered support for the organizations. For example, all organizations have a strong group of followers on Facebook, which is one of the well-known social networking sites. In addition, the partnerships and collaborations offer all organizations ways to replicate and reach out to the far-flung areas with their approach and processes.

It is found that all the organizations studied are open to replicate their ideas through other organizations. In the process, they are eager to network or partner with other organizations in both national and international domains in order to reach out to the excluded in other localities. The underlying observation across the cases is to scale or replicate the initiatives with the help from local partners. While the area-based organizations are interested in growth and scaling of their organizations, the issue-based organizations are just interested to grow as an idea. Yet, all the organizations are open for partnerships and replication through such partnerships. For example, Barefoot College has spread its wings in different states of the country in addition to working in several other countries through vibrant partnerships with other organizations which can replicate the idea. The same goes with Gram Vikas where it wants to spread as an organization and, at the same time, create different organizations which will stand on their own within the given time-frame.

On the other hand, the issue-based social enterprises are more interested in growing as an idea and building awareness among communities, and partnering with organizations through which their processes, ideas and activities can be replicated. However, Goonj collaborates with about a couple of hundred organizations across the country to reach out to the most poor and excluded. In addition, Anshu claims that he does not want to grow beyond 1,000 employees or 12 cities. It becomes tough for a social organization to manage its operations in case if it grows bigger. Enable India is also interested in replication through partnerships created in the process. The other reason projected by Enable India is that integrating with different cultures in a variety of geographical locations may take much time if the organization plans to scale up, whereas in case of replication through collaboration with other organizations that already exist in different areas, social value creation would be enhanced with limited efforts. As Dipesh narrates:

> You can't simply get into a village in Maharashtra having your office in Bangalore, or it will take few years or decades to build trust if you start one on your own. So we want to avoid this delay and rather we will enable local organizations or NGOs so that they can carry forward the work in their respectable regions. This approach gages a significant impact.

It is to state that all social enterprises are keen in partnership building. They work with multiple organizations at different locations in order to replicate their innovations.

It is revealed that social enterprises at all spectrums undertake merit-based lobbying in order to acquire new resources, connections and partnerships in the process of social value creation. However, such lobbying is just restricted to promote what social entrepreneurs believe instead of deploying favour from the external groups. For example, Gram Vikas has so far carried out lobbying with government to spread out the importance of full sanitation and water supply in different places of the country. It is largely due to its belief in the sanitation structures that it has been so far associated with. Enable India takes up lobbying as a structural procedure in order to acquire relevant partnerships with various potential employers. Its strategy is embedded within the organizational structures where (a) collaborative training, (b) peer competition, (c) testing and probing and (d) opening up with the potential employers occupy most of the lobbying it carries out. Barefoot College does lobbying with various government agencies, especially with ministries and departments which deal with the activities it undertakes. Its international collaborations are largely supported by the federal government. On the other hand, Goonj has been lobbying with various communities, a few corporate companies and Indian military in order to use their resources while reaching out to the poor and the marginalized. While all social enterprises studied have had their roles evolved in lobbying with various social and institutional mechanisms who, in turn, expected to offer resources and support largely required for nurturing the field, they all restricted themselves to the merit-based lobbying which has evolved to reach out to the target groups.

Collaboration with the Government

As discussed earlier, the role of social enterprises in using resources offered by government and to persuade it to replicate the successful ideas developed by them in different contexts is amplified in this research. Especially, such collaborations are useful for the social entrepreneurship movement in two crucial ways: (a) gaining relevant resources required to carry out various developmental activities and (b) reaching out to more needy under various methods and policies existing with the government. This also includes, but is not limited to, spreading the ideas that social entrepreneurs have innovated. Collaboration with various governments is the easiest way to reach out to numerous needy groups and spread the impact. For example, innovative curriculum developed by Barefoot night schools has been spread across Rajasthan state with government intervention. Enable India has been constantly looking forward to work with the government, and is collaborating with SBI is one such activity. Goonj mechanism is especially reaching out to the needy during natural disasters with greater support from State, whereas Gram Vikas has pioneered in undertaking State-sponsored projects and activities. Nevertheless, it is imperative to denote that all the organizations studied in this research have shown keen interest in collaborating with the government. Furthermore, it is to remind as Joe propelled that the social good they envisage has to be otherwise taken care of by the government. Hence, it is their right to seek involvement of the government in various activities they undertake.

Ecosystem

As discussed in the second chapter, out of the seven pillars of ecosystem, a few of them have played a crucial role, some have played a passive role, and the remaining institutions have played no role. For example, government is quite supportive of the social entrepreneurship sector in terms of offering monetary support under various schemes and programmes that it undertakes. However, it has failed to offer proper legal mechanisms for social enterprises to thrive. Though academia has not played any direct role, volunteers from academic institutions play a key role in organizational building. The role volunteers play in Goonj is a classic example. In addition, Jagriti Yatra provides a rich learning environment about three cases discussed in this research including Goonj, Barefoot College and Gram Vikas. Students who participate in the yatra, take back rich knowledge and experience. While institutional and non-institutional actors, including communities, donors and philanthropists, play a crucial role, international collaborations and partnerships also offer necessary recognition and awards which substitute a part of the financial resources required for running the ventures. In the absence of a dedicated legal system and policy mechanism for social entrepreneurship, social enterprises find it difficult to operate mission-centric entrepreneurial ventures. It is found that social enterprises have overlooked the options available to initiate mission-centric enterprises. However, lack of support from legal systems is somehow disturbing the growth of the social entrepreneurship sector. When it comes to incubation systems, it is also found that none of the cases studied in this research were in need of any incubator support. In fact, when these ventures started to develop, there was no concept of social incubator. In addition, it is found that impact investing has played no role in these institutions. This could be partly because all the four cases in this research have not represented an ideal business case for investments.

Social Value Creation

The social value created addresses problems related to multiple social groups in the process. Hence, it does not isolate various groups that often experience multiple exclusions or social re-exclusion. The innovative service delivery and process employed by the area-based social enterprises is certainly worth mentioning in this context. Especially in the case of avoiding the caste- and community-based social taboos, they have adopted innovative methods where people from across the sections have been benefited. The innovative service delivery processes employed frequently are crucial to achieve such transformation. For example, when both Barefoot College and Gram Vikas realized that addressing concerns of communities which often experience multiple exclusions may not be an easy task due to the domination from other sections, they adopted a 'larger picture' in their operations in order to include the excluded sections which face multiple exclusions. Barefoot College and Gram Vikas had to explicitly take poverty curve for their deprivation measure in order to have the caste-based deprived covered under the activities they undertake. It is partly due to the fact that most of the Dalits and tribes are poor and deprived. However, it is further found that though they could reach out to the Dalits and tribals, they were unable to annihilate caste hierarchies existing in the society, which is a way more tough challenge. In addition, both the area-based organizations have shown remarkable commitment in order to address the issues related to women. Especially, encouraging SHGs in the rural areas is one of the key issues for their success.

In case of Goonj, it has tackled one of the significant social issues related to women—sanitary napkins. Due to the predominant backwardness that prevails among women, efforts to address all their necessary needs are not undertaken due to the nature of many such needs which are rooted in a culture which does not allow women to talk about them in public. One such issue Goonj has brought into the forefront is about the usage of sanitary napkins for women coming from deprived backgrounds. The incremental innovations Goonj has undertaken over a period of last one-and-a-half decade have widened its prospects from mere distributing old cloths to recent sanitary napkins and many more. The involvement of Enable India in empowering and enriching the participation of PwDs in mainstream has implications for social value creation in terms of enhancing their social well-being.

Social Entrepreneurship and Neoliberal Sanctuary

It is also found that the active social entrepreneurship sector may reduce the role of the State in the areas where social enterprises operate. The role of the State is minimized or the State opts out from the welfare activities that are carried out by social entrepreneurs. For example, in the case of Gram Vikas, it is proven that the State does not bother to directly involve in developmental activities in 1,090 villages where Gram Vikas undertakes its activities. As a result, people in these areas pay for availing basic services that are available to them. However, the State which has later entered into basic service provision in nearby areas has ignored the areas under operation of Gram Vikas. Though social enterprises claimed to adhere to creation of social good through enhancing social value, in the process, it may reduce the role of State where basic commodities become part of market orientation. Especially, this aspect needs further research which will be contemplated to understand the role of social entrepreneurship in reducing the role of State and promoting communities to pay for the basic services which otherwise should be part of the State developmental agenda. In the case of Goonj, undertaking construction of bridges, Enable India promoting the rights of PwDs and various initiatives of Barefoot College including education initiatives are few indicators to prove such a scenario. Due to these experiments and increased welfare offered by these organizations, which is otherwise a sole responsibility of the State, it is realized that State has taken a lenient stand and restricts its own participation in the provision of welfare activities.

Fostering Alternative Social Realities

It is evident throughout the cases studied that social entrepreneurs create and foster alternative social realities through questioning the status-quo and social hierarchies. The reality in the pre-existence of social enterprises has had hard social implications for certain social groups whose participation in social and market life was overpowered by their backwardness and exclusion. Emerging with innovative solutions for such social problems faced by these groups, social enterprises search for alternative methods, processes, structures and institutions in order to create alternative social realities where all social groups take equal participation. In the process, the innovation and community participation have emerged key for the success in terms of pushing different factors together to realize the dreams of those targeted by these initiatives. In case of area-based social enterprises studied, Barefoot College and Gram Vikas have addressed problems related to the people who were in the vicious circle of poverty and backwardness whose interest were bypassed by existing institutions. Both the organizations have taken various innovative structures in order to create an alternative reality where people affected by problems themselves came forward to solve them. As a result, today, they lead a dignified life. With regard to the issue-based social enterprises studied, Enable India and Goonj have addressed unique problems faced by various deprived sections. Similar to the area-based social enterprises, these organizations have also evolved in terms of addressing the problems of the target groups and have projected alternative realities.

This book has attempted to understand and highlight various processes and innovations employed by selected social enterprises in India in order to create greater inclusiveness through addressing various social problems faced by different social groups with service and product delivery. The heterogeneity of social enterprises studied as part of the research and their institutional environment offer rich comparison and understanding of different ways of addressing social problems within the ambiguity of intuition-based reasoning of social entrepreneurs (Schumpeter 1934/2002; Zahra, Rawhouser, Bhawe, Neubaum, and Hayton 2009). The research offers rich analysis of social transformation and building a framework to explain the process of social entrepreneurship. The research further opens up a debate to understand whether the increased role of social entrepreneurship reduces the role of State in offering social welfare and provision of basic services? Another core area of research interest that can be derived from this research involves understanding social innovations employed within the resource constraint and social uncertain environment in order to achieve envisaged social transformation. Further, the research opens a space to look into whether social entrepreneur like his entrepreneur counterpart, as Schumpeter denoted, seizes to act as an entrepreneur upon creating the venture or continues to act as a social entrepreneur due to multiple complex systems involved in the process. These three issues are capable of emerging as strong research areas that can be further taken up by interested researchers in the subject area.

The widening exclusion space, withdrawal of State from basic service provision and reduced funding for welfare activities enhance the adoption of innovations in different levels by organizations working in the field. In such a context, the current book offers comprehensive understanding about the context of social value creation and building greater inclusiveness through usage of innovative methods and institutional forms under the broader agenda of social entrepreneurship. This study identifies that the field of social entrepreneurship requires thorough recognition and support from various players in the ecosystem in order to enhance its visibility and achieve systematic social change. The well-established cases as studied in this research managed to succeed despite the existence of prevalent environment. In fact, there are a plenty of such social innovations or entrepreneurial ventures that, despite their promise to create alternative social realities, fail to move forward due to several constraints that come in the process, which include personal, financial, legal and policy restrictions. Thus, it is expected that the successful processes described in this book and the various phases and stages explained in the social entrepreneurial framework could offer useful knowledge for the practitioners to build their ventures successfully and create alternative social realities. What matters the most in the contemporary context is that a significant number of social start-ups are being initiated by youth who, I am sure, will not give up until their passion takes them to achieve their ambition of transforming social settings. It remains our responsibility to support all such endeavours in order to rewrite social realities and create social inclusiveness. I believe that this book, in such direction, is an attempt to build necessary knowledge that can help budding social entrepreneurs and other enthusiasts in the field.

Bibliography

ADB. *India Social Enterprise Landscape Report*. Manila: Asian Development Bank, 2012.

Adler, N. 'The Arts and Leadership: Now That We Can do Anything, What Will We Do?' *Academy of Management Learning and Education* 5, no. 4 (2006): 486–99.

Aldaba, F., P. Antezana, M. Valderrama and A. Fowler. 'NGO Strategies Beyond Aid: Perspectives from Central and South American and the Philippines'. *Third World Quarterly* 21, no. 4 (2000): 669–83.

Alter, S.K. 'Case Studies in Social Enterprises'. 2002. Available at: http://www.virtueventures.com/files/cicases.pdf (accessed 16 November 2012).

———. *Case Studies in Social Entrepreneurship*. Washington, DC: Counterpart International, 2006.

Alvord, S.H., L.D. Brown and C.W. Letts, 'Social Entrepreneurship and Societal Transformation'. *Journal of Applied Behavioural Science* 40, no. 3 (2004): 260–82.

Amin, A., A. Cameron and R. Hudson. *Placing the Social Economy*. London: Routledge, 2002.

Anderson, B. and G. Dees. 'Chapter 7: Rhetoric, Reality, and Research: Building a Solid Foundation for the Practice of Social Entrepreneurship'. In *Social Entrepreneurship: New Models of Sustainable Social Change*, edited by A. Nicholls, 144–68. Oxford: Oxford University Press, 2006.

Anheier, H. *Nonprofit Organisations: Theory Management, Policy*. London: Routledge, 2005.

Archer, G., T. Baker and R. Mauer. 'Towards an Alternative Theory of Entrepreneurial Success; Integrating Bricolage, Effectuation and Improvisation'. *Frontiers of Entrepreneurship Research* 29, no. 6 (2009): 4.

Armato, M. and N. Caren. 'Mobilizing the Single Case Study: Doug McAdam's Political Process and the Development of Black Insurgency, 1930-'970'. *Qualitative Sociology* 25, no. 1 (2002): 93–103.

Auerswald, P. 'Creating Social Value'. *Stanford Social Innovation Review* 7, no. 2 (2009): 51–55.

Austin, J., H. Stevenson and J. Wei-Skillern. 'Social and Commercial Entrepreneurship: Same, Different or Both?' *Entrepreneurship, Theory and Practice* 30, no. 1 (2003): 1–22.

Austin, J., R. Gutierrez, E. Ogliastri and E. Reficco. *Effective Management of Social Enterprises: Lessons from Business and Civil Society Organisations in Iberoamerica*. Cambridge, MA: Harvard University Press, 2006.

Austin, J.E. *The Collaboration Challenge: How Nonprofits and Businesses Succeeded Through Strategic Alliances.* San Francisco, CA: Jossey-Bass, 2000.

Autin, J.E., Leonard, H.B., Stevenson, H.H. and Wei-Skillern, J.C. *Entrepreneurship in the Social Sector.* Los Angeles: SAGE, 2007.

Backman, E.V. and S.R. Smith. 'Healthy Organisations, Unhealthy Communities?' *Nonprofit Management and Leadership* 10, no. 4 (2000): 355–71.

Bakshi, N. and B. Baron. 'Enabling Indian Diaspora Philanthropy'. 2011. Available at: http://www.give2asia.org/documents/Give2Asia-IndiaDiasporaGiving-Report.pdf (accessed 4 February 2012).

Balakrishnan, R. 'By the Power of Cloth: How Goonj Transforms Villages Through its Cloth for Work'. In *The Poor and the Public Sector: Public Private Community Partnerships*, edited by R. Shobha. New Delhi: Purple Communications, 2009.

Banks, J.A. *The Sociology of Social Movements.* London: Macmillan, 1972.

Barendsen, L. and H. Gardner. 'Is the Social Entrepreneur a New Type of Leader?' *Leader to Leader* 2004, no. 34 (2004): 43–50.

Barney, J.B. 'Firm Resources and Sustained Competitive Advantage'. *Journal of Management* 17, no. 1 (1991): 99–120.

Baviskar, B.S. 'NGOs and Civil Society in India'. *Sociological Bulletin* 50, no. 1 (2001): 3–15.

Bhowmick, N. 'Accountability of India's Nonprofits Under Scrutiny'. 2010. Available at: http://content.time.com/time/world/article/0,8599,2036307,00.html (accessed 10 December 2015).

Bishop, M. 'The Rise of the Social Entrepreneur: Whatever He May Be'. *The Economist* 378, no. 8466 (2006): 11–13.

Blowfield, M. *Business and Sustainability.* Oxford: Oxford University Press, 2013.

Bornstein, D. *How to Change the World: Social Entrepreneurs and the Power of New Ideas.* New York: Oxford University Press, 2004.

Borzaga, C. and J. Defourny. *The Emergence of Social Enterprise.* London: Routledge, 2001.

Borzaga, C. and M. Loss. 'Work Integration Social Enterprises in Italy. Trends and Issues'. EMES Working Paper 02/02, 2002. Available at: http://www.emes.net/site/wp-content/uploads/PERSE_WP_02-02_I.pdf (accessed 19 June 2013).

Boschee, J. 'Social Entrepreneurship'. *Across the Board* 32, no. 3 (1995, March): 20–25.

———. 'Merging Mission and Money: A Board Member's Guide to Social Entrepreneurship'. 1998. Available at: http://www.socialent.org/pdfs/MergingMission.pdf (accessed 9 March 2011).

———. 'Eight Basic Principles for Nonprofit Entrepreneurs'. *Nonprofit World* 19, no. 4 (2001, July–August): 15–18.

———. *Migrating from Innovation to Entrepreneurship: How Nonprofits Are Moving Toward Sustainability and Self-sufficiency.* Dallas, TX: The Institute for Social Entrepreneurs, Section 2, 2006.

———. '"Social Innovation" and "Social Enterprise": A Powerful Combination'. 2007. Available at: http://www.socialent.org/documents/SOCIALINNOVATIONANDSOCIALENTERPRISE--APOWERFULCOMBINATION.pdf (accessed 19 June 2015).

———. 'A Key Lesson Business Can Teach Charities'. In *The Chronicle of Philanthropy.* 18 September 2008. Available at: http://www.socialent.org/documents/AKEYLESSONBUSINESSCANTEACHCHARITIES.pdf (accessed 14 December 2013).

Boschee, J. and J. McClurg. *Toward a Better Understanding of Social Entrepreneurship: Some Important Distinctions*. St Paul, MN: Institute for Social Entrepreneurs, 2003.

Brandenburg, M. 'Making the Case for Social Metrics and Impact Investing'. *Community Development Investment Review* 6, no. 1 (2010): 47–49.

Brundtland Commission. 'Report of the World Commission on Environment and Development: Our Common Future', 2002. Available at: http://www.un-documents.net/our-common-future.pdf (accessed 8 March 2012).

Bridges, C.M. and W.B. Wilhelm. 'Going Beyond Green: The "Why and How" of Integrating Sustainability into the Marketing Curriculum'. *Journal of Marketing Education* 30, no. 1 (2008): 33–46.

————. 'Is Social Enterprise at a Crossroads?' n.d. Available at: http://www.cabinetoffice.gov.uk/~/media/assets/www.cabinetoffice.gov.uk/third_sector/COI%20 SE%20presentation%20FINAL%20pdf.ashx (accessed 14 May 2011).

Brooks, A.C. *Social Entrepreneurship: A Modern Approach to Social Value Creation*. Upper Saddle River, NJ: Pearson Prentice Hall, 2009.

Brown, L.D. and M.H. Moore. 'Accountability, Strategy, and Non-Governmental Organisations'. Hauser Center for NonProfit Organisations Working Paper 7, 2007. Available at: http://papers.ssrn.com/sol3/papers.cfm?abstract_id=269362 (accessed 8 December 2011).

Burt, R.S. *Structural Holes: The Social Structure of Competition*. Cambridge, MA: Harvard University Press, 1992.

Cannon, L. 'Chapter 26: Defining Sustainability'. In *The Earthscan Reader on NGO Management*, edited by M. Edwards and A. Fowler, 363–65. London: Earthscan, 2002.

Cantillon, R. *Essay on the Nature of Trade in General*. New York: A.M. Kelley, 1755/1964.

CASE. 'Developing the field of social entrepreneurship'. 2008. Available at: http:// entrepreneurship.saddleback.edu/Resources/Social%20Entrepreneurship%20/ Field%20of%20Social%20Entrepreneurs.pdf (accessed 18 June 2012).

CSIM. 'Social Accounts Report: March 2008–April 2010'. 2010. Available at: http:// san-india.org/downloads/2013/EnAbleIndia.pdf (accessed 29 November 2014).

Certo, S.T. and T. Miller. 'Social Entrepreneurship: Key Issues and Concepts'. *Business Horizons* 51, no. 4 (2008): 267–71.

Chell, E. 'Social Enterprise and Entrepreneurship'. *International Small Business Journal* 25, no. 1 (2007): 5–26.

Cho, A.H. 'Politics, Values and Social Entrepreneurship'. *International Small Business Journal* 25, no. 1 (2006): 5–26.

Choi, N. and S. Majumdar. 'Social Entrepreneurship as an Essentially Contested Concept: Opening a New Avenue for Systematic Future Research'. *Journal of Business Venturing* 29, no. 3 (2014): 363–76.

Christopoulos, D. and S. Vogl. 'The Motivation of Social Entrepreneurs: The Roles, Agendas and Relations of Altruistic Economic Actors'. *Journal of Social Entrepreneurship* 6, no. 1 (2015): 1–30.

Clinton, L. 'Is India Really a Hotbed for Social Enterprise?' 2010. Available at: http://magazine.good.is/articles/is-india-really-a-hotbed-for-social-enterprise (accessed 10 February 2014).

Cohen, E. *Echoing Green: Building Institutions, Impacting Policy, Creating Community*. New York: Echoing Green, 1995.

Coles, P. 'Time to Rethink Everything'. 2002. Available at: http://www.barefootcol-lege.org/Barefoot%20Pioneers.pdf (accessed on 14 March 2009).

Collier, D., F.D. Hidalgo and A.O. Maciuceanu. 'Essentially Contested Concepts: Debates and Applications'. *Journal of Political Idealogies* 11, no. 3 (2006): 211–46.

Collins, J. *Good to Great and the Social Sectors: A Monograph to Accompany Good to Great*. New York: Collins, 2005.

Crabtree, B.F. and Miller. W.L. *Doing Qualitative Research*. CA: SAGE Publications, 1992.

Creswell, J.W. *Qualitative Inquiry and Research Design: Choosing Among Five Approaches*. Thousand Oaks, CA: SAGE Publications, 2007.

Curtis, T. 'Finding that Grit Makes a Pearl: A Critical Re-Reading of Research into Social Enterprise'. *International Journal of Entrepreneurial Behavior & Research* 14, no. 5 (2008): 276–90.

Dacin, P.A., M.T. Dacin and M. Matear. 'Social Entrepreneurship: Why We Don't Need a New Theory and How We Move Forward From Here'. *Academy of Management Perspectives* 24, nò. 2 (2010): 36–56.

Das, K. 'Issues in Promoting Rural Infrastructure in India'. Gujarat Institute of Development Research. Admedabad, India 2001. Available at: http://ged.ubor-deaux4.fr/ceddt67.pdf (accessed 8 November 2013).

Davis, S. 'Social Entrepreneurship: Towards an Entrepreneurial Culture for Social and Economic Development', *Conference Proceedings of Youth Employment Summit*, 7–11 September 2002. Available at: https://www.ashoka.org/files/yespa-per.pdf (accessed 8 October 2009).

Davister, C., J. Defourny and O. Gregoire. 'Work Integration Social Enterprises in the European Union: An Overview of Existing Models'. EMES Working Paper 04/04, 2004. Available at: http://emes.net/content/uploads/publications/PERSE_04_04_Trans-ENG.pdf (accessed 3 August 2011).

Dawn, R. 'Challenges in the Employment of Persons with Disability'. *Economic and Political Weekly* XLVII, no. 36 (2012): 20–21.

Dees, A.G. and B.B. Anderson. 'Framing a Theory of Social Entrepreneurship: Building on Two Schools of Practice and Thought'. *ARNOVA Occasional Paper Series: Research in Social Entrepreneurship* 1, no. 3 (2006): 39–66.

Dees, J.G. 'The Meaning of "Social Entrepreneurship"'. 1998. Available at: heep://the-ef-org/resources-Dees103198.html (accessed 18 May 2011).

Dees, J.G. and B.B. Anderson. 'Framing a Theory of Social Entrepreneurship: Building on Two Schools of Practice and Thought'. *ARNOVA Occasional Paper Series: Research in Social Entrepreneurship* 1, no. 3 (2006): 39–66.

Defourny, J. and M. Nyssens. 'Social Enterprise Europe: Recent Trends and Developments'. *Social Enterprise Journal* 4, no. 3 (2008): 202–28.

———. 'Conceptions of Social Enterprise and Social Entrepreneurship in Europe and the United States: Convergences and Divergences'. *Journal of Social Entrepreneurship* 1, no. 1 (2010): 32–53.

Devine, J. 'The Paradox of Sustainability: Reflections of NGOs in Bangladesh'. *Annals of the American Academy of Political and Social Science* 590, no. 1 (2003): 227–42.

Drayton, B. 'Everyone a Changemaker: Social Entrepreneurs Ultimate Goal'. *Innovations* (winter), 2006: 1–14.

Drayton, W. 'The Citizen Sector: Becoming as Entrepreneurial and Competitive as Business'. *California Management Review* 44, no. 3 (2002): 120–32.

Drucker, P. *Innovation and Entrepreneurship*. Oxford: Butterworth-Heinemann, 1999.

Dul, J. and T. Hak. *Case Study Methodology in Business Research*. Oxford: Elsevier, 2008.

Eade, D. *Capacity Building: An Approach to People-Center Development*. Oxford: Oxfam, 1997.

Ebrahim, A. 'Making Sense of Accountability: Conceptual Perspectives for Northern and Southern Nonprofits'. *Nonprofit Management and Leadership* 14, no. 2 (2003): 191–212.

———. 'The Many Faces of Nonprofit Accountability'. Working Paper 10-069. Boston: Harvard Business School, 2010.

Eisenhardt, K.M. 'Theory Building from Cases: Opportunities and Challenges'. *Academy of Management Journal* 51, no. 1 (2007): 25–32.

Elkington, J. and Hartigan, P. *The Power of Unreasonable People: How Social Entrepreneurs Create Markets that Change the World*. Boston: Harvard Business Press, 2008.

Feagin, J.R., A.M. Orum and G. Shoberg. *A Case for the Case Study*. London: University of North Carolina Press, 1991.

Fedela, A. and R. Miniaci. 'Do Social Enterprises Finance Their Investments Differently from For-Profit Firms? The Case of Social Residential Services in Italy'. *Journal of Social Entrepreneurship* 1, 2 (2010): 174–89.

Floyd, D. 'Social Impact: Can it be demonstrated?' 2014. Available at: http://www.theguardian.com/social-enterprise-network/2013/may/13/mythbusting-demon-strate-social-impact (accessed 30 April 2014).

Fowler, A. 'Assessing the Performance of Non Governmental Organisations in Sustainable Development: The Case for Quality and Not Quality in International Aid'. *Discourse* 2, no. 2 (1999): 121.

———. 'NGDOs as a Moment in History: Beyond Aid to Social Entrepreneurship or Civic Innovation?' *Third World Quarterly* 21, no. 4 (2000a): 637–54.

———. 'The Quality of Aid and Development Partnerships'. *Focus* 63 (2000b): 220–32.

Frank, R. 'World's Richest Man: "Charity Doesn't Solve Anything"'. *Wall Street Journal* (15 October 2010). Available at: http://blogs.wsj.com/wealth/2010/10/15/worlds-richest-man-charity-doesnt-solve-anything/

Fuglasang, M., Melisa, K., Marthe, N., Tony, P. and Rodney, S. 'Growing the Social Economy in a Fiscal Crisis'. Istanbul, Turkey: Conference Paper, Global Economic Symposium, 2010. Available at: http://www.econstor.eu/bitstream/10419/79128/1/729563421.pdf (accessed 8 September 2015).

Gallie, W.B. 'Essentially Contested Concepts'. *Proceedings of the Aristotelian Society* 56 (1956): 167–98.

Garia, N. 'India Makes Some Progress on Poverty'. *Wall Street Journal*. 11 July 2011. Available at: http://blogs.wsj.com/indiarealtime/2011/07/11/india-makes-some-progress-in-reducing-poverty/ (accessed 8 March 2012).

Gartner, W.B. 'Is there an Elephant in Entrepreneurship? Blind Assumption in Theory Development'. *Entrepreneurship Theory and Practice* 25, no. 4 (2001): 27–39.

GEM. '2009 Report on Social Entrepreneurship'. 2009. Available at: http://www.gemconsortium.org/assets/uploads/1349344229GEM_2009_Social_Entrepreneurship_Report.pdf (accessed 8 October 2012).

GIZ. 'Responsible Finance: A Catalyst for Responsible Business—International and Indian Trends and Challenges in Responsible Finance'. 2012. Available at: http://responsible-business.in/sites/default/files/Responsibe%20Finance%20GIZ%202012.pdf (accessed 23 May 2014).

Gould, D.J. and J.A. Amaro-Reyes. 'The Effects of Corruption on Administrative Performance: Illustration from Developing Countries'. World Bank Staff Working Paper 580, Management and Development Series Number 7. Washington DC: The World Bank, 1983.

Government of India (GoI). 'Census 2001 Data'. 2001. Available at: http://www.censusindia.gov.in/Census_Data (accessed 24 September 2010).

Government of Orissa. 'Human Development Report 2004'. 2004. Planning and Coordination Department, Government of Orissa.

Granovetter, M. 'The Strength of Weak Ties'. *The American Journal of Sociology* 78, no. 6 (1973): 1360–80.

Guclu, A., J.G. Dees and B.B. Anderson. *The Process of Social Entrepreneurship: Creating Opportunities Worthy of Serious Pursuit.* Durham, NC: Center for the Advancement of Social Entrepreneurship, Fuqua School of Business, Duke University, 2002.

Hammersley, M. *What's Wrong with Ethnography?* London: Longman Publishing House, 1992.

Harding, R. *Social Entrepreneurship Monitor.* London: London Business School. 2006. Available at: http://www.london.edu/assets/documents/PDF/Gem_Soc_Ent_web.pdf (accessed 6 April 2011).

Haugh, H. 'Community-led Social Venture Creation'. *Entrepreneurship: Theory and Practice* 31, no. 2 (2007): 161–82.

Haugh, H. and P. Tracey. 'The Role of Social Enterprise in Regional Development'. In *Social Enterprise and Regional Development Conference,* edited by Cambridge-MIT Institute. Cambridge: Cambridge–MIT Institute, 16 September 2004.

Haugh, H.M. and A. Talwar. 'How Do Corporations Embed Sustainability Across the Organisation?' *Academy of Management Learning and Education* 9, no. 3 (2010): 384–96.

Hibbert, S., G. Hogg and T. Quinn. 'Consumer Response to Social Entrepreneurship: The Case of the Big Issue in Scotland'. *International Journal of Nonprofit and Voluntary Sector Marketing* 7, no. 3 (2002): 288–301.

Hill, T.L., T.H. Kothari and N. Shea. 'Patterns of Meaning in the Social Entrepreneurship Literature: A Research Platform'. *Journal of Social Entrepreneurship* 1, no. 1 (2010): 5–31.

Hirway, I. 'Inclusive Growth Under a Neoliberal Framework: Some Critical Questions'. *Economic and Political Weekly* 47, no. 20 (2012): 64–72.

Hockerts, K. 'Entrepreneurial Opportunity in Social Purpose Business Ventures'. In *Social Entrepreneurship,* edited by J. Mair, J. Robinson and K. Hockerts, 142–53. Basingstoke: Palgrave Macmillan, 2006.

Huppé, G.A. 'Building Impact Investment Readiness: A New Approach to Unlocking Institutional Investment Globally'. *Stanford Social Innovation Review*. 2014. Available at: http://www.global-economic-symposium.org/knowledgebase/ The-Future-of-Social-Impact-Investing/virtual-library/building-impact-invest-ment-readiness-a-new-approach-to-unlocking-institutional-investment-globally-stanford-social-innovation-review/at_download/file (accessed 15 August 2014).

The Indian Express. 'First Official Estimate: An NGO for Every 400 People in India'. 2010. Available at: http://www.indianexpress.com/news/first-official-estimate-an-ngo-for-every-400-people-in-india/643302/ (accessed 20 November 2010).

Intellecap. 'Indian Social Enterprise Landscape Survey'. 2010. Available at: http://beyondprofit.com/tag/survey/ (accessed 9 March 2013).

———. 'On the Path to Sustainability and Scale: A Study of India's Social Enterprise Landscape'. 2012. Available at: http://intellecap.com/sites/default/files/publica-tions/intellecap_landscape_report_web.pdf (accessed 18 March 2013).

International Disability Rights Monitor. 'Regional Report of Asia'. 2005. Available at: http://www.ideanet.org/cir/uploads/File/CIR_IDRM_Asia_05.pdf (accessed 20 November 2013).

Irena, B., Marika, A., Giovanni, A. and Mario, C. 'Indicators and Metrics for Social Business: A Review of Current Approaches'. *Journal of Social Entrepreneurship* 7, no. 1 (2016): 1–24.

Jack, S.L. and A.R. Anderson. 'The Effects of Embeddedness on the Entrepreneurial Process'. *Journal of Business Venturing* 17, no. 5 (2002): 467–87.

Jazairy, I., M. Alamgir and T. Panuccio. *The State of World Rural Poverty: An Enquiry into Its Causes and Consequences*. New York: International Fund for Agricultural Development, 1992.

Koppl, R. 'Entrepreneurial Behaviour as a Human Universal'. In *Entrepreneurship: The Engine of Growth*, edited by M. Minniti, vol. 1: People, 1–19. Westport, CT: Praeger Publishers.

Kramer, M.R. *Measuring Innovation: Evaluation in the Field of Social Entrepreneurship*. Boston, MA: Skoll Foundation by Foundation Strategy Group, 2005.

Krishnan, M. 'India has Most Innovative Social Entrepreneurs: Schwab'. *Hindustan Times*. 31 October 2006. Available at: http://www.hindustantimes.com/ news-feed/nm19/india-has-most-innovative-social-entrepreneurs-schwab/arti-cle1-176602.aspx (accessed 14 March 2013).

Kummitha, R.K.R. 'Rehabilitation or Re-Exclusion'. *Indian Journal of Political Science* LXIX, 3 (2008): 505–18.

———. *Social Entrepreneurship and Social Inclusion: A Study of a Rural Social Enterprise*, PhD thesis, University of Hyderabad, Hyderabad, 2011.

———. 'Social exclusion: The European Concept for the Indian Social Realities'. *Social Change* 45, no. 1 (2015): 1–23.

———. 'Social Entrepreneurship as a Tool to Remedy Social Exclusion: A Win-Win Scenario.' *South Asia Research*, 36, no. 1 (2016): 61–79.

Kummitha, R.K.R. and S. Majumdar. 'Dynamic Curriculum Development on Social Entrepreneurship—A Case Study of TISS'. *The International Journal of Management Education* 13, no. 3 (2015): 260–67.

Lasprogata, G.A. and M.N. Cotten. 'Contemplating "Enterprise": The Business and Legal Challenges of Social Entrepreneurship'. *American Business Law Journal* 41, no. 1 (2003): 67–113.

Leadbeater, C. *The Rise of Social Entrepreneur*. London: Demos, 1997.

———. *Social Enterprise and Social Innovation: Strategies for the Next Ten Years*, Cabinet Office of the Third Sector. 2007. Available at: http://www.charles-leadbeater.net/cms/xstandard/social_enterprise_innovation.pdf (accessed on 18 June 2013).

Lehner, O.M. 'The Phenomenon of Social Enterprise in Austria: A Triangulated Descriptive Study'. *Journal of Social Entrepreneurship* 2, no. 1 (2011): 53–78.

Letts, C.W., W. Ryan and A. Grossman. 'Virtuous Capital: What Foundations Can Learn from Venture Capitalists?' *Harvard Business Review* 75, no. 2 (1997): 36–44.

Leveau-Vallier, A. 'Networks of Social Entrepreneurs in India'. 2011. Available at: http://appli6.hec.fr/amo/Public/Files/Docs/236_en.pdf (accessed 9 January 2013).

Light, P.C. 'Reshaping Social Entrepreneurship'. *Stanford Social Innovation Review* 4, no. 3 (2006, Fall): 47–51.

Lincoln, Y.S. and Guba, E.G. *Naturalistic Inquiry*. Beverly Hills, CA: SAGE Publications, 1985.

Mair, J. 'Social Entrepreneurship: Taking Stock and Looking Ahead'. IESE Working Paper 888, November 2010. Available at: http://iese.edu/research/pdfs/DI-0888-E.pdf (accessed 9 May 2013).

Mair, J. and I. Marti. 'Social Entrepreneurship Research: A Source of Explanation, Prediction, and Delight'. *Journal of World Business* 41, no. 1 (2006): 36–44.

Mair, J., J. Robinson and K. Hockerts. 'Introduction'. In *Social Entrepreneurship*, edited by J. Mair, J. Robinson and K. Hockerts, 1–14. Basingstoke: Palgrave Macmillan, 2006.

Martin, R.L. and S. Osberg. 'Social Entrepreneurship: The Case for Definition'. *Stanford Social Innovation Review* 5, no. 2 (2007, Spring).

Mashelkar, R.A. *Goonj: Its Inspiring Innovations, Innovations for Inspiration Awards 2010*. Mariko Innovation Foundation, Erehwon Innovation Consulting, 2010.

Meyskens, M., Robb-Post, C., Stamp, J.A., Carsrud, A.L. and Reynolds, P.D. 'Social Ventures from a Resource-Based Perspective: An Exploratory Study Assessing Global Ashoka Fellows'. *Entrepreneurship Theory and Practice* 34, no. 4 (2010): 661–680.

Miles, M.B., Huberman, A.M. and Saldana, J. *Qualitative Data Analysis: A Methods Sourcebook*. CA: SAGE Publications, 2013.

Miller, R. and K. Hall. 'Social Return on Investment (SROI) and Performance Measurement: The Opportunities and Barriers for Social Enterprises in Health and Social Care'. *Public Management Review* 15, no. 6 (2012): 923–41.

Mishra, A.K. and R. Gupta. 'Disability Index: A Measure of Deprivation Among Disabled'. *Economic and Political Weekly* XLI, no. 38 (2006): 4026–29.

Monitor Institute. 'Investing for Social and Environmental Impact: A Design for Catalyzing an Emerging Industry'. 2009. Available at: http://monitorinstitute.com/downloads/what-we-think/impact-investing/Impact_Investing.pdf (accessed 18 September 2012).

Mort, S.G., J. Weerawardena and K. Carnegie. 'Social Entrepreneurship Towards Conceptualisation'. *International Journal of Nonprofit and Voluntary Sector Marketing* 8, no. 1 (2003): 76–88.

Mueller, S., L. Nazarkina, C. Volkmann and C. Blank. 'Social Entrepreneurship Research as a Means of Transformation: A Vision for the Year 2028'. *Journal of Social Entrepreneurship* 2, no. 1 (2011): 112–20.

Mulgan, G. 'Cultivating the Other Invisible Hand of Social Entrepreneurship: Comparative Advantage, Public Policy, and Future Research Priorities'. In *Social Entrepreneurship: New Models of Sustainable Social Change*, edited by A. Nicholls, 74–96. Oxford University Press: Oxford, 2006.

Mulgan, G., S. Tucker, R. Ali and B. Sanders. *Social Innovation. What it is, Why it Matters and How it Can Be Accelerated*. London: Young Foundation, 2007.

Murray, R., Caulier-Grice, J. and Mulgan, E. 'The open book of social innovation'. 2010. Available at: http://youngfoundation.org/wp-content/uploads/2012/10/The-Open-Book-of-Social-Innovationg.pdf (accessed on 28 August 2015).

Nanath, K. 'Goonj: The Power of Cloth'. *Emerald Emerging Markets Case Studies* 1, no. 4 (2011): 1–12.

National Center for Charitable Statistics. 'Number of Nonprofit Organisations in the United States 1996–2006', National Center for Charitable Statistics. 2007. Available at: http://nccsdataweb.urban.org/PubApps/profile1.php?state=US (accessed 24 February 2009).

Nelson. R. 'Co-evolution of Technology, Industrial Structure, and Supporting Institutions'. *Industrial and Corporate Change* 3, no. 1 (1994): 47–63.

Nicholls, A., ed. *Social Entrepreneurship, New Models of Sustainable Social Change*. Oxford: Oxford University Press, 2006.

———. 'Playing the Field; A New Approach to the Meaning of Social Entrepreneurship'. *Social Enterprise Journal* 2, no. 1 (2006a): 1–5.

———. 'Introduction'. In *Social Entrepreneurship: New Models of Sustainable Social Change*, edited by A. Nicholls, 1–35. Oxford: Oxford University Press, 2006b.

———. 'What is the Future of Social Enterprise in Ethical Markets?' Office of the Third Sector. 2007. Available at: http://webarchive.nationalarchives.gov.uk/+/http:/www.cabinetoffice.gov.uk/media/cabinetoffice/third_sector/assets/future_social_enterprise_ethical_markets.pdf (accessed 23 February 2012).

———. 'The Institutionalisation of Social Investment: The Interplay of Investment Logics and Investor Rationalities'. *Journal of Social Entrepreneurship* 1, no. 1 (2010): 70–100.

Nicholls, A. and Cho, A. 'Social Entrepreneurship: The Structuration of a Field'. In *Social Entrepreneurship: New Models of Sustainable Social Change*, edited by A. Nicholls, 99–118. New York: Oxford University Press, 2006.

Nwankwo, E., N. Philips and P. Tracey. 'Social Investment Through Community Enterprise: The Case of Multinational Corporation Involvement in the Development of Nigerian Water Resources'. *Journal of Business Ethics* 73, no. 1 (2007): 91–101.

O'Brein, D., J. Wilkes, Ad. Haan and S. Maxwell. 'Poverty and Social Exclusion in North and South'. IDS Working Paper 55, Institute of Development Studies and Poverty Research Unit, University of Sussex, Brighton, 1997.

O'Brien, C. 'Education for Sustainable Community Development: Barefoot College, Tilonia, India'. 1997. Available at: http://digitool.library.mcgill.ca/webclient/StreamGate?folder_id=0&dvs=1404879704768~409 (accessed 13 August 2009).

Ormiston, J. and R. Seymour. 'Understanding Value Creation in Social Entrepreneurship: The Importance of Aligning Mission, Strategy and Impact Measurement'. *Journal of Social Entrepreneurship* 2, no. 2 (2011): 125–50.

Oster, S.M., C.W. Massarsky and S.L. Beinhacker. *Generating and Sustaining Non-Profit Earned Income. A Guide to Successful Enterprise Strategies.* San Francisco, CA: Jossy-Bass, 2004.

Parkinson, C. and C. Howorth. 'The Language of Social Entrepreneurs'. *Entrepreneurship Theory and Regional Development* 20, no. 3 (2008): 285–309.

Patton, M.Q. *Qualitative Evaluation and Research Methods*, 2nd ed. Newbury Park, CA: SAGE Publications, 1990.

Pearce, J. *Managing and Measuring Social Enterprises.* London: SAGE Publications, 2003.

Pearce, J. and A. Kay. *Social Enterprise in Anytown:* London: Calouste Gulbenkian Foundation, 2003.

Pearce, J. and J.P. Doh. 'The High Impact of Collaborative Social Initiatives'. *MIT Solan Management Review* 44, no. 1 (2005): 67–74.

Peredo, A.M. and J.J. Chrisman. 'Toward a Theory of Community-Based Enterprise'. *Academy of Management Review* 31, no. 2 (2006): 309–28.

Peredo, A.M. and M. McLean. 'Social Entrepreneurship: A Critical Review of the Concept'. *Journal of World Business* 41, no. 1 (2006): 56–65.

Perrini, F. 'Social Entrepreneurship Domain: Setting Boundaries'. In *The New Social Entrepreneurship*, edited by F. Perrini, 1–25. Cheltenham: Edward Elgar, 2006.

Planning Commission. 'Faster, Sustainable and More Inclusive Growth: An Approach to the Twelfth Five Year Plan'. 2011. Available at: http://planning-commission.nic.in/plans/planrel/12appdrft/approach_12plan.pdf (accessed 8 November 2013).

Poon, D. 'The Emergence and Development of Social Enterprise Sectors'. *Social Impact Research Experience Journal.* 2011. Available at: http://repository.upenn.edu/cgi/viewcontent.cgi?article=1010&context=sire (accessed 24 August 2013).

Prabhu, G.N. 'Social Entrepreneurship Leadership'. *Career Development International* 4, no. 3 (1999): 140–45.

Prahlad, C.K. *The Fortune at the Bottom of the Pyramid.* Upper Saddle River, NJ: Wharton School Publishing, 2006.

Pruthi, S. 'Process of Social Entrepreneurship in India: The Case of GOONJ'. In *Social and Sustainable Enterprise: Changing the Nature of Business*, edited by S. Underwood, R. Blundel, F. Lyon, A. Schaefer, 1–23. Bingley: Emrald Group Publishing, 2012.

Raina, R.S. 'Policies and the Evolution of Social Entrepreneurship in India: Tight-Rope Walk to a Potential Runway'. Villgro Research Paper. 2013. Available at: http://www.villgro.org/research-papers (accessed 17 June 2014).

Rajan, T.A. and S. Hari. 'Innovation in Social Enterprises: The Role of Venture Investors'. Villgro Research Paper. 2013. Available at: http://www.villgro.org/research-papers (accessed 15 June 2014).

Rajasekhar, D. and S. Satpathy. 'An Assessment of a Major Anti-Poverty Programme (SGSY) for Women in India'. In *Poverty, Poverty Alleviation and Social Disadvantage*, edited by C. Tisdell, 490–517, vol. 2. New Delhi: Serials Publications, 2007.

Ray, S. 'Incubating Social Entrepreneurship as Part of Corporate Social Responsibility'. Villgro Research Paper. 2013. Available at: http://www.villgro.org/research-papers (accessed 17 June 2014).

Roy, B. S. 'Barefoot College: Its Experiences'. 2005.Available at: http://archiv.ub.uni-heidelberg.de/savifadok/2741/1/20_Rethinking.pdf (accessed 17 June 2010).

———. 'Demystifying Professionalism: The Barefoot Approach', *Proceedings of 2011 Blue Planet Prize Commemorative Lectures 2011*. 2011. Available at: http://www.af-info.or.jp/en/blueplanet/doc/list/2011lect-barefoot.pdf (accessed 16 December 2014).

Roy, B. and J. Hartigan. 'Empowering the Rural Poor to Develop Themselves: The Barefoot Approach'. *Innovations* 3, no. 2 (2008, Spring): 67–93.

Saltuk, Y., A. Bouri and G. Leung. *Insight into the Impact Investment Market: An In-depth Analysis of Investor Perspective and over 2,200 Transactions*. JP Morgan. 2011. Available at: http://www.jpmorganchase.com/corporate/social-finance/document/Insight_into_the_Impact_Investment_Market.pdf (accessed 14 November 2013).

Salvado, J.C. 'Social Enterprise Models and SPO Financial Sustainability: The Case of BRAC'. *Journal of Social Entrepreneurship* 2, no. 1 (2011): 79–98.

Santos, F. 'A Positive Theory of Social Entrepreneurship'. Working Paper Series. Fontainebleau: INSEAD, 2009.

Sarasvathy, S.D. *Effectuation: Elements of Entrepreneurial Expertise*. Cheltenham: Edward Elgar Publishing, 2008.

Sarriot, E.G., P.J. Winch, L.J. Ryan, J. Bowie, M. Kouletion, E. Swedberg, K. LeBan, J. Edison, R. Welch and M.C. Pacque. 'A Methodological Approach and Framework for Sustainability Assessment in NGO-Implemented Primary Health Care Programs'. *International Journal of Health Planning and Management* 19, no. 1 (2004): 23–41.

Schumpeter, J.A. *The Theory of Economic Development: An Inquiry into Profits, Capital, Credit, Interest, and the Business Cycle*. New Brunswick, NJ: Transaction Publishers, 1934/2002.

Seelos, C. and Mair, J. 'Social Entrepreneurship: The Contribution of Individual Entrepreneurs to Sustainable Development'. Working Paper 553. Spain: IESE Business School, 2004.

———. 'Sustainable Development: How Social Entrepreneurs Make It Happen'. Working Paper 611. Spain: IESE Business School, 2005.

———. 'Profitable Business Models and Market Creation in the Context of Deep Poverty: A Strategic View'. *Academy of Management Perspectives* 21, no. 4 (2007): 49–63.

Shaw, E. and E. Carter. 'Social Entrepreneurship. Theoretical Antecedents and Empirical Analysis of Entrepreneurial Processes and Outcomes. *Journal of Small Business and Enterprise Development* 14, no. 3 (2007): 418–434.

Shockley, G.E. and P.M. Frank. 'Schumpeter, Kirzner, and the Field of Social Entrepreneurship'. *Journal of Social Entrepreneurship* 2, no. 1 (2011): 6–26.

Short, J.C., T.W. Moss and G.T. Lumpkin. 'Research in Social Entrepreneurship: Past Contributions and Future Opportunities'. *Strategic Entrepreneurship Journal* 3, no. 2 (2009): 161–94.

Silver, H. 'Social Exclusion and Social Solidarity: Three Paradigms'. *International Labour Review* 133 (1994): 531–78.

Silver, H. and S.M. Miller. 'Social Exclusion: The European Approach to Social Disadvantage', *Indicators* 2, no. 2 (2003): 1–17.

Silverthorne, S. 'Putting Entrepreneurship in the Social Sector', *Harvard Business School Working Knowledge.* 2008. Available at: http://hbswk.hbs.edu/items/5782.html (accessed 28 September 2010).

Smith, A. *The Wealth of Nations.* London: W. Strahan and T. Cadell, 1776.

Spear, R. 'National Profiles of Work Integration Social Enterprises'. Working paper no. 02/06, 2002. Available at: http://emes.net/content/uploads/publications/ELEXIES_WP_02-06_UK.pdf (accessed 4 January 2016).

———. 'Social Entrepreneurship: A Different Model?' *International Journal of Social Economics* 33, no. 5/6 (2006): 399–410.

Spear, R., M. Aiken, A. Noya and E. Clarence. 'Boosting Social Entrepreneurship and Social Enterprise Creation in the Republic of Serbia'. OECD Local Economic and Employment Development (LEED) Working Paper 2013/12. OECD Publishing. 2013. Available at: http://dx.doi.org/10.1787/5k3xz6lswcwl-en (accessed 14 August 2015).

Srivastava, S.S. and R. Tandon. *Invisible, Yet Widespread: The Non-Profit Sector in India.* New Delhi: PRIA, 2002.

Stake, R.E. *The Art of the Case Study Research.* Thousand Oaks, CA: SAGE Publications, 1995.

Steyaert, C. and D. Hjorth. *Entrepreneurship as a Social Change, A Third Movement in Entrepreneurship book.* Cheltenham: Edward Elgar, 2006.

Stryjan, Y. 'Sweden: Social Enterprises within a Universal Welfare State Model'. In *Social Enterprise—At the Crossroads of Market, Public Policies and Civil Society* edited by M. Nyssens, 206–21. London: Routledge, 2006.

Tan, W., J. Williams and T. Tan. 'Defining the "Social" in "Social Entrepreneurship": Altruism and Entrepreneurship'. *International Entrepreneurship and Management Journal* 1, no. 3 (2005): 353–65.

Thake, S. and S. Zadek. *Practical People, Noble Causes: How to Support Community-based Social Entrepreneurs.* London: New Economists Foundation, 1997.

The Economist. 'Batting the Babu Raj'. 2008. Available at http://www.economist.com/node/10804248 (accessed 29 March 2012).

The World Bank. *People with Disabilities in India: From Commitments to Outcomes*, 1–186. Human Development Unit, South Asia Region, the World Bank, 2009. Available at: http://www- wds.worldbank.org/external/default/WDSContentServer/WDSP/IB/2009/09/02/000334955_20090902041543/Rendered/PDF/502090WP0Peopl1Box0342042B01PUBLIC1.pdf.

———. 'Ease of Doing Business in India'. 2011. Available at: http://www.doingbusiness.org/data/exploreeconomies/india/ (accessed 29 September 2012).

Thomas, J. and R.K.R. Kummitha. 'Evolution of Social Entrepreneurship Education Programmes in India'. Villgro Research Paper. 2013. Available at: http://www.villgro.org/research-papers (accessed 17 June 2014).

Thompson, J. and B. Doherty. 'The Diverse World of Social Enterprise: A Collection of Social Enterprise Stories'. *International Journal of Social Economics* 33 no. 5–6 (2006): 361–75.

Thompson, J., G. Alvy and A. Lees. 'Social Entrepreneurship: A New Look at the People and the Potential', *Management Decision* 38, no. 5 (2000): 328–38.

Thompson, J.L. 'The World of the Social Entrepreneur'. *International Journal of Public Sector Management* 15, no. 5 (2002): 412–31.

Townsend, D.M. and T.A. Hart. 'Perceived Institutional Ambiguity and the Choice of Organisational form in Social Entrepreneurial Ventures'. *Entrepreneurship, Theory and Practice* 32, no. 4 (2008): 685–700.

Trexler, J. 'Social Entrepreneurship as Algorithm: Is Social Enterprise Sustainable?' *E:Co Issue* 10, no. 3 (2008): 65–85.

United Nations. *Word Population to 2010.* New York: United Nations, 2004.

———. *Analysing and Measuring Social Inclusion in a Global Context.* New York: United Nations, 2010.

Urbano, D., N. Toledano and D.R. Soriano. 'Analyzing Social Entrepreneurship from an Institutional Perspective: Evidence from Spain'. *Journal of Social Entrepreneurship* 1, no. 1 (2010): 54–69.

USAID. *Fundamentals of NGO Financial Sustainability.* Bethesda: Abt Associates, 2000.

———. 'Financial capacity building for NGO Sustainability, Program Brief no. 12'. 2008. Available at: http://pdf.usaid.gov/pdf_docs/Pnadn555.pdf (accessed 13 January 2014).

Venneson, P. 'Case Studies and Process Tracing: Theories and Practices'. In *Approaches and Methodologies in Social Sciences: A Pluralist Perspective* edited by D. Della Porta and M. Keating, 223–39. Cambridge: Cambridge University Press, 2008.

Verschuren, P. 'Case Study as a Research Strategy: Some Ambiguities and Opportunities'. *International Journal of Social Research Methodology* 6, no. 2 (2003): 121–39.

Waddock, S.A. and J.E. Post. 'Social Entrepreneurs and Catalytic Change'. *Public Administration Review* 51, no. 5 (1991): 393–401.

Wallace, S.L. 'Social Entrepreneurship: The Role of Social Purpose Enterprises in Facilitating Community Economic Development'. *Journal of Developmental Entrepreneurship* 4, no. 2 (1999): 153–74.

Wallace, T. 'NGO Dilemmas: Trojan Horses for Global Neoliberalism'. *Social Register* 40 (2003): 202–19.

Wallace, T. and J. Chapman. 'Some Realities Behind The Rhetoric of Downward Accountability'. Working Paper presented at Interact 5th Evaluation Conference, Holland. 1 April 2003. Available at: http://www.managingforimpact.org/sites/default/files/resource/some_realities_behind_the_rhetoric_of_downward_accountability.pdf (accessed 10 December 2015).

Weerawardena, J. and G. Sullivan Mort. 'Investigating Social Entrepreneurship: A Multidimensional Model'. *Journal of World Business* 41, no. 1 (2006): 21–35.

Westall, A. and D. Chalkley. 'Social Enterprise Futures'. 2007. Available at: http://www.smith-institute.org.uk/pdfs/social_enterprise.pdf (accessed 4 November 2010).

White, H. and L. Woestman. 'Aid Quality: Measuring Trends in Donor Performance'. *Development and Change* 25 (1994, July): 527–54.

Wolcott, H.F. *Transforming Qualitative Data: Description, Analysis and Interpretation.* Thousand Oaks, CA: SAGE Publications, 1994.

Wong, L. and J. Tang. 'Dilemmas Confronting Social Entrepreneurs: Care Homes for Elderly People in Chinese Cities'. *Pacific Affairs* 79, no. 4 (2006/2007): 623–40.

Yin, R. *Case Study Research.* Beverly Hills, CA: SAGE Publication, 1984.

————. *Case Study Research: Design and Methods.* Beverly Hills, CA: SAGE Publication, 2013.

Young, R. 'For What it is Worth: Social Value and the Future of Social Entrepreneurship'. In *Social Entrepreneurship: New Models of Sustainable Social Change*, edited by A. Nicholls, 56–73. Oxford: Oxford University Press, 2006.

Yunus, M. 'Nobel Lecture by Muhammad Yunus'. 2006. Available at: http://www.nobelprize.org/nobel_prizes/peace/laureates/2006/yunus-lecture-en.html (accessed 10 June 2013).

Zahra, S., H. Rawhouser, N. Bhawe, D. Neubaum and J. Hayton. 'Globalisation of Social Entrepreneurship Opportunities'. *Strategic Entrepreneurship Journal* 2 (2008): 117–31.

Zeyen, A., M. Beckmann, S. Mueller, J.G. Dees, D. Khanin, N. Krueger, P.J. Murphy, F. Santos, M. Scarlata, J. Walske and A. Zacharakis. 'Social Entrepreneurship and Broader Theories: Shedding New Light on the "Bigger Picture"'. *Journal of Social Entrepreneurship* 4, no. 1 (2012): 1–20.

Index

About the Author

Rama Krishna Reddy Kummitha is UNU-JSPS Fellow with the Institute for the Advanced Study of Sustainability at the United Nations University in Tokyo, Japan. He is also a visiting scholar with the National Graduate Institute for Policy Studies, Tokyo. Dr Kummitha has worked as an assistant professor at the Center for Social Entrepreneurship, Tata Institute of Social Sciences, Mumbai. He has been actively involved in research related to social entrepreneurship, social innovation, civil society, social exclusion and management strategy. He was earlier awarded the Indira Gandhi Merit Award by the Government of India and the Junior Scientist Award by Bonn University, Germany, for his academic contributions. He has received his PhD from the University of Hyderabad, India.